David S G Godfrey

EXPLORATIONS IN RECONCILIATION

This book represents the next generation in studies on social reconciliation. Until now much of the writing has been filled with 'shoulds' and 'oughts' – prescriptions for what might be done at some future point. This book, however, is built on a great deal of experience with the difficult work of reconciliation. It recognises the difficult balancing acts that reconciliation entails in the real world, and the necessity of seeing both sides of issues at the same time. This book is a genuine milestone that will give orientation to efforts at reconciliation for the future.

Robert Schreiter

Author of *Reconciliation: Mission and Ministry in a Changing Social Order*

Theologians and scholars of religion draw on rich resources to address the complex issues raised by political reconciliation in the Middle East, the former Yugoslavia, South Africa, Northern Ireland and elsewhere. The questions addressed include: Can truth set a person, or a society, free? How is political forgiveness possible? Are political, personal and spiritual reconciliation essentially related?

Explorations in Reconciliation brings Catholic, Protestant, Mennonite, Jewish and Islamic perspectives together within a single volume to present some of the most relevant theological work today.

Explorations in Reconciliation

New Directions in Theology

Edited by
DAVID TOMBS
Trinity College Dublin, Ireland
and
JOSEPH LIECHTY
Goshen College, USA

ASHGATE

Published by
Ashgate Publishing Limited
Gower House
Croft Road
Aldershot
Hants GU11 3HR
England

Ashgate Publishing Company
Suite 420
101 Cherry Street
Burlington, VT 05401-4405
USA

Ashgate website: http://www.ashgate.com

British Library Cataloguing in Publication Data
Explorations in Reconciliation: New Directions in
    Theology
    1. Reconciliation – Religious aspects – Christianity
    2. Reconciliation – Religious aspects – Islam
    I. Tombs, David, 1965– II. Liechty, Joseph
    201.7

Library of Congress Cataloging-in-Publication Data
Explorations in reconciliation : new directions in theology / edited by David Tombs and Joseph Liechty.
        p. cm.
    Includes index.
    ISBN 0-7546-5184-3 (alk. paper)
    1. Reconciliation–Religious aspects–Christianity. 2. Reconciliation–Religious aspects–Islam. I. Tombs, David, 1965– II. Liechty, Joseph.

    BT738.27. E97 2005
    201'.7–dc22

                                                                            2004030289

ISBN 0 7546 5184 3

Typeset by IML Typogaphers, Birkenhead, Merseyside
Printed and bound in Great Britain by Athenæum Press Ltd, Gateshead, Tyne & Weir

This book is dedicated to our colleagues at the Irish School of Ecumenics, and especially to the former Directors, Geraldine Smyth OP and Kenneth Kearon, who initiated the Belfast programme in Reconciliation Studies.

Contents

List of Contributors

Cecelia Clegg is Associate Director of the Centre for Theology and Public Issues, University of Edinburgh and Lecturer in Reconciliation Studies on the Belfast-based M.Phil. in Reconciliation Studies for Trinity College Dublin, Irish School of Ecumenics. She is the author, with Joseph Liechty, of *Moving Beyond Sectarianism: Religion, Conflict, and Reconciliation in Northern Ireland* (2001).

Marc Gopin is an Orthodox rabbi and conflict resolution specialist, currently serving as Visiting Associate Professor of International Diplomacy at the Fletcher School, Tufts University. His publications include *Holy War, Holy Peace: How Religion Can Bring Peace to the Middle East* (2002) and *Between Eden and Armageddon: The Future of Religions, Violence, and Peacemaking* (2000).

David Herbert is a sociologist of religion and Lecturer on the Belfast-based M.Phil. in Reconciliation Studies for Trinity College Dublin, Irish School of Ecumenics. He is author of *Religion and Civil Society* (Ashgate 2003) and editor of *Religion and Social Transformations* (Ashgate 2001).

Ada María Isasi-Díaz is Professor of Ethics and Theology at the Theological and Graduate Schools of Drew University, New Jersey. Born and raised in Cuba, she is a well-known *mujerista* theologian and author of *En La Lucha: Elaborating a Mujerista Theology* (2003 [1993]) and, with Yolanda Torango, *Hispanic Women: Prophetic Voice in the Church* (2004 [1988]).

Joseph Liechty is Plowshares Professor of Peace Studies at Goshen College, Indiana. He is the author, with Cecelia Clegg, of *Moving Beyond Sectarianism: Religion, Conflict, and Reconciliation in Northern Ireland* (2001) and the editor, with Alan Falconer, of *Reconciling Memories* (1998 [1988]).

Geraldine Smyth OP is a former leader of the Irish Dominicans and their international work and a past Director of the Irish School of Ecumenics, where she continues to teach in the area of ecumenical social ethics. She is the author of *A Way of Transformation: A Theological Evaluation of the Justice, Peace, and Integrity of Creation Process* (1995).

David Tombs is a political theologian and co-ordinator of the Belfast-based M.Phil. in Reconciliation Studies for Trinity College Dublin, Irish School of

Ecumenics. He is author of *Latin American Liberation Theology* (2002) and editor with Michael Hayes of *Truth and Freedom: The Church and Human Rights in El Salvador and Guatemala* (2001).

Wilhelm Verwoerd is a former lecturer in the Department of Philosophy, University of Stellenbosch, South Africa, and a researcher within the South African Truth and Reconciliation Commission. He is currently a programme co-ordinator at the Glencree Centre for Reconciliation, Co. Wicklow, Ireland. He is editor, with Charles Villa-Vicencio, of *Looking Back, Reaching Forward: Reflections on the South African Truth and Reconciliation Commission* (2000).

Miroslav Volf is originally from Croatia and now teaches at Yale Divinity School, where he is the Henry B. Wright Professor of Theology. He is well known for his book *Exclusion and Embrace: A Theological Exploration of Identity, Otherness, and Reconciliation* (1996).

Acknowledgements

The contributors to this collection are all in some ways practitioners of reconciliation and write in the light of their practical experience in South Africa, Croatia, Ireland, Bosnia, Latin America and elsewhere. For this reason some of the chapters were first offered to a specific audience at a conference or public lecture and have subsequently been revised for publication here. Gopin, Volf and Smyth's chapters have been revised from papers first written for the 'Boundaries and Bonds' conference of the Irish School of Ecumenics in Belfast, 1997. Wilhelm Verwoerd's chapter is a revised version of his John Whyte Memorial Lecture, University College Dublin (20 November 2003). The chapter by Ada María Isasi-Díaz is a slightly modified version of an article that originally appeared in the *Journal of Hispanic/Latino Theology* 8.4 (May 2001) and is reprinted with kind permission. Likewise the chapter by Cecelia Clegg was presented first in the Margaret Beaufort Lecture Series, University of Cambridge, England, November 2002, and subsequently published as 'Between Embrace and Exclusion', *New Blackfriars* 85 (January 2004). It has been revised and reprinted with the kind permission of the Dominican order. The cartoon on page 113 is reprinted with permission from *Truths Drawn in Jest*, edited by Wilhelm Verwoerd and Mahlubi 'Chief' Mabizela (Cape Town: New Africa Books, 2000). As editors we are grateful to all concerned for making this possible. We must also give special thanks to Emily Hersberger and Caroline Clarke for help in preparing the manuscript and to Sarah Lloyd and the staff of Ashgate Publishing for their professional and friendly assistance in bringing it to fruition.

Introduction

David Tombs and Joseph Liechty

The urgent need to prevent, end and recover from the ethnic, religious and nationalist conflicts that have multiplied since the end of the Cold War provides the context for new explorations in the theology of reconciliation. In recent years a number of important books in political science, jurisprudence and ethics have debated the challenges of reconciliation, peace-building and transitional justice in societies emerging from sustained and often bloody conflicts. This literature raises ethical and other questions for theologians and scholars of religion to work with when addressing the complex issues raised in the Middle East, the former Yugoslavia, South Africa, Rwanda, Latin America, Northern Ireland and elsewhere. It includes questions like: can truth set a person, or a society, free? How is political forgiveness possible? What need is there for repentance and for justice? Is reconciliation, especially the aspect of forgiveness, compatible with justice? Are political, social, personal and spiritual reconciliation essentially related?

From the writings of the apostle Paul onwards, Christian thinkers have struggled to read the signs of the times and reflect theologically in response to political events. A constructive engagement between theology and politics is as necessary now as it has ever been. For Christian theologians to take up the political challenges of reconciliation is particularly appropriate because these raise so many related theological questions.

Paul says, 'All this is from God, who reconciled us to himself through Christ, and has given us the ministry of reconciliation; that is, in Christ God was reconciling the world to himself, not counting their trespasses against them, and entrusting the message of reconciliation to us' (2 Cor. 5:18–19). For Paul himself there was an immediate political relevance to this message, as shown in the radical egalitarianism of his vision of being reconciled in Christ: 'There is no longer Jew or Greek, there is no longer slave or free, there is no longer male and female; for all of you are one in Christ' (Gal. 3:28). However, Paul also shows elsewhere in his writing, understanding the radical implications of such a message is not always easy. Since Constantine, the Church has tended to focus on the sacramental and personal aspects of reconciliation, and generally neglected the political and social dimensions. Fortunately, in recent years this has started to change. Christian theologians, ethicists and biblical scholars have started to address old questions in new ways and the political relevance of reconciliation has become both a demanding challenge and an exciting opportunity for theology.

This book, written by scholars working in varied contexts, draws together key developments in this new work and extends them further. A first group of essays considers religious resources for reconciliation, a theme that was vital long before the tragedy of 9/11, but undeniably so since then. The first author, Marc Gopin, has been a passionate advocate of the idea that every religious tradition, although sometimes, frequently or even currently associated with violence, has resources for making peace that are drawn from the particularities of its traditions, texts and practices, and the search for peace can never bypass these resources.[1] Here the theorist turns practitioner, as Gopin offers from the depths of his Jewish tradition an extended and intimate reflection on the theme of the stranger in the Hebrew Bible and what it can teach us about the relationship of the self and the Other. He also takes on the additional task of considering how these scriptural and theological insights might be integrated with theories of conflict analysis and resolution in the context of complex cultural situations.

In the second essay, Miroslav Volf amplifies themes he had earlier developed in his highly regarded book *Exclusion and Embrace: A Theological Exploration of Identity, Otherness, and Reconciliation*, presenting God's call to embrace (reconciliation) as revealed in the cross of Christ. As a Croatian offering a theologically grounded response to the practices of exclusion that generate political and social conflicts in the Balkans and around the world, Volf speaks here as a Christian to Christians, and yet readers from diverse perspectives will find much to consider and act upon.

In one sense, David Herbert's chapter on 'Islam and Reconciliation' is the exception in this first section, because he writes as a sociologist and from outside the faith tradition. However, Herbert uses this stance to write a carefully nuanced account, making the case, in parallel with Gopin and Volf, for searching out resources for peace within the varied traditions of Islam. As he draws attention to aspects of Islam likely to be positive for conflict resolution, he also offers a corrective to those scholars who would settle for an essentialist and therefore simplistic reading of Islam. In contrast to most of the other chapters in the collection, he also does more to examine reconciliation in the context of international relations, not only conflicts within states. The controversy still swirling around Samuel Huntington's 'clash of civilisations' thesis makes this international approach important, especially in relation to Islam.[2]

---

[1] See Marc Gopin, *From Eden to Armageddon: The Future of World Religions, Violence, and Peacemaking* (New York: Oxford University Press, 2000).

[2] Samuel P. Huntington, 'The Clash of Civilisations?', *Foreign Affairs* 72.3 (Summer 1993), 22–49. A shorter version appeared as 'The Coming Clash of Civilizations or, The West Against the Rest', *New York Times* (6 June 1993), E.19; a later expanded version appeared as *The Clash of Civilisations and the Remaking of the World Order* (New York: Simon and Schuster, 1996).

A second section of three chapters focuses on the dynamics of reconciliation and Christian theology. Joseph Liechty, writing out of his long experience of reconciliation work in Northern Ireland, notes that the fresh surge of post-Cold War writing on reconciliation is sometimes hampered by the lack of an agreed set of terms and definitions. He proposes an approach to definition through an account of the internal dynamics of reconciliation and in the process gives particular attention to problems and complexities around the understanding and practice of forgiveness. He argues that if the different aspects of the Christian forgiveness process are identified and distinguished more clearly, it can help to resolve the often unhelpfully general debates such as whether repentance must precede forgiveness or vice versa.

Ada María Isasi-Díaz writes as a *mujerista* theologian born and raised in Cuba and now working in the United States. She presents reconciliation as a religious, social and civic virtue in which the practice of reconciliation links God to human beings and human beings to each other in ways that embody a spirituality of peace and justice. Her chapter illustrates how the emergence of contextual political theologies can give new relevance to traditional theological teaching.

David Tombs describes the work of the Interdiocesan 'Recovery of Historical Memory' (REMHI) project in Guatemala as a practical outworking of a prophetic political theology. As a Church-sponsored 'truth commission' to support an official UN initiative, the REMHI project was a remarkable achievement in confronting painful truths. Yet at a practical level, the project also exposed the difficulties that remain in the pursuit of justice when perpetrators enjoy impunity and those in power frustrate political reforms. Tombs points to this dilemma as an ongoing challenge that a political theology of reconciliation cannot ignore.

The third part of the book, 'The Ongoing Challenge of Reconciliation', looks at the continuing practical challenges that the churches and society face in making reconciliation a reality in everyday life.

Wilhelm Verwoerd draws on his background as a political philosopher, his experience with the South African Truth and Reconciliation Commission and his work in Northern Ireland with former combatants to develop a philosophical approach to the significance of inclusive memory that embraces the humanity of all. Whilst not directly addressed to religious questions, the issues that arise from this in relation to sectarianism and religious identity, will be obvious to those interested in the application of 'inclusive memory' to social and religious identities in South Africa, Northern Ireland, the Balkans and elsewhere.

Cecelia Clegg draws on the findings of the 'Moving Beyond Sectarianism' project – a major six-year research project in Northern Ireland – and the notion of 'embrace' in Miroslav Volf's work to address the sectarian divisions between Catholics and Protestants in Ireland. Drawing on her training in psychology and psychotherapy, and guided by the need to 'speak the truth in love to the churches', Clegg offers a pastoral challenge for churches and other faith communities to respond to in addressing the continuing legacies of conflict.

Geraldine Smyth starts with Brian Keenan's reflections in *An Evil Cradling* on his time in Beirut, and his experience in crossing cultural boundaries. Keenan's words are shown to have a special relevance to the politics of identity in his native Belfast. She goes on to look at Jesus' crossing of the Jordan to show how Jesus' frequent crossing and recrossing of boundaries (between Jews and Samaritans, Jews and Gentiles, men and women, rich and poor) offers a theological resource for creating and maintaining right relationships.

Whilst the chapters have a common concern – the challenges and opportunities that arise from the inter-relationships between social identity, religious faith and political reconciliation – each author addresses their own social context and reflects on their own experiences. They do not speak with a single voice, but they all recognise the complexities of reconciliation and offer an engaged commitment to exploring how this might be understood more deeply.

PART I

RELIGIOUS RESOURCES FOR RECONCILIATION

CHAPTER 1

The Heart of the Stranger[1]

Marc Gopin

The concept of stranger in human experience is relevant to almost all relationships. We human beings constantly create both very large and very small societies in which someone is a stranger to that society. Simultaneously we ourselves frequently experience varying degrees of estrangement in one setting or another. From a religious point of view, there is always the question hovering over our experience as to whether we are in close relation to or estranged from God at any given time.

The centrality of the stranger in both law and metaphor in biblical religions is at least one key to how a believer is supposed to love the other who is different and how the believer may also be loved by others or by God. The idea of a stranger who is also beloved holds in tension the ethical experience of love together with the ontological reality of human differences and separation. The concept of stranger, the living reality of strangers, and the laws obligating love for the stranger are therefore highly suggestive as to how believers can create community without consuming unique identities, how we can be both strangers to each other in our uniqueness and differences but also beloved, and how we, through our ability to meet and coexist, thereby embrace and welcome home the ultimate Stranger to this world, the Divine Presence. The God of the Bible seems to be occasionally at home in the midst of human beings and occasionally alienated by our abominable behaviour, but always hoping that our own embrace of strangers becomes the basis for welcoming the Divine stranger into the community of human beings.

In this chapter I explore the theological centrality of the stranger or sojourner, the *ger*, in the Hebrew Bible. I also explore theological approaches to boundaries between self and the ultimate Other, the Divine Presence, and the nature of coexistence between different beings. These themes are all dealt with extensively in the Hebrew Bible. It is a Bible that Jews and Christians share, even if I see it through the overarching lens of rabbinic Judaism's 2000-year-old religious constructs whereas Christians see it through the lens of the New Testament and 2000 years of Christian traditions. In the final pages I turn to some pragmatic integration of these theological

---

[1] The first version of this chapter was presented to the 1997 'Boundaries and Bonds' conference, held in Belfast, Northern Ireland, and organised by the 'Moving Beyond Sectarianism' project of the Irish School of Ecumenics.

concepts with theories of conflict analysis and resolution in the context of complex cultural situations.

God, the Stranger, and the Boundaries of Coexistence

When I use the term 'the Other' I am, of course, engaged with Martin Buber, Emmanuel Levinas and many others attempting to understand this space or boundary between the individual and the person or the world, including the God or the Sacred, that the individual encounters. In addition, much of what I say about the self and the Other refers to collective selves as well, to whole ethnic, religious or national groups in their encounters with 'other' distinct groups. I acknowledge, of course, that identity in the real world is more ambiguous than any of these categories; we see ourselves as part of more than one collective identity – the human race, the nation, the clan, the family, the religion – and this complicates the question of self, other and boundaries.

The biblical creation story in Genesis is perhaps the most fundamental blueprint of biblically based cultures for everything that is right and wrong about human existence. It offers us a window into the biblical version of how, as human beings, we can create or destroy, construct society anew or perpetuate a morass of violence. The creation story also reveals God as Creator from out of this world, as the first biblical stranger who reaches across impassable boundaries to give birth, to nurture life, even as He or She is not completely part of it but rather in some undefined relationship.

Before we explore God the Stranger, however, we must engage a more fundamental discussion about of the nature of God. We think so often of an expansive and limitless concept of God, both in time and in space. Traditional Judaism, through the Hebrew Bible, shared with the world the concepts of a Divine Being who is prior to the universe, a Creator who is eternal and beyond this world. And yet we cannot conceive of divinity without reference to this very universe.

When we say something is limitless we delimit it by adjectives of space and time. Thus, every traditional name of God refers in some way to a Divine relationship to the physical world. Even the most obscure name, *eyn-sof*, literally 'without end', used in classical Jewish mysticism, Kabbalah, to refer to the utterly unknowable aspect of God, is conditioned by concepts of space and time. Talk of limitlessness has as its referent the limitations of physical dimensions.

Nevertheless, tradition does affirm a concept of God beyond physical existence. Maimonides, certainly, was the most keenly aware of the problematic nature of Divine address and attribution precisely because that attribution cannot move beyond the physical universe. In his *The Guide for the Perplexed*, Maimonides realised that the attribution of positive qualities to

God, such as kindness, implies a kind of limitation of God to the physical universe. And he was very conscious that a Jewish God cannot be collapsed into the universe.

It appears, then, that we have an inescapable paradox in the relationship of God to the world. This has been encapsulated traditionally by the terms 'immanence' and 'transcendence'. But this is an uncomfortable paradox and each term or way of describing God is fraught with problems. God as transcendent means little, because we have no way to intellectualise what is beyond space and time. God as immanent is scandalous when analysed carefully, at least from a strictly Jewish monotheistic view; it seems to either justify earthly idolatry, or render the concepts of Creation and Creator meaningless. How can a Creator create Himself if He is immanent in the universe? How can an Immanent Presence, solely defined in such a way, and completely identified with an object, be itself the Creator of that object? Furthermore, traditional Jewish philosophy and Kabbalah have understood well the perils of over-identifying God and the world. If God is defined only as immanent in the world or identified with it, then the entire conception of good and evil, virtue and sin, falls apart. In the modern period, no one understood as well as Hermann Cohen, the German idealist philosopher, that the ethical 'ought' has no reality, and the political ought of messianic Judaism, that is, the ideal of creating the good society on earth, has no reality unless they are distinguished from the immanent 'is'. God must be the source of the ethical ought and the political ought, and in order to play that role, to give those oughts ontological reality, God must be even more transcendent than those very oughts. The dream of what should take place in the human relationship to the universe must have reality if virtue and sin, *mitsvah* and *averah*, are to be meaningful categories. But they cannot be real unless they are given a source in Transcendence. Either the dream of what is not yet real has reality or it is simply the play of neural transmitters, synapses and the reconstruction of emotional states. If it is the latter one could argue that this can make no serious claim on the human conscience. In order for it to be more than that, it must in some way reflect what is not quite of this world. If God exists in Transcendence then it is possible for Good to exist in Transcendence, and then it can make a claim on the physical world. It can say to members of the physical world, 'Strive to reach beyond yourselves and your current moral level of behaviour.'

Here is the paradox, however. If God is not immanent in at least some sense of that term then the practice and experience of religion – as the vast majority of human beings have understood it – is impossible. If God is not immanent then prayer means nothing because no one is listening in any real sense; the soul as an image of God, or an expression of Divine Presence, is a figment of the imagination; hope in Divine aid to change oneself or change the world is foolhardy; and the idea of Divine truths occurring to human minds at some critical juncture, in the forms of prophecy or inspiration, is a pipe dream. This does not preclude a serious commitment to the idea of the Good (or to the idea of *mitsvah* and *averah*, which emanate from a concept of the Good) that emerges from a posited faith in or knowledge of Divine transcendence. But most of deep religious experience is gone, leaving the emotional life of the individual without spiritual moorings.

There is one way to solve this dilemma, and that is to hold Divine Immanence and Divine Transcendence in dramatic tension. Since at least one pole of that dramatic tension involves a reality that is unknowable then the only way to understand this is by use of metaphor, which the Torah (meant here as the Hebrew Bible, but also the texts of rabbinic Judaism) provides through one of its most prominent themes and concerns: the sojourner or guest, also called a stranger or the *ger*. From Abraham to Ruth, from the Exodus stories to countless laws of interpersonal aid, from remonstrations in the five books of Moses to the social criticism of the prophets, there is no person of greater concern in the Bible than the stranger who is with us but not with us, whom we know but do not know, who is a source of great mystery and yet ancestral familiarity, whose treatment by us is ultimately a litmus test of whether we and our culture have succeeded or not in the eyes of God, and whose experience is essentially a yardstick of our moral stature. If we love the stranger, protect him and see to his needs, then our society passes a kind of Divine test, and we also have the emotional and spiritual fulfilment of identifying completely with an echo of ourselves. The admonition in Exodus 23:9 to not oppress the stranger is given poignant emotional depth by saying to the listeners that you know the heart of the stranger having been strangers in the Land of Egypt, having experienced what the worst kind of estrangement is when one human being makes another into an object, into a slave. Loving the stranger in the present becomes an opportunity to heal yourselves, heal your history, and also heal others through the existential meeting with and moral care for the Other who lives across a clear cultural, economic or political boundary.

The stranger or sojourner is the classic Other in monotheism. The sojourner is also, I would argue, a not so thinly veiled metaphor for God in this world. The God of the Bible loves the stranger intensely because it is He/She. In Jewish theology the *she'khinah*, the Divine Presence, can be both part of the innermost workings of our physical existence, and yet simultaneously hold from view Her mysterious identity. The *she'khinah* is immanent even though the true nature of God is distant, unknowable and estranged. We cannot find God or see God or even know how to do so without meeting the human stranger through love. The stranger is the key to the Divine paradox.

Before we can fully understand the relationship between God and the concept of stranger, however, we must ask, what is a stranger? A stranger is one who is foreign to us in many ways, utterly unknowable in some fashion, and yet is in some potential relation to us at the same time – someone who I at least begin to know in some way. We pass a stranger on the street, and we have no idea who she is; in the crowded cities we pass thousands of people whom we will never know; at the airport in some foreign city we will never know these strangers whom we have seen in a fleeting glimpse. We will never know their history, their habits, their dreams and their failures, no matter how we may long to know them. But at some moment we occupy the same space and time of the stranger. If a spectacular event had occurred as we passed these strangers, if the building had been hit by an earthquake and we had been trapped together, or if we together had helped save the life of a person suddenly gone into cardiac arrest, we might have created an intimate relationship transforming us from complete strangers into lifelong friends. But such is usually not meant to be. There is some element of tragedy in the fleeting encounter with strangers: an opportunity lost perhaps for the greater unity of the human spirit on this earth that is achieved when strangers become committed to each other through some shared experience. In Jewish theology there is an element of the Divine in every human being, in every stranger, and at the moment of the brief encounter of strangers who meet is the possibility of the reunion of the Divine with itself, but it remains unfulfilled. There is some element of divine tragedy in strangers who have failed to be reunited, though the reunion seemed so possible at that instant. But the public space – between families and groups, at the border of the lives of strangers, especially where there is tragedy – also presents an immense opportunity for spiritual discovery and ultimate moral fulfilment.

Estrangement is insidiously pervasive in human experience. Let's return to the strangers passing in the airport. Even if we had met those strangers in the airport, would they have ever ceased completely to be strangers? Who knows another human being so well that he cannot say of the other that he is a stranger? I have lived with and loved my wife for twenty years now, and I have not begun to recount to her all the events of my life, and it is not for lack of trying. If she cannot see all that I see in my mind's eye, if she cannot have my memories, feel my longings and my traumas, feel my sources of shame or see the history of my fantasies (thank God!), will she ever really know me? Do I ever completely cease to be a stranger?

There is an elastic quality to the concept of stranger that allows it to elude definition. For example, can you love a stranger? The biblical tradition repeatedly demands the most intimate care for the *ger*, the stranger, including the command to love the *ger* (Deut. 10:19). But how can we feel these love emotions even as we are estranged from another, or even as we perceive the other as stranger? It seems logical on a certain level that at the moment in which we experience love for the stranger, the category of stranger must become absurd. Yet the biblical text holds love and the stranger in paradoxical tension. As we quoted earlier, 'And do not oppress the stranger, for you know the heart of the stranger, having been strangers in the land of Egypt'

(Ex. 23:9). Somehow, it must be possible to retain the title of stranger and still be loved.

Love of God is at the heart of monotheistic religion, and yet God is the quintessential stranger to this world in the pull and tug of Jewish theology. God must remain a stranger at the doorstep of physical reality. If we invite God too far inside we end up worshipping something else – not God, but ourselves quite often, or a piece of land – and in idolising a physical object and thinking it to be God we actually destroy the very Divine Presence that we sought to invite into our reality. We make sanctification of place a dangerous enterprise.

If we do not, however, open the door to this extraordinary Stranger then we risk an existence bereft of meaning, of spiritual and emotional depth. It will also be bereft of the hope that comes from the knowledge that virtue is real, that virtue shares in some way an ideal realm with an existing God.

The reality of something as abstract as virtue has depended through much of intellectual history on the reality of God. Virtue's actualisation in the religious mind is therefore a pregnant possibility, always luring the human heart one step further towards fulfilment. Virtue's existence is at the heart of the Jewish understanding of Revelation, while the dream of virtue's realisation in human political community is the distant dream of messianic Redemption. Virtue is never completely actualised, however. We human beings are grossly imperfect, and yet we are good enough to aspire toward virtue's actualisation both in our personal ethical life and in political life.

Ger encapsulates and symbolises the fundamental relation of humanity to the world and beyond. It also characterises and defines for us the essential link between God and world, God and the human being, God and the soul. It allows God to exist in abstraction or transcendence, but also in immediate relationship. It is a being who we can love with great intensity without fearing that our human narcissistic tendency to overwhelm, to consume and imperialistically strangle the things we love might destroy an authentic and morally independent understanding of God. We all know of love that helps the other grow and love that strangles. We learn to distinguish love that is unconditional from love that is self-serving, love that liberates, ennobles and empowers from love that stifles and tortures. It is the same with love of the Divine. The danger in monotheism has always been that the love of God, this invitation of the Sacred into human existence, has turned out to be a vehicle of self-love, strangling the very presence of God through self-worship, through idolisation of land, nation and states.

It is not scandalous in Jewish theology to reflect that God, the stranger, needs the human being to be looking out of existence toward God even as God is looking in. If there is no one looking out, even as God looks in, then the door between God and the world ceases to exist. The door must be *perceived* as a door on both its sides. Authentic relationship occurs only through the consciousness that the Divine Sojourner, this visitor from transcendent realms, has an identity in this world and also the possibility of loving and being loved.

The concept of the human being created in the image of God is crucial for the foundation of Jewish ethics, but it also serves as the critical existential linkage of God and the human being as two parallel strangers in the drama of Creation. Both of them yearn and succeed – in different ways – to negotiate their estrangement and their discovery of relationship.

There are many bases of Jewish ethical behaviour. Few of those arguments challenge monotheistic human beings as profoundly as the idea that the God we fear and love happens to reside in the image, the *tselem*, of the other human being – the other who now transforms into a sacred Other. Arguments for love and compassion, or the duties owed to another person, are frequent in biblical literature. But it is hard to expect love or compassion, or even a sense of legal duty, to another with whom one is at war, or who hates you or abuses you. And yet Judaism does demand such leaps of conscience. The concept of *tselem* is crucial for this moral leap to take place.

The idea that God resides in the image of the other person who, therefore, becomes a sacred Other is startling, and it is inextricable from the odyssey of the religious psyche towards Divine encounter. No religious human being lives without the longing for Divine encounter. Torah texts in various places have the audacity to redirect that longing toward the Other, to place the 'image' of that God in the human Other, no matter who that Other is: a difficult father perhaps, whom one must nevertheless honour; or an enemy to whom one must offer a means of escape in the heat of battle and to whom one offers peace; or an enemy who hates you to whom the Bible insists you must offer help to when he is struggling with a burden, like the burden of bad leadership. It is as if a Divine voice says perpetually to the inner self who is conscious of the sacred laws of morality, 'You want to find Me? You want to fast and suppress your body, or engage in any number of demonstrations of devotion in order to locate Me or conjure Me? Fine, go right ahead, but you have only to look and really see the stranger or estranged Other who walks past you every day. And the more that you truly see him or her the more you will find Me.'

An image, however, is elusive by definition. It recalls the original of which it is a copy, but it is not the original, and it must not be. The door that opens between God and the world, Transcendence and Immanence, can allow an image to pass through, reflected in the universe, and reflected in the face of the human being. But, once again, the image and the reality remain separate.

The image of the Transcendent Being inside the human being is testimony to the phenomenon of sojourning across boundaries at the very core of God's relation to the world. Just as God the Creator in the Genesis story sees the human being, Adam, as alone in the Garden of Eden in need of a partner, He too saw Himself as alone, in need of the universe, but, in particular, in need of the conversant and communicative human being. The consciousness of the human being who is alone, who cannot communicate with others, who has no *ezer ke'negdo*, no partner confronting him, is not true consciousness. The fully conscious human being is a communicative human being, empathically related to the living beings around him. God is in need of this conscious, communicative being. It is possible then that *ezer ke'negdo* did not just refer to the creation of the full human pair of man and woman, but was self-referential. God realised that He had created an *ezer ke'negdo* for Himself, namely the human being. The human being is a helpmate that stands with God but also apart from God in the drama of the Creation story, fulfilling the crucial task of taking care of the Garden of Eden, taking care of the earth. But the human being is also an *ezer* who is *ke'negdo*, opposite God or separate from God because of his finitude and capacity to fail.

The human being could never be wholly communicative with a transcendent Being. Ultimately God cannot have the intimacy and intertwining of self and Other that is possible for physical lovers. The splitting of the human into the male and female is a crucial moment of creating the reality of aloneness but also the possibility of companionship of indescribable physical and spiritual intimacy. When these two human beings enter the story, the Divine engagement with the world becomes immediately more indirect, oblique, dependent to some degree on the human being who now carries the image of God. The Garden of Eden story shifts toward the essential questions facing the human interaction with the world and away from the immediacy of Divine action in the world. But the image of God in the human being is conscious self-awareness and communication. Estrangement between the human and the Divine is answered or alleviated by sharing this consciousness, this communication among human beings, especially between lover and beloved.

As we communicate fully with each other through thoughts, emotions, empathy and altruism, especially in the drama of lovers' intimacy, we complete who we are as images of God. No ideas are true until they can be articulated; no feelings are true feelings until they are communicated by deed, by dialogue, or in some non-verbal fashion. In completing communication with each other we complete communication with the Other. Communication is the ultimate fulfilment of consciousness for strangers. As we communicate we not only complete human consciousness in the act and experience of love, we complete the image of God and overcome His estrangement as well as our own. It is as if the image of God is activated in us in its fullest sense as we love and come to know intimately the other being who is our *ezer ke'negdo*. In so doing, we also allow the door to Transcendence to be fully opened. We give

God a way to be in the world through His image and a way to overcome the austere and awesome estrangement of creating the world alone.

Transcendence and Immanence in the Divine relationship to the world have their parallel in the human choices of aloneness and engagement. The stranger is in the place in between these two dramatically different places. He is at the gateway waiting to enter or not to enter, should we choose to invite him in. But there is another choice available to the Other who is not yet engaged. It is a sinister choice that can and should be called evil. It is the choice of consumption. Consumption lies at the heart of both human existence and human destructiveness, life-giving and death-giving. The need to be all-consuming, to leave no space in which one does not consume, is the real key to human evil.

The relationship between over-consumption and the destruction of a natural environment is self-evident when it is seen in its ecological expression. Certainly our generation more than any other knows the consequences of over-consumption. Or perhaps not enough of us see it clearly enough to stop our own destruction. What is clear is that the loss of boundary between the human and the one tree that was off limits in the Garden of Eden is the story of over-consumption and breaking boundaries – not in order to meet the other, to engage and appreciate the tree, but in order to consume and thus destroy it. Appreciation of the Other must respect boundaries of separate existence. Where there is no boundary there is no recognition of anything but the self. Where there is nothing but the self there is only demonic destruction and self-worship.

The Edenic story, however, is not just about the boundary between the self and a natural universe that calls for care and respect. It is also about the fundamental relationship of the human being to all other beings. When Adam reached for the tree his motives may have been the purest in the world. He may have felt that the world will be redeemed if only he can bring his Divine image into every space of the Garden, and thus know the entire garden. Yet in his rapaciousness, his inability to resist the one tree out of many, Adam embraced the greed that cost him his ability to maintain a boundary. By consuming rather than meeting the Other, he practised ultimate alienation from the sacred aspect of the Other in the world. So have all zealots of history, religious or otherwise, felt as they blazed a path of destructive consumption, with the result of millions of lives wasted in brutal warfare. So too have many political, ideological and religious systems failed to understand that no matter how pure the motive, the reach for every last piece of territory grossly violates the keys to true knowledge and wisdom: humility and self-limitation.

Adam's rapaciousness, the key to the Eden story, is thus the key to the question of the sojourner, the *ger*, and boundaries. It raises the fundamental questions – indeed, the essential challenge that so many political, ideological and religious systems have failed to address – of how to relate without consuming, how to meet others and not destroy them in the name of trying to meet. This is exactly why the stranger is the essential metaphor of biblical experience and why it is the key to its ethical stance.

It is precisely because Adam and Eve were guilty of the consumption of the Other, of the destruction of boundaries and the elimination of the viable existence of the different and the strange, that they lost their son at the hands of their other son. Jealous murder is the ultimate consequence of the deadly side of human consumption, and children often accentuate the nascent tendencies of their parents. That is, I would argue, the intent of the biblical theme regarding the sins of the fathers being visited upon the sons. A society that in one generation dehumanises and takes advantage of a stranger or a minority, consuming him in some sense, can easily commit genocide in the next generation. Cain did not commit genocide, but he took the first step towards it.

Nothing calls into question the worthiness of the human race more than the phenomenon of massive violence. It is precisely the actions of Cain that set in motion a series of events over generations that led to Divine regret at the creation of the human race. This is the essence of the Flood symbolism in Genesis. The Flood is a Divine gesture to the world of exactly what the world, in turn, had gestured to God: random destructiveness. Thus, the metaphorical framing of the question of boundaries between and recognition of the self and the Other leads eventually to a radical questioning of the worth of the human race in the hands of the biblical story.

What is crucial about the Flood story is naturally Noah. Noah is the single one. Noah is lonely and isolated. Noah stands against a generation, and in so doing he evokes the image of a stranger, outside the boundaries of his generation. But Noah also evokes the most important paradox associated with the strange Other, the single one. It is the stranger, be it God, Noah or some other leader, who, while standing outside the bounds of physical reality or even sociological reality, is able to be a creator, even a nurturer. It is the curious destiny of the stranger to be both nurturing of life but also outside of it, even necessarily outside of it. Peculiarity is the destiny of the stranger. But the peculiarity nurtures and creates or recreates life on a universal scale. Noah embodied this nurturing: as a stranger with a radical respect for boundaries, he did not consume the world around him but nurtured it and was chosen to recreate the world.

The Noah episode is the first indication we have that a fundamental paradox of disengagement with the world will be wedded to a nurturing care for the all of humanity. Further, it suggests that radical unity of the world, the breaking of all boundaries between selves, is not constructive in and of itself. In fact, this kind of universalism, as powerfully symbolised by the peoples of the Tower of Babel, is destructive, antithetical to the conception of God, and therefore the Good, that biblical Judaism is seeking to convey to all of humanity.

This sets the stage for the destiny of the stranger, the particular Other, who remains in his particularity, but who relates to God as one of two strangers united in their common love of and commitment to the world in its entirety. The stranger is loved but not consumed. The stranger continues to be different but is loved nevertheless. The boundary remains. And the love travels across the boundary day to day like light from the sun. But it does not consume and is not consumed. Both remain vibrant and effluent, and the metaphor of Divine relationship to and love for the world is re-enacted in the relationship of self and other, in the ethical relationship of meeting across boundaries that are never destroyed.

Abraham, the father of the Hebrew people, but also the traditional father of Islamic peoples and an important figure of faith in Christian tradition, is singular in his peculiar relationship to God. At the same time, however, with all of his distinct rites and ceremonies and his unique storyline, he is also a man through whom all nations will be blessed (Gen. 12:3) and who follows the ways of God which involve a universal commitment to justice and righteousness. The latter are expressed truly in their most radically universalist sense, because Abraham will use these very Divine characteristics to defend even the most vile community of rapists and murderers in Sodom, demanding before God that the innocent should never be swept away with the guilty (Gen. 18:22–33).

Nothing like the following verse defines more precisely the exquisite paradox of the sanctified life of the stranger, a blend of radical particularity in a morally challenging world, together with an acute commitment to the same world. God says, 'For I have singled him out, that he may instruct his children and his posterity to keep the way of the Eternal God, to practice righteousness and justice, in order that the Eternal God may bring about for Abraham what He has promised him' (Gen. 18:19). The act of singling out and making promises to a particular clan are clear evidence of the valuation of boundaries. But this simultaneously frames a commitment to a universal set of ideas whose radical universalism will become clear just four verses later when Abraham extends these ideals even to the most corrupt inhabitants of Sodom. Thus it is out of a place of *particularity*, of being a sojourner who nevertheless crosses boundaries with a universal concern, that Abraham presents an ideal model of engagement with the world, without consuming that world or allowing it to consume him. Relation becomes possible without violence, while the spiritual mission of interrelationship is not only maintained but is realised on a far deeper level than would be thought possible.

There is no easy solution to the problem of the boundary between self and Other, nor to the pitfalls of both universal pretensions and particular identities. It seems that violence has emerged in the history of religious traditions, especially monotheistic traditions, from a universalist stance bent on consuming or exterminating all things and people in its path. But violence has also emerged from particularist stances that do not care for or do not value the existence of others who are not members of one's clan or sect.

One of the essential dangers of monotheistic notions of particularity and mission has been the concept of chosenness, essentially the beloved relationship of the stranger with God, with her own agreement and arrangement with God as to what she is called upon to do in the world. It is nothing less than the chosenness of a child by a parent who loves all her children, and gives each of them a special task to accomplish. The successes and failures of that agreement and relationship are a strictly internal affair, between a person or a group and God, not a litmus test of global success or domination.

There is no question that this concept as it has been appropriated by all three traditions, as far as I can tell, has been one of the most destructive and misinterpreted conceptions in the history of monotheism. For the Prophets of Israel this chosenness was just as frequently framed as a chosenness for special punishment as special rewards, and most often a chosenness for obligation and mission. How anyone in their right mind could have read the Prophets of Israel and come to the conclusion that chosenness meant superiority or privilege is beyond me. And yet I continue to be amazed at how any religious idea, no matter how good or decent, can be reinterpreted in some historical period by the highest of authorities for the lowest of purposes. The number of groups that, in the name of monotheism, have used the chosenness metaphor to destroy indigenous peoples physically or emotionally in the past millennium defies the imagination. Such is our burden in being inheritors of historical religions and historical mistakes.

Till now, I have addressed these issues on a theological plane. Now, however, I would like to integrate this with consideration of the empirical questions facing humanity: questions relating to sectarianism, boundaries and the role of religion in peace and conflict.

Organised religion, especially in its more uncompromising forms, generally denies the fluidity of identity in religious life. But from the vantage point of conflict and violence, there are various ways in which religious communities are evolving all the time, sometimes for better and sometimes for worse. Of the key factors involved in this process, some are external to the community and the individual and some are internal. The external factors involve economic, political, social, psychological, ethnic, military and security matters that deeply affect us every day of our lives. These factors interact in complex ways both with the inner life of religious individuals, be they simple parishioners, leading clergy, religious institutions and their hierarchies. This in turn causes an inner and ever-evolving process of interpreting the spiritual and moral priorities of the religious traditions (or, in some interpretations, the spirit of God) as to how to react to these new circumstances. It also evokes struggle over institutional change.

There is also an unmistakable complexity to all of this in the fact that education and many other factors make the depth of someone's religious identity and sense of self extremely variable. Each person sees some fundamental elements of their religious world-view as non-negotiable. Often, however, there is great identity confusion in many parts of the world, particularly among those who are violent in the name of religion, as to what their religious identity really is as an in-depth experience. Thus in conflictual situations we tend to take a binary approach to the world: we practise negative identity and define ourselves by who we are not.

This negative identity is not very pleasant. It needs conflict and misery in order to sustain itself, and it puts the human being or the community that experiences it, or has significant elements of it, in an impossible position. On the one hand, much evidence suggests that the normal human reaction to the world is to renounce violence. Most people, especially mothers, would rather not bury their children and would do anything to avoid that horror. I feel that reality more than ever before as a father. On the other hand, the need for identity is so powerful a force in human life that millions of people over the millennia of human civilisation have been willing to die for this negative identity, or kill for it, or both. If identity is essentially negative, if there is deep doubt or lack of vision for conceiving of a substantive identity without the enemy, then there is no choice but to recreate the circumstances in which conflict with an enemy is necessary.

Another factor that drives this process of negative identity particularly concerns eras of human life in which the nature of civilisation pushes the average person towards a loss of deep identity, or positive identity. The irony here is that the liberal state, the noble effort (to which I wholeheartedly subscribe) to create a state in which everyone has civil rights without regard to religion or ethnicity, has led to an effort to homogenise culture. Above all, however, it is an unlimited form of capitalism, or the drive to expand the sale of goods by whatever means, that has led to an onslaught of common and homogenising experience, of clothing, entertainment, food, language and many other things. This has led to a massive level of identity poverty and/or ambiguity, which, in turn, has made representatives of all the major religions desperate to recapture identity through chauvinism and exclusivity, even to the point of developing completely new religious rules – which they claim as ancient – in order to solidify the negative identity of these homogenised millions of vaguely religious, but positively lost individuals around the globe.

As is often the case, we members of the human race are victims of our own noble efforts to improve the world, in this case our efforts for enlightenment and industrialisation. We have not wasted our time in trying, however. In the last few centuries we have substantially improved the quality of life for millions of people. But our arrogance prevents us from seeing what we have destroyed in the process and where we have erred. George Soros, the billionaire philanthropist, has noted that communism failed because it could not face its flaws, and that capitalism will fail also if it does not recognise its major flaws. This is very wise.

Yet it is in understanding the depth and the sources of religious violence and conflict that we understand its solutions. Correcting one of the fundamental errors of modern civilisation – namely, the tendency to ignore the importance of cultural particularity for the individual and for the community, and failing to integrate it into the meaning structures of modern society – is not a simple task. Concretely, it means we cannot enter as peacemakers into a culture or a religious society with a pre-programmed, homogenised set of values and principles, unless those principles are accompanied by an embrace of the unique identity of groups and individuals. It means we can no longer afford to bury the individual in a sea of universal principles. It requires us to express the depth of identity, including religious identity, in a way that embraces its own uniqueness but also shares with the whole society a set of shared meanings. Yet recognising this delicate combination, and seeking it in an evolving world that comprises multiple cultures and religious expressions, brings us closer to ending religious violence.

What has this to do with the biblical stranger? Everything. The stranger as the paradigm of particularity but also universalism is exactly what I am proposing for complex civilisations and for peacemaking. We must learn how to embrace our particularities and honour them. We should cease to build cultural life based solely on homogenised identities that deeply threaten so many people's commitments to their past, their families and their very sense of self. We must construct ways of relating, ways of envisioning and constructing our futures, ways of healing our pain and solving our social problems and conflicts, which embrace the particular. But that particular identity, or the identity of the stranger, cannot be one that is over against the larger world; it must see itself as *in service of the world*, as Abraham did. It must see a society that is not threatening because it does not promise to consume the minority or those who are different. This society merely calls for members to care for it, each in their own way, through the expression of their own values and customs. And the society, in turn, will set up a mode of interaction that has as its challenging task a way of negotiating and including these different contributions to an envisioned future.

It goes without saying that we, who are all strangers to each other, have our past injuries, all of them deep and important. Strangers who have the strength of deep identity, and who are not threatened with loss by society, are not as prone to reject the pain of the other. It is the deeply felt mortal threat to existence that usually shuts off the possibility of healing, contrition, even forgiveness, more than pride or stubbornness, at least in my observations. In frustration, we label lack of contrition for mistakes as stupidity, stubbornness, arrogance and the like. But, in truth, we must understand the sense of mortal threat that lies at the bottom of an angry soul. It is this threat to the soul of the strange Other that we have insufficiently seen, heard and felt. And it does not matter whether that stranger is rich or poor, powerful or weak. The dangerous alienation is the same. We have not devised our strategies of peacemaking in such a way as to heal the mortal threat to identity which, in turn, creates virulent forms of sectarianism.

Thus the particular identity is not a challenge or threat to peaceful civilisation. On the contrary, it is increasingly attractive to people all over the world. It is sectarianism based on negative identity that is most deeply threatening, a kind of sectarianism that cannot see itself as a biblical stranger in the company of strangers, all inhabiting this earth before God, capable of loving and being beloved, capable of helping and being helped, capable of seeing the Divine in the strange Other, while holding fast to the depth of one's own unique, special love relationship with God.

Resolving Conflicts

The theology of identity that I am proposing may offer much to the tragedies surrounding the conflict in Israel and Palestine, and especially the inner workings of Israeli society. Understanding this tragedy means recognising the role that sub-conflicts play in the perpetuation of the larger conflict. Often large human groups perpetuate a conflict in order to avoid facing problems that are even more terrifying than current conflicts. Secular Jewish Israel and religious Jewish Israel have been at war with each other for most of this century, but due to the convenient presence of the larger conflict with the Arab world, the war has been muted or stalemated. The fact is that anti-Semitism, the Holocaust, and the mixture of actual and perceived threats of hostile Arab states to Israeli existence have held together a people radically injured and confused by the events of the twentieth century. In addition, they are reeling, as we all are, from the advent of modern culture. Israel is experiencing a crisis in positive identity, and I would argue that Palestine has been experiencing it also. This leads to negative identity and often to a secret need to perpetuate the circumstances creating the negative identity, rather than face the deeper questions of who we are. Negative identity involves a need to abuse the stranger, emerging out of one's own experience of being a stranger. If the rule of deep identity of the stranger is 'love your neighbour as you love yourself' (Lev. 19:18), then the rule of superficial identity or negative identity is 'do unto others what they have done unto you, or before they do it unto you again'.

In Israel, the religious world and the secular, liberal world have an uncanny capacity to abuse each other and guarantee that there will be no real ability to create a society together. Thus these worlds are held together only by war with larger enemies. That is not to say that Israel has not had dangerous enemies; it has. But major parts of the electorate have perpetuated the existence of the enemy by the way in which they treat the Palestinians, without realising the deep injuries and identity crises that perpetuate this abuse.

I have tried in various ways to get each side of this sub-conflict to engage in basic conflict resolution gestures. I have especially tried to suggest conflict resolution measures that explicitly embrace and utilise all the cultures that are involved in the conflict. This is vital to the healing of the destructive element in sectarianism, and some of this work is going on in Israel, at least on the popular level. But even as the high-level peace processes with Arab and Palestinian leaders continue, deep religious rifts in both Jewish and Arab society extend a stubborn resistance to this process. This is the case despite the plain evidence that religiously motivated violence on both the Arab and the Jewish side, including bombings, random violence and assassination of high leaders, is one of the most blatant characteristics of the derailing of the Oslo accords. Why the resistance to facing the importance of religion? It has much to do with stubborn commitments on all sides to negative identities formed over against another. Furthermore, there is a fear of creating a future in which no side plays an undisputed hegemony over the culture. There is, I believe, a mortal fear of the future, because there is a mortal fear of the future of both secular and religious identities.

In addition to the secular/religious rift, it seems clear to outsiders that a flourishing culture in Israel will have to have Jewish elements and Arab elements, secular elements and religious elements. Israel will have no future without embracing the Jewish cultural and religious identity of its people. But there is also no future for an Israel that does not embrace the liberal values of civil rights, separation of synagogue and state, and freedom of religion. There is also no future for an Israel that does not embrace its indigenous culture, the culture of the Palestinians, and embrace Palestinians' role in the future of their own state, as well as in the future of Israel. Finally, there is no good future for a Palestinian state without the cultural understanding that its land is also dear on a religious level to Jewish people all over the world. Both countries will need to incorporate the love of the stranger, or Other, as social policy, making space, and even honouring the presence of the Other. This, essentially, is the embrace of the stranger, the acceptance of a marriage between the particular and the universal in the context of a civilised state of the future.

I remember once having a chance encounter with a young Jordanian Palestinian, whom I immediately liked. We engaged in conversation, and I remember how much I wanted to escape my identity as a Jew and simply meet him beyond ethnic and religious identities, beyond the wars in which the people he loved killed the people that I loved. But as I devised a basic conflict resolution strategy, that is, as I thought about how to reach out to him, all of the Jewish religious values that I had been taught as a child kept coming to mind. I ran to get him a seat, because I remembered the rabbinic text that says, 'Who is honoured? He who honours his fellow human being.' As he said things in anger, that made me angry, I remembered the ancient advice, 'Do not approach a man in his hour of anger', and 'The key to wisdom is silence.' And when I had the opportunity to help him, but hesitated, the words of Exodus 23 sprang to mind, on helping an enemy with his burden. But, above all, as he sat before me and I looked into his eyes, I imagined what he must have looked like as a child, I imagined his parents, and then I dreamed of all the places in the Torah, where God speaks of all human beings as His children. All the anger in my heart melted, even despite myself. I realised that I met him as a stranger, as an Other, who is nevertheless beloved. And I made peace with him, not just as a homogenised, universal citizen of the planet, but mainly as a Jew in all my outrageous peculiarity, meeting him with all of his peculiarities, in the presence of the Eternal Stranger.

I have also come to realise that there are so many overt symbols of my identity in my religious life. Kosher and Sabbath restrictions, my blessings obligations and all the verses and texts running through my head, give structure and identity to my moral and cognitive universe. So when I meet the Other who is somewhat like me, when I meet the Other who has been my enemy, I easily embrace him. But when I am weak in my identity I deeply fear these meetings and usually fail at them. When my identity is strong then there is no mortal threat to my Jewish identity because the structure of my identity is clear. It frees my mind and heart to enter into the Other without fear of dissolution.

Each time I engage in difficult meetings with the Christian Other, for example, a voice inside me says that I am a traitor, stepping on the graves of millions of innocent Jews throughout history who were tortured, killed or made to live miserable lives simply because they would not utter the name Jesus as a name of God. I have to live with that voice always, and I see those poor Jewish victims before my eyes all the time; I feel it much more deeply than the anger I may have at the Islamic world, despite the past forty years. I have three choices in response to that voice. I can live a life of Jewish substance and spirituality and stay completely away from the Christian world. Or I can leave the Jewish world, follow this passion I have for peacemaking, and care for all of humanity, all the while living with the guilt of that voice. Or I can give as much nourishment to the boundaries of my Jewish identity as I can without losing my vision of the love of a stranger, learning to live with that mournful voice of parents and community inside, and hoping that over time I will be able to embrace the angry voice inside as yet another beloved stranger.

The confusion I have just described inside my soul drives many of us towards no identity at all. By contrast, it is important to realise that war gives structure to identity in the absence of one, even for the best of us, even for the peacemakers. When war decreases, domestic violence increases, because the structure of identity is threatened. The answer to this is not less identity but more identity – an identity that embraces the Other in the spirit of the highest ideals of my culture or religion. But asking the questions, 'Who would I be without the war? Could I cope with life without this conflict?' becomes important. We all must ask these questions and reflect on our answers every day in order to keep conflict and war from becoming something we unconsciously perpetuate as a substitute identity.

Besides Israel, intractable conflicts involving religious identities are taking place in Bosnia, the former USSR, Sri Lanka, India, the United States, Canada and other places. Each situation requires its own answers. But the common underlying principle is that those committed to peace and broad liberal ideals may in fact be undermining their own goals by not listening to their adversaries and attempting to include them in a vision of the future. When adversaries, religious or otherwise, cannot envision themselves in the future, and if we have not tried mightily to help them envision themselves in that future, then violence seems like a viable option. It becomes a way of 'going out in a blaze of glory' as long as one expects to die anyway.

'The boundary', it seems, is a surprisingly important spiritual value and of profound importance sociologically as well. But the uses to which the boundary has been put in human history have been on the whole quite dismal. Conversely, the attempt at coercive nullification of boundaries has seen an equally evil history, to which the Jewish people can easily attest. The negotiation of the nature of the boundary, however, and the steady work on the guidelines of crossing the boundary – of embracing the stranger in all her particularity – is the key to the creation of deep and meaningful human identity.

The *ger* philosophy that I have suggested here is a theological framework for negotiating a position *vis-à-vis* the Other that makes neither the universalist, all-consuming error nor the particularist error of chauvinistic dehumanisation of the Other. It is a philosophy of seeing others and oneself as sojourners with God on this earthly plane. One loves the sojourner, joins him, but sees the boundary; and then, far from recoiling, becomes even more enamoured of the stranger by virtue of the boundary. The boundary makes one a lover and also beloved, offering love in its highest expression: as ultimate valuation of the other as an independent and treasured being. To summarise texts in both the Bible and the Koran, one thanks God and praises God for His manifold creation, for the creation of so many distinct beings and peoples, who in their very differences speak to the aesthetic and moral genius of the Creator, whose only hope for an end to estrangement is in the love that He witnesses and partakes in between the many strangers and sojourners of this sacred earth.

CHAPTER 2

A Theology of Embrace for a World of Exclusion[1]

Miroslav Volf

In his recent memoirs, *All Rivers Run to the Sea*, Elie Wiesel called the poem quoted below 'magnificent'.[2] It was written more than fifty years ago in Bucharest by a young Jewish poet little over twenty-five years of age. Listen to the unpredictable rhythms of its provocative metaphors and to the mixture of tenderness and brutality in the story it tells:

> Black milk of daybreak we drink it at evening
> we drink it at midday and morning we drink it at night
> we drink and we drink
> we shovel a grave in the air there you won't lie too cramped
> A man lives in the house he plays with his vipers he writes
> he writes when it grows dark to Deutschland your golden hair
>   Margareta
> he writes it and steps out of doors and the stars are all sparkling
>   he whistles his hounds to come close
> he whistles his Jews into rows has them shovel a grave in the ground
> he commands us play up for the dance …
>
> Black milk of daybreak we drink you at night
> we drink you at midday Death is a master aus Deutschland
> we drink you at evening and morning we drink and we drink
> this Death is ein Meister aus Deutschland his eye is blue
> he shoots you with shot made of lead shoots you level and true
> a man lives in the house your goldenes Haar Margarete
> he loses his hound on us grants us a grave in the air
> he plays with his vipers and daydreams der Tod ist ein Meister aus
>   Deutschland
> dein goldenes Haar Margarete
> dein aschenes Haar Shulamith.

You might recognise in the dark music of this poetry the first and the last stanzas of what must be one of the most remarkable literary creations about

---

[1] This essay was presented to the 1997 'Boundaries and Bonds' conference, held in Belfast, Northern Ireland, and organised by the 'Moving Beyond Sectarianism' project of the Irish School of Ecumenics.

[2] Elie Wiesel, *All Rivers Run to the Sea: Memoirs* (New York: Alfred A. Knopf, 1995), 356.

the most infamous event in the twentieth century. The event is the Holocaust; the poem is Paul Celan's 'Deathfugue'.[3] Behind the outlandish lyric about digging graves 'in the air' and 'in the ground' and about 'playing up for the dance' lies a brutal reality. It was a common practice in Nazi concentration camps to order one group of prisoners to play or sing nostalgic tunes while others dug graves or were executed. Young German men cultivated enough to occupy themselves with writing and tender enough to daydream about their girlfriends' golden hair were masters of death: they committed mass murders in cold blood and were cynical enough to grace the atrocity with music.

The Holocaust may be unique in its perpretrators' combination of barbarity and cultivation, primitivism and sophistication; it may be unique in the sheer number of murders committed; and it may be unique in the single-mindedness and technological skill with which the Nazis directed genocidal intentions against a single people, the Jews. But in many respects, a holocaust is not an anomaly in the world we live in, not a violent intruder into the otherwise peaceful house of contemporary. Death is not just a blue-eyed master 'aus Deutschland'. Rivers of blood and mountains of corpses – most recently in Bosnia and Rwanda – are a horrifying testimony to the fact that in many places in our world, the most brutal forms of exclusion are the order of the day.

What is more, there are no signs that the practice of exclusion is a short dark tunnel with the bright light of social harmony shining at its end. Rapid population growth, diminishing resources, unemployment, migration to shanty cities, and lack of education are steadily increasing the pressure on the many social faultlines of our globe. In the wake of the demise of the bi-polar world defined by socialism in the East and capitalism in the West, the tectonic plates that underlie society are defined less by ideology than by culture. As Samuel Huntington argues, 'the faultlines between major civilisations – the broadest level of cultural identity people have – will be the lines along which future battles are fought'. Though we cannot predict exactly when and where social quakes will occur or how powerful they will be, we can be sure that the earth will shake. Conditions are ripe for more Rwandas and Bosnias. In many places in the world, the soil has been well prepared and the seed of the bitter fruit of exclusion has been profusely sown. Many a person will find her cup filled with the black milk of daybreak.

In this chapter I want, first, to look briefly at the practice and, more specifically, the character of exclusion. Second, I want to offer a vision of

---

[3] Paul Celan, known for his Holocaust poetry, first published 'Deathfugue', or *'Todesfuge'*, in German in a collection of poetry entitled 'Poppy and Memories', or *Mohn und Gedachnis* (Stuttgart: Deutsche Verlags-Anstalt GmbH, 1952). Extracts cited are from John Felstiner, *Poet Survivor, Jew* (New Haven, CT: Yale University Press, 1995), 31–2.
Editors' Note: Felstiner refers to the two characters as 'Margareta' and 'Shulamith' in English, but preserves Celan's 'Margarete' and 'Sulamith' when quoting the German original. The same convention is followed in the discussion below.

embrace inspired by the character of God as revealed on the cross of Christ. Third, by building on a story from Sarajevo, I will offer some reflections on what good, if any, a soft embrace can do in the harsh world of exclusion. In conclusion, I will return to Celan's Margarete and Shulamith.

The World of Exclusion

The mad world of exclusion is too complex for me even to attempt to describe fully in the scope of this paper. I will concentrate on what one may call its inner logic, that is, on how we think and act as we exclude. I use the first-person plural when I say this because I believe the practice of exclusion is not just something that the evil and barbaric others do out there; exclusion is also what we, the good and the civilised people, do right here where we are. True, most of us do not 'whistle our Jews' and command them to sing while shovelling their own graves. Yet the tendency to exclude lurks in the dark regions of all our hearts, seeking an opportunity to find a victim.

As the term 'ethnic cleansing' – the most powerful recent metaphor for exclusion – suggests, the logic of exclusion is a logic of purity. Blood must be pure: German blood alone should run through German veins, free from all non-Aryan contamination. Territory must be pure: Serbian soil must belong to Serbs alone, cleansed of all non-Serbian intruders. Our origins must be pure: we must go back to the pristine purity of our linguistic, religious, or cultural past, shake away the dirt of otherness collected on our march through history. The goal must be pure: we must let the light of reason shine into every dark corner, or we must create a world of total virtue so as to render all moral effort unnecessary. The origins and the goal, the inside and the outside, everything must be pure: plurality and heterogeneity must give way to homogeneity and the unity of one people, one culture, one language, one book, one goal. Anything that does not fall under this all-encompassing 'one' is considered ambivalent, polluting and dangerous. It must be removed. To have a pure world, we push others out. To be pure within, we eject otherness from inside ourselves. Implicit in the drive for purity is a whole programme for arranging our social worlds – from the inner worlds of our selves to the outer worlds of our families, neighbourhoods and nations. It is a dangerous programme because it is totalitarian and governed by a logic that reduces, ejects and segregates.

In the extreme cases, we kill and drive out. To ensure that the vengeance of the dead will not be visited upon us in their progeny, we destroy their habitations and their cultural monuments. Like the robbers in the story of the Good Samaritan, we strip, beat and dump people somewhere outside our own proper space, leaving them half-dead (Luke 10:30). This is exclusion by elimination, which was at work with such shameless brutality in Stalin's Soviet Union and Hitler's Third Reich. The more subtle side of exclusion by elimination is exclusion by assimilation. You can survive, even thrive, among us, if you become like us; you can keep your life, if you give up your identity. Using the notions developed by Claude Levi-Strauss in *A World on the Wane*, we can say that exclusion by assimilation rests on a deal: we will refrain from vomiting you out if you let us swallow you up.[4]

The second, more benign, strategy of exclusion is to assign others the status of inferior beings. We make sure that they cannot live in our neighbourhoods, get certain kinds of jobs, receive equal pay or honour; they must stay in their proper place, which is to say, the place we have assigned for them. As Lucas Beauchamp's neighbours put it in William Faulkner's *Intruder in the Dust*, they must be 'niggers' first, and then we may be prepared to treat them as human beings.[5] We subjugate them so we can exploit them in order to increase our wealth or simply inflate our egos. This is exclusion by domination, spread all over the globe in more or less diffuse forms but existing most glaringly in the caste system in India and in the former apartheid policies of South Africa.

A third form of exclusion is becoming increasingly prevalent not only in the way in which the rich of the West and North relate to the poor of the South but in the way that suburbs relate to inner cities, or the jet-setting 'creators of high value' relate to the rabble beneath them. It is exclusion as abandonment. Like the priest and the Levite in the story of the Good Samaritan, we simply cross to the other side and pass by, minding our own business (Luke 10:31). If others neither have goods we want nor can perform services we need, we make sure to keep them at a safe distance. We close ourselves off from them so that their emaciated and tortured bodies can make no inordinate claims on us.

The practice of exclusion goes hand-in-hand with a whole array of emotional responses to the other, ranging from hatred to indifference. Before Israeli Prime Minister Itzaak Rabin was murdered in 1995, right-wing Israeli demonstrators carried large posters portraying him like Yasser Arafat, with *keffiyeh* on his head and blood dripping from his hands. The image was designed to generate hate, that revulsion for the other that feeds on the sense of harm or wrong suffered and is fuelled by the humiliation of not having been able to prevent it. Some of the most brutal acts of exclusion depend on hatred, and if the common shared history of individuals and communities does not contain enough reasons to hate, masters of exclusion will rewrite those histories and fabricate injuries in order to manufacture hatred.

Strangely enough, the havoc wreaked by indifference may be even greater than that brought by hatred as it is felt, lived and practised. In *Modernity and the Holocaust*, Zygmunt Bauman notes that the mass destruction of Jews in

---

[4] Claude Levi-Strauss, *A World on the Wane* (trans. John Russell; New York: Criterion Books, 1961).

[5] William Faulkner, *Intruder in the Dust* (New York: Random House, 1948), 18.

the Second World War 'was accompanied not by the uproar of emotions, but the dead silence of unconcern'.[6] Especially within a larger geographical frame of reference, where others live at a distance from us, indifference can be more deadly than hate. Whereas the fire of hatred flares up in proximity to the other and then dies down, we can sustain cold indifference over time, especially in contemporary societies. I turn my eyes away and I go about my own business. Numbed by the seeming inevitability of exclusionary practices taking place outside of my will, I start to view horror and my implication in it as normal. I reason that the road from Jerusalem to Jericho will always be littered with people beaten and left half dead; I can pass by – I *must* pass by – without much concern. The indifference that led to the prophecy of a road strewn with bodies carries within it its own fulfilment.

A Vision of Embrace

Then how should we respond to the practice of exclusion? In my book *Exclusion and Embrace*, I have suggested that as Christians we should respond by developing a theology and a practice of embrace.[7] But what is embrace? Let me try to explicate the meaning of this metaphor by briefly exploring a notion that is central to both Scripture and modern political philosophy: that of a covenant. And in order to get a handle on the covenant, I need to look briefly at the idea of 'social contracts'.

Political liberalism, which conceives life as essentially about individual self-interest, has promoted the contract as the master metaphor for social life. Plagued by fear of harm and driven by desire for comfort, individuals enter into contracts that favour them with security and gain. Contracts let each person achieve with the help of others what none could achieve alone. Civil society emerges as the offspring of such contractual interaction. But are the shoulders of contract broad enough to carry the social burden placed on it?

The social utility of contracts is indisputable; without them, life in modern societies would be nearly impossible. But will contract do as the master metaphor for social life as a whole? Does it suggest a vision of how we *should* live, a vision of the good life? To the contrary, along with a chorus of other thinkers, Robert Bellah has argued in his best-selling book *Habits of the Heart* that contractual relations render all commitments unstable and undermine social life. In order to counter the damage created by a contractual

---

[6] Zygmunt Bauman, *Modernity and the Holocaust* (New York: Cornell University Press, 1989), 74.

[7] Miroslav Volf, *Exclusion and Embrace: A Theological Exxploration of Identity, Otherness, and Reconciliation* (Nashville, TN: Abingdon Press, 1996).

understanding of human relations, he suggested we need to retrieve the covenant as the alternative master metaphor for social life.[8] With its origins in the world of religious commitments rather than business transactions, covenantal relations better express the communal and moral dimensions of human life.

The understanding of social life as covenantal has its roots in early Calvinism's so-called Calvinist monarchomachs – the fighters against monarchy. For them, the covenant between human beings was based on and preserved by God's covenant with them, and the covenant's moral foundations were supplied by the covenant-making God. The duties of human beings as God's covenant partners were expressed in the 'moral law', the Decalogue, which mapped a moral order that extended as far as the rule of the one God did and encompassed the whole of human community. So 'covenant' became a useful political category because it was first a moral category, and it became a moral category because it was at its core a theological category. It embodied the understanding that all human covenants, from family and neighbourhood to state, must be subordinate to God's inclusive covenant that encompasses the whole of humanity and is guided by substantive values.

I want to suggest, however, that for Christian reflection on social issues the new covenant of Jesus Christ is much more significant than the original covenant of God with God's people. First, the new covenant was a response to a persistent pattern of humans breaking the original covenant; because Israel has broken God's covenant, God offered a new one. In social terms, then, a covenant emerges from a backdrop of enmity, understood not as some fictive state of nature, but as a pervasive social dynamic between the people who already belong to the covenant but fail to keep it. Second, the new covenant raises the fundamental issue of how to transcribe the covenant's moral demands from 'tablets of stone' onto 'hearts of flesh' (Jer. 31:31ff.). In social terms, the new covenant suggests that we need more than rules and regulations. Rather, it is essential for covenant partners to be shaped by the covenants, they have formed so that they do not betray and tyrannise one another.

If Christian theologians want to explore the social meaning of the new covenant, they need to turn to the cross of Jesus Christ, on which they see what God did to renew the covenant that humanity broke. We can learn three things from the cross about how to renew a covenant: how to strengthen covenants that are fragile, repair those that are broken, and keep covenants from being completely undone.

First, on the cross God renews the covenant by *making space* for humanity in God's very self. The open arms of Christ on the cross are a sign that God

---

[8] Robert Bellah, *Habits of the Heart: Individualism and Commitment in American Life* (Berkeley: University of California Press, 1985).

does not want to be a God without humanity; God suffers humanity's violence in order to embrace it. What could this divine 'making-space-in-oneself' imply for our mutual relations?

I argued earlier that unlike a contract, a covenant is not simply a relationship of mutual utility but of moral commitment. We have to go a step further, however, for covenant partners are not simply moral agents who have certain duties to one another within the framework of a long-standing relationship. Precisely because a covenant is lasting, it does not allow us merely to be separate individuals, unaffected by one another or even proud of our independence. To the contrary, the very identity of each of us is formed through our relation to others. I, Miroslav Volf, am who I am not only because I am distinct from Judy Gundry-Volf, my wife, but also because over the past fifteen years I have been profoundly shaped by a relationship with her. Similarly, to be 'black' in the United States means to be in a certain relationship – all too often, an unpleasant one – to 'whites'. Our identities are shaped by others with whom we are in relationship.

For these reasons, renewing a covenant asks us to transcend the perspective of our own side and take into account the complementary view of the other. Even more, renewing a covenant means attending to shifts in the other's identity, to make space for the changing other in ourselves and to be willing to renegotiate our own identity in interaction with those of others. Each person in a covenant must understand her own behaviour and identity as complementary to the behaviour and identity of her covenantal partners. Without such complementarity and the continual readjustment of dynamic identities, moral bonds alone will not guard against the stresses a pluralistic context puts onto a convenantal relationship. Sustaining and renewing covenants require those involved to mutually work to 'make space for the other in the self' and to reshape the self in light of the other.

Second, renewing a covenant entails *self-giving*. On the cross, the new covenant was made 'in blood' (Luke 22:20). Notice that the blood of the new covenant was not the blood of a third party (an animal), shed to establish a fictive blood relation between the parties of the covenant and dramatise the consequences of breaking it. In this respect the new covenant is profoundly different from the first covenant God made with Abraham. In Genesis 15, Abraham cut the sacrificial animals in two, and 'a smoking fire pot and a flaming torch' – both symbols of theophany – passed between the halves (15:17). This unique ritual act performed by God was a pledge that God would rather 'die', much like the animals through which God passed, than break the covenant. The thought of a living God dying is difficult enough – as difficult as the thought of a faithful God breaking the covenant. At the foot of the cross, however, that difficulty widens into unbelievability. For the narrative of the cross is not a self-contradictory story about the God who died because God broke the covenant, but a truly incredible story about the God who did what God should have been neither able nor willing to do: to die because God's covenantal partner, humanity, broke the covenant.

The blood in which the new covenant was made is the blood of self-giving, even self-sacrifice. One party had broken the covenant, and the other suffered the breach because it would not let the covenant be undone. If such innocent suffering strikes us as unjust, in an important sense it *is* unjust. Yet injustice is precisely what it takes to renew a covenant. One of the biggest obstacles to repairing broken covenants in families, neighbourhoods and nations is that broken covenants invariably produce deep disagreements over what constitutes a breach and who is responsible for it. Partly because of the desire to shirk the responsibilities that accepting guilt involves, those who break a covenant do not or will not recognise that they have broken it. In a world of clashing perspectives and strenuous self-justifications, in a world of crumbling commitments and aggressive animosities, covenants are kept and renewed because those who, from their perspective, have not broken the covenant are willing to do the hard work of repairing it. Such work is self-sacrificial; something of the individual or communal self dies performing it. Yet the self by no means perishes, but is renewed as the truly communal self, fashioned in the image of the triune God who will not be without the other.

Third, the new covenant is *eternal*. God's self-giving on the cross is a consequence of the fact that the covenant is everlasting. And the covenant is everlasting because God is unable to give up the partner who has broken it. 'How can I hand you over, O Israel?' Hosea's God asks rhetorically, with 'compassion grown warm and tender' (Hos. 11:8). Bound to Israel with 'bonds of love', God cannot hand over Israel; God's commitment is irrevocable and God's covenant indestructible. Similarly, while a political covenant may be dissolved, a broader social covenant is strictly unconditional and therefore 'eternal'. It can be broken, but it cannot be undone. Every breach of such a covenant still takes place within its ongoing life, and the struggle for justice and truth on behalf of the victims of the breach takes place within that context. Nobody is outside a social covenant, and no deed is imaginable that would put someone beyond its borders. The will to give ourselves to others and to welcome them, to readjust our identities to make space for them, comes before any judgement about them other than that of simply identifying them as human. The will to embrace precedes any truth about others and any construction of our sense of justice. This will is absolutely indiscriminate and strictly immutable. It transcends our efforts to map good and evil onto our social world.

Here, then, is a vision of a new covenant that is foremost a vision of embrace: to embrace, we need to keep readjusting our complementary identities, we need to keep repairing covenants even if we have not broken them, and we need to keep refusing to let covenants ever be undone. This is exactly what the Father in the story of the Prodigal Son did when he embraced his returning son. God's new covenant was God's embrace of the humanity that keeps breaking the covenant; our covenants, modelled on God's new one, are our way of embracing one another – even our enemies.

Embrace Instead of Exclusion

Someone might object that the practice of embrace – never giving up on the other, sacrificing the self, and cultivating a willingness to rethink our thoughts and reshape our very identities in response to the other – will be not only inefficient but positively harmful in the harsh world of exclusion. Let me respond by commenting on a story found in one of the most profound reflections on the war in Bosnia, Zlatko Dizdarevic's *Sarajevo: A War Journal*. Here is the story as he tells it:

> In Sarajevo a three-year-old girl playing outside her home is hit by a sniper's bullet. Her horrified father carries her to the hospital. Bleeding, she hovers between life and death. Only after her father, a big hulk of a man, has found a doctor to care for her does he allow himself to burst into tears. The television camera records his words. These words, every one of them belong in an anthology of humanism, helplessness, and forgiveness at its most extreme – not so much forgiving the criminal who shot a three-year-old child, as forgiving the wild beasts for being wild beasts, for being debased by an evil that destroys every human impulse. Two of his sentences give rise to thoughts that will linger long past today or tomorrow. The first comes when the stricken father invites the unknown assassin to *have a cup of coffee with him so that he [the assassin] can tell him, like a human being, what has brought him to do such a thing.* Then he says, aware that this question may not elicit any *human response*: 'One day her tears will catch up with him …'

After relating this story, Dizdarevic offers the following comment, surprising in its negative assessment of the father's offer and of its implications for the future of Bosnia:

> There is absolutely nothing to be done for this nation. It will never attain justice and happiness if it cannot bring itself to recognise an executioner as an executioner, a murderer as a murderer, a criminal as a criminal. If the most barbaric act imaginable in this war, a sniper shooting at a three-year-old girl playing in front of her own home, elicits only an invitation to a cup of coffee and hope for forgiveness, then Bosnia-Herzegovina doesn't stand much chance to survive.[9]

The murderous act of deliberately shooting a three-year-old, explicable only in terms of the radical evil of the perpetrator, demands a strict and unmerciful punishment, not an offer of understanding and forgiveness, reasons Dizdarevic. Wild beasts – those with every human impulse destroyed by evil –

---

[9] Zlatko Dizdarevic, *Sarajevo: A War Journal* (New York: Fromm International, 1993), 15–16, original emphasis.

must be tracked down and then either killed or driven out, not invited to participate in a ritual of friendship. Without punishment of the evildoers and banishment of wild beasts, argues Dizdarevic, Bosnia will attain neither justice nor happiness. From this perspective, that big hulk of a man who wants to share a cup of coffee with the assassin was a sentimental fool who, if he had things his way, would have hurled any nation into perdition.

I want to propose a different reading of this story than the one Dizdarevic offers. I am not about to suggest that the executioner should not be recognised and named as executioner. Murder cannot simply be disregarded. Truth must be told, and justice must be established. Neither am I about to suggest that the perpetrators should not be stopped, that they should be allowed to continue with their atrocities until they are 'somehow' persuaded by the power of forgiveness. The instruments of evil must be taken out of their hands. But I do want to suggest that the best way – the Christian way – to respond to iron and blood is not with iron and blood. The hope for Bosnia, indeed the hope for a whole world infested by the evil of exclusion, lies precisely in men and women who, despite the outrage committed against them, will muster enough strength to want to invite the perpetrator for a cup of coffee and inquire of him, as a human being, what has 'brought him to do such a thing'. The hope of Bosnia lies in those who believe in the power of tears to catch up with the enemy because they are persuaded, as E.M. Cioran puts it, that tears are not 'swallowed up by the earth' but that 'by paths unknown to us, they all go upwards'. The hope of Bosnia and of our whole world, wrecked by exclusion, lies in those who, despite enduring humiliation and suffering, have not given up on the will to embrace the enemy.

Why should one start walking the difficult road toward embrace in the midst of raging exclusion? Because we must resist being sucked into the vortex of inhumanity. 'The rifle butt in the back', writes Dizdarevic elsewhere in the book, 'shatters everything civilisation has ever accomplished, removes all finer human sentiments, and wipes out any sense of justice, compassion, and forgiveness.'[10] If the rifle butt in the back creates inhumanity, then the hope for Bosnia cannot lie in a rifle butt in the back of the perpetrator. For this would only ensure that a sense 'of justice, compassion, and forgiveness' will forever be replaced by the rage of revenge and hatred. Though Dizdarevic seems to expect 'justice and happiness' from unforgiveness, at times he is aware of the way in which people who find themselves helpless and enraged can become caught in self-fulfilling cyles of hatred and fear. He writes, 'But what we'll neither forgive nor forget is that they have broken what is the best in us; they have taught us to hate.'[11] As hate leads to unforgiveness and unforgiveness reinforces the hate, the downward spiral of despair keeps

---

[10] Dizdarevic, *Sarajevo*, 54.
[11] Dizdarevic, *Sarajevo*, 34.

turning. The hope of Bosnia, the hope of our world, lies with men and women who are determined to fight evil every step of the way while at the same refusing to let the rifle butt do its work on their souls after it is finished doing its work on their bodies.

The refusal of victims to let violence committed against them contaminate their souls must be one of the most difficult and most heroic acts a human being is capable of. Dizdarevic slights it by describing the response of the father in his story as 'only an invitation to a cup of coffee and hope for forgiveness'. Does he think that the father does not condemn the act? Does he think that no rage had to be attended to before the invitation could be offered? Does he not see what a superhuman effort it would take to look the assassin in the eyes and ask 'why' instead of letting the flood of legitimate accusations flow? Without such heroism, which seeks to offer forgiveness without dispensing it glibly, strives to establish communion without condoning evil, and reflects the very heart of the triune God, we may be doomed, in Paul Celan's words, to drink the black milk of daybreak, to 'drink it at evening', to 'drink it at midday and morning', to 'drink it at night'.

Margareta and Shulamith

'Deathfugue' ends with the following lines: 'dein goldenes Haar Margarete/ dein aschenes Haar Sulamith'. Margareta is the blonde-haired German girl – the romantic ideal drawn from Goethe's poetry – of whom the SS executioner tenderly daydreams. Shulamith is no 'ash blond but the "black and comely" maiden in the Song of Songs ... Shulamith is the beloved par excellence and is seen as the Jewish people itself,' writes Celan's biographer John Felstiner. At the end of his comments on 'Deathfugue', he notes that when Celan twins Shulamith and Margareta, 'nothing can reconcile them. Celan's word *aschenes* [the ashen hair of Shulamith] tells why'.[12]

No one can blame Celan for leaving Margareta and Shulamith unreconciled, side-by-side, as symbols of the unbridgeable gulf between the Jews and the Germans created by unspeakable evil. When he wrote 'Deathfugue' in 1947, the ovens that had sent millions of his compatriots, including his parents, to their 'grave in the air' had barely cooled down. But what about followers of Jesus Christ, the Messiah who, as the Apostle Paul writes, died for us, the ungodly and the enemies? 'Deathfugue' is a kind of mission statement in reverse, a poetic narration of what we do when, instead of seeking to anticipate a world in which love of God and of neighbour will reign, we are bent on anticipating hell. A testimony of atrocity and grief, 'Deathfugue' is a powerful reminder that in a world of exclusion – a world we

---

[12] John Felstiner, *Poet, Survivor, Jew*, 38.

ourselves are part of and have helped create – we must engage in the arduous task of reconciliation.

Reconciliation between God and humanity is at the heart of the Gospel we proclaim; reconciliation between human beings estranged on account of injustice, deception and violence must be at the centre of the mission we pursue. This difficult task of reconciliation should command our imagination, our intelligence and our resources. We should not rest until Margareta and Shulamith, blacks and whites, Bosnians, Croats and Serbs have extended their arms to each other in joyful embrace.

CHAPTER 3

Islam and Reconciliation:
A Hermeneutical and Sociological
Approach

David Herbert

The Believers are a single Brotherhood: so make peace and reconciliation between your two (contending) brothers: and fear Allah, that ye may receive mercy.

(Qur'an, Sura 49:10)

Allah fills with peace and faith the heart of one who swallows his anger, even though he is in a position to give vent to it.

(Qur'an, Sura 42:37)

The rejection of non-violent methods is [partly] related to the threat associated with the global invasion of Islamic communities by modernization, including industrial and urban lifestyles. Unfortunately, in the minds of many Muslims and non-Muslims [in the Middle East], non-violence is associated with Western Christian philosophy. As a result, they assume that a 'de-authentication' of Islamic culture and tradition will ensue from a Muslim embrace of non-violence. Underlying such an approach is a misconception that conflates non-violence with Christianity and modernization.[1]

I have ... never heard a phrase used in Arabic that would translate, however idiomatically, as 'the system failed' – whether it be applied to the legal system or any other part of the political structure. Indeed, the idea of institutional failure is virtually unimaginable when persons ... take up all the space of institutions.[2]

In the aftermath of 11 September 2001, the mobilisation of Islam as a political ideology by a range of state and non-state groups across the world, and the increased suspicion and hostility towards Islam heightened by these events, one approaches the topic of 'Islam and reconciliation' with some trepidation. In this chapter I aim to do three things. First, I will consider some ways in which Islamic texts are used in the contemporary Muslim-majority world, and, in this context, explore some of the hermeneutic arguments that have developed among predominantly Muslim scholars over texts which bear on attitudes towards and understandings of reconciliation amongst Muslims. As the first two quotations make clear, there are resources at the heart of the

---

[1] M. Abu Nimer, *Nonviolence and Peace Building in Islam: Theory and Practice* (Gainesville, FL: University Press of Florida, 2003), 121.
[2] L. Rosen, *The Culture of Islam* (Chicago, IL: University of Chicago Press, 2002), 71.

Islamic textual tradition which appear to be highly supportive of an ethos of reconciliation; but there is dispute over the scope of applicability and meaning of these texts in view of the broader scriptural tradition and conditions of contemporary interpretation.

Second, I will consider some examples of reconciling practices in contemporary Muslim communities, both those of a more traditional nature and those influenced or instigated by Western agencies. In reality these two sets of practices overlap, but it is important to consider them separately from an analytic standpoint. As indicated in the third quotation above, this is partly because of the kind of obstacles that inhibit adoption of methods perceived as Western in origin, and partly because the character of some traditional practices raises questions about their suitability in contemporary contexts. As one participant in a traditional third-party mediation process in Gaza put it: 'You can be certain that the outcome is not going to be in favour of the poor, even if justice requires it.'[3]

Third, I will consider these arguments and practices against a broader socio-cultural background of arguments about the character and structure of Muslim communities and societies, and about the relationship between Islam, civil society, democracy and human rights. If reconciliation is fundamentally a social practice, that is, something enacted in the spaces and connections between individuals, communities and nations, then teasing out these relationships is fundamental to developing an understanding of what reconciliation can mean in Muslim societies and in situations involving Muslim participants. I have described the approach here as both hermeneutical and sociological, because I believe that it is important to understand both the meaning of reconciliation for social actors involved, and the cultural and structural constraints acting on them.

One point of particular importance brought to light by recent ethnographic work is that whereas it may once have been assumed that patterns of social order, authority and meaning associated with traditional Muslim societies (such as tribalism, charismatic religious leadership and Sufi religious practices) would inevitably be weakened by modernisation, it now appears that such patterns and practices are much more capable of adapting to modern conditions than was once thought. Hence the range of possible trajectories for cultural traditions (and hence patterns of intercultural transaction) contingent on modernisation has greatly increased. In these circumstances, reconciliation cannot be assumed to mean convergence on Western cultural norms of, for example, individual human rights, the bearer of which is a self readily divisible from his or her social roles. This is because such a conception of the self has limited influence in Muslim-majority societies, even ones strongly influenced by urbanisation and other aspects of

---

[3] Abu Nimer, *Nonviolence and Peace Building in Islam*, 207.

modernisation.[4] As the final quotation above suggests, social processes of reconciliation may need to be thought about differently in highly personalised cultures. However, this kind of generalisation about cultures is also problematic.

This is clearly a lot of ground to cover in a single chapter, making the risk of over-simplification considerable. Muslim-majority societies are not uniform, and many Muslims now live in Western countries where they are a minority. Many of their assumptions relevant to their understandings of reconciliation – the social and political role of religion, the scope of private choice, and of obligations to kinship networks – are influenced by that context, whether in the direction of convergence, reaction or various forms of hybrid. Given the global influence of modern systems, institutions and connectivity, not least amongst migrant groups, distinctions between West and non-West are also problematic, as many scholars have argued.[5] In particular, generalisations about cultural systems – such as the absence of the differentiated self, personalisation of social networks and problems of building depersonalised institutions, as found by Rosen in his studies of North African Muslim-majority societies – appear to run counter to universal humanist assumptions that arguably underlie much work in reconciliation studies. They may smack of the kind of cultural essentialism famously attacked by Said.[6]

However, a range of ethnographic studies, both of Muslim culture in general and of peace-building activities in particular, continue to throw up evidence of persistent and evolving cultural difference, as well as increasing recognition of and ambivalence towards Western norms such as human rights and gender equality.[7] Thus we simply must find ways to deal with this mottled pattern of both universality and difference, regardless of perceptions of political correctness.

First, then, I turn to an examination of some of the ways and contexts in which Islamic textual sources are currently interpreted, and hence to a consideration of resources for reconciliation in the Islamic textual tradition.

Contexts for the Interpretation of Islamic Texts

The major textual sources of Islam are the Qur'an and *hadith* (traditions), especially traditions about the Prophet (*sunna*). The former consists of

---

[4] See Rosen, *The Culture of Islam*, and G. Starrett, *Putting Islam to Work: Education, Politics and Religious Transformation in Egypt* (Berkeley, Los Angeles and London: University of California Press, 1998).

[5] R. King, *Orientalism and Religion* (London: Routledge, 1999).

[6] E. Said, *Orientalism* (London: Penguin, 1978).

[7] K. Dwyer, *Arab Voices: the Human Rights Debate in the Middle East* (London: Routledge, 1991); A. Karam, *Women, Islamisms and the State: Contemporary Feminisms in Egypt* (London: Macmillan, 1998).

revelations to Muhammad and was collated to reach its final textual form within thirty years or so of his death.[8] The *hadith* were passed on by oral and written traditions, and collated into major collections about 250–300 years after the death of the Prophet.[9] These collectors established a system for discerning the authenticity of this vast collection of material based on the reliability of the chain of transmission (*isnad*) from the Prophet or his companions. The Qur'an and *sunna* are two of four recognised sources of Islamic law (*sharia*) in Sunni tradition, the others being *qiyas* (reasoning by analogy from the former two sources) and *ijma* ('consensus'), which has for most of history been understood as the consensus of religious scholars (*ulama*), who issue *fatawa*, 'legal judgements' (or *fatwas* in post-Rushdie Anglicised form), on controversial issues.

Historically the *ulama* have tended to be supportive of the state while retaining a certain amount of independence from it, an autonomy materially based (as with medieval Christian monasticism) on property endowments (*waqf*). But since the expansion of the modern state, often including much nationalisation of property, governments have had more direct influence over the *ulama*, and have often sought to use them to legitimise state action. This process of co-option has somewhat undermined their credibility, perhaps especially amongst the more Western-influenced elite.[10] Arguably, the absence of a central religious authority (compared with Rome for Roman Catholicism) has also weakened the resistance of the *ulama* to state influence (although Al-Azhar university in Cairo has played a significant transnational leadership role in the Sunni world, and also Qom in the Shi'ite world). Recent surveys in some societies enable us to gauge the extent of erosion of confidence in the *ulama*. In fact, in spite of increased criticism, the *ulama* remain quite widely respected across Muslim societies, depending on national and local political conditions. A recent study in the three most populous Muslim-majority societies found that just over half of respondents in Egypt and Indonesia (53 and 55 per cent, respectively) and 40 per cent in Pakistan expressed 'a lot of trust' in the *ulama*, while only about a fifth (19, 18 and 21 per cent, respectively) said they had 'no trust' in them.[11]

However, while public trust in the *ulama* may remain fairly high (and this must be seen in a context in which the credibility of state institutions has been substantially undermined), the *ulama*'s monopoly on the interpretation of

---

[8] A. Rippin, *Muslims: Their Religious Beliefs and Practices. Volume 1: The Formative Period* (London: Routledge, 1990), 24.

[9] Rippin, *Muslims*, 37.

[10] I. Abu-Rabi, 'A Post-September 11 Critical Assessment of Modern Islamic History', in I. Markham and I. Abu-Rabi (eds), *11 September: Religious Perspectives on the Causes and Consequences* (Oxford: Oneworld, 2001), 32–3.

[11] R. Hassan, *Faithlines: Muslim Conceptions of Islam and Society* (Oxford: Oxford University Press, 2002), 158.

Islam's sacred texts has been considerably eroded and subjected to a variety of challenges. Thus modernist critics have argued that the *ulama*'s traditional education ill equips them to face the challenges of the modern world.[12] Feminist scholars such as the Moroccan Fatima Mernissi have acquired knowledge of the *hadith* tradition and used it to challenge the basis of popular sayings used to limit the public role of women.[13] But most significantly, unprecedented levels of literacy, a state education which teaches children to read Islamic tradition as a source of practical knowledge, the growth of private mosques and the spread of communications technologies which enable the rapid spread of a range of views and are difficult to regulate have culmulatively produced a proliferation of interpretations of these sources.[14] In a process analogous to the Protestant Reformation in Christianity, each person becomes their own interpreter, and a range of views are able to become popular, or at least influential for some. As one commentator writes, 'The upshot of all these changes is that at the beginning of the twenty-first century, Islamic authority has badly fragmented and competing *fatawa* [legal opinions] are flying thick and fast.'[15]

One notorious example of the exercise of this interpretative freedom and opportunity for dissemination is the story of Muhammed Abd al-Salam al-Faraj, a self-styled handyman preacher in a family-built mosque in Cairo's slums, who produced a pamphlet in the late 1970s. This simplified the argument of Islamic radical Sayyid Qutb who posited that unjust Muslim rulers should be regarded as illegitimate, and developed its own, based on a novel reading of a thirteenth-century Islamic scholar ibn Taimiyya. Faraj drew the conclusion that 'We have to establish the rule of God's religion in our country first ... There is no doubt that the first battlefield for *jihad* is the extermination of these infidel leaders.'[16] Inspired by the pamphlet, a young army officer, Islambuli, approached Faraj with a plot to assassinate Anwar Sadat, Egypt's president since 1970. On 26 September 1981, Islambuli and three accomplices halted an armoured car they were parading in past the President, and hurled grenades supplied by Faraj at Sadat, killing him and several of his entourage.[17]

---

[12] Abu-Rabi, 'A Post-September 11 Critical Assessment of Modern Islamic History', 35.

[13] F. Mernissi, *Women and Islam: An Historical and Theological Inquiry* (Oxford: Blackwell, 1988), 1–15.

[14] G. Starrett, *Putting Islam to Work: Education, Politics and Religious Transformation in Egypt* (Berkeley, Los Angeles and London: University of California Press, 1998); E. Abdo, *No God But God: Egypt and the Triumph of Islam* (Oxford: Oxford University Press, 2000).

[15] C. Murphy, *Passion for Islam: Shaping the Modern Middle East: The Egyptian Experience* (London: Scribner, 2002), 197–8.

[16] A. Shadid, *The Legacy of the Prophet* (Oxford: Westview, 2002), 76.

[17] Shadid, *The Legacy of the Prophet*, 78.

Islamic textual sources are then open to interpretations that legitimise violence against the state. On the other hand, they are also used to support violence on behalf of the state (at least by a Muslim ruler), and, as we shall see, to support nonviolent approaches to conflict. This openness of ancient textual sources, and the success of political groups of all persuasions in co-opting them, has led one sceptical commentator to argue that 'No ... essential Islam exists: as one Iranian thinker put it, Islam is a sea in which it is possible to catch any fish one wants ... [T]he answer as to why this or that interpretation [is] put on Islam resides ... not in the religion and its texts but in the contemporary needs of those articulating an Islamic politics.'[18]

This context is important for assessing the potential for these sources to be used as a resource for reconciliation. However, I would argue that while textual sources underdetermine contemporary meanings – or you can argue with interpreters who fundamentally disagree until the cows come home, and never secure agreement – this means neither that all hermeneutics are pointless, nor that texts are simply the unresisting victims of their interpreters. Rather, making the hermeneutical argument for nonviolent, reconciliation-friendly readings matters because hermeneutical arguments, albeit indirectly, have social consequences. In addition, texts offer what might be articulated as a kind of 'resistance' to their interpreters; they are not infinitely plastic, and they offer a hermeneutical horizon of images, tropes and stories which subtly influence their readers even if they do not determine particular readings.

Furthermore, Halliday's scepticism is expressed in an international context in which powerful voices both in the West and in the Muslim-majority world argue the exact opposite. That is, they advocate 'essentialist' concepts of Islam, meaning they support the idea that the tradition has one single correct meaning or position on any matter, and that all other interpretations are deviant. Essentialist tendencies in the West include media presentations of Islam as a homogeneous 'Other', especially in the post-Cold War period.[19] The increasing dominance of television as a global communication medium, and its tendency to favour clear, simple presentation of information over complex argument, leads to a propensity to reinforce existing stereotypes. There have been attempts to counter this tendency by presenting a diverse picture of Islam as, for example, the British media has done since *The Satanic Verses* controversy (1988–90). But the fact that conflict is often more 'newsworthy' than cooperation means that images of conflict tend to outnumber and outweigh more harmonious images and stories.[20] Beyond the mass media,

---

[18] F. Halliday, *Nation and Religion in the Middle East* (London: Saqi, 2000), 134.

[19] E. Said, *Covering Islam* (London: Penguin, 1997 [1981]).

[20] T. Liebes, *Reporting the Arab–Israeli Conflict* (London: Routledge, 1997).

international relations and popular philosophy literatures also tend to oversimplify the diversity of Islamic groups.[21]

In Muslim-majority societies essentialist voices include authoritarian governments keen to assert official versions of Islam, and Islamists – a broad term denoting those who argue that a return to Islam is central to Muslim revival in all areas of life – keen to challenge their authority. States have tended to use their control of the mass media to reinforce their message, with Islamist groups countering through 'micro media', such as videos and audio tapes. Recently, rapidly expanding satellite networks such as al-Jazeera, founded in 1996, have increased access to television for Islamist voices – witness the broadcast of bin Laden's videos – hence Arab audiences' access to Arabic and other language media sources from across the region and internationally.[22] However, in spite of this diversification, Islamist and state sources predominate, and both tend to convey stereotypical images of the West.

Yet accepting that there are strong forces favouring an over-unified presentation of Islam is not the same as embracing Halliday's apparent position: that Islam is purely at the mercy of its interpreters and exerts no shaping force at all on the modern politics pursued in its name. Rather, between essentialist readings and total relativisation of its meanings, it is important to articulate a position which asserts that there are a plurality of possible readings of the Islamic textual tradition, including strands that strongly support a reconciling ethos. Hence, acknowledging that there are many Muslim voices and histories, and that the presentation of Islam both in the West and the Muslim-majority world is prone to bias and distortion, I shall attempt to present a balanced view of a small sample of Islamic textual traditions relevant to the topic of reconciliation.

Abu-Nimer sees three main strands of interpretation in a rapidly growing academic literature 'that addresses the question of whether and how Islam as a religion supports principles and values of non-violence, peace and war'.[23] The first group sees Islamic tradition as basically war-like, and emphasises military interpretations of the concept of *jihad*. Some of these commentators, like Gilles Kepel and Bernard Lewis, have been quite influential amongst Western audiences.[24] A second group argues that Islam only legitimises the use of violence under quite clearly defined conditions, and this literature

---

[21] S. Huntington, *The Clash of Civilizations and the Remaking of the World Order* (New York: Simon and Schuster, 1996); P. Berman, *Terror and Liberalism* (London: Norton, 2002).

[22] M. Steger, *Globalization: A Very Short Introduction* (Oxford: Oxford University Press, 2003), 7.

[23] Abu Nimer, *Nonviolence and Peace Building in Islam*, 25.

[24] G. Kepel, *The Revenge of God: The Resurgence of Islam, Christianity and Judaism in the Modern World* (Cambridge: Polity, 1994); B. Lewis, *The Crisis of Islam* (London: Weidenfeld and Nicholson, 2003).

tends to argue for a position approximating to the just war tradition in Christianity.[25] Although the concept is not necessarily central when thinking about Islam and reconciliation, the issue of *jihad* dominates the literature; its proper interpretation is likely to be in the background of many discussions, and so warrants some consideration here. Finally, a third group of scholars argue for a strong nonviolent, reconciliation-supportive strand to the tradition.

Jihad and the Problematic Assumption of Muslim Political Domination

The concept of *jihad* ('struggle') is central to Islamic legitimisation of the use of force, and has been subject to a range of interpretations. While discussion in this section will focus on the external meanings of *jihad* which sanction the use of physical force, it should be noted that *jihad* also presents an internal imperative to overcome temptation, develop spiritual life and struggle for social justice without physical conflict. In this latter sense *jihad* can be a powerful resource not only for nonviolent resistance but for reconciliation, especially in so far as the latter involves a struggle to overcome one's desire for vengeance and struggles to make peace.

Interpretations of the external *jihad* range from an insistence that *jihad* is properly only a defensive war launched with the aim of 'establishing justice, equity and protecting basic human rights'[26] to the view that it is properly understood as 'armed struggle for the defence *or advancement* of Muslim power ... until all the world either adopts the Muslim faith or submits to Muslim rule'.[27] Given this range of interpretation, it is particularly important to understand the development of the extrinsic sense of *jihad* in the context of early Islamic history.

One of the main thrusts of the Qur'an is a hatred of the *fitna* (civil war or strife) endemic amongst the nomadic tribes of the Arabian Peninsula into which Muhammad was born. Against this anarchy, Islam asserts strict limits on what is permissible in warfare. Overall, the solution to *fitna* which the Qur'an proposes is the unification of warring factions in submission to Allah. This solution was highly effective in that time and place, but ironically, however, was also perhaps one of the reasons for Muslim involvement in conflict in the modern period. From the time of the *hijra* (622 CE), when Muhammad's persecuted followers fled Mecca and negotiated themselves

---

[25] H. Zawati, *Is Jihad a Just War?* (Lampeter: Edwin Mellen, 2002); A. Sachidena, 'The Justification of Violence in Islam', in J.P. Burns (ed.), *War and its Discontents: Pacifism and Quietism in the Abrahamic Traditions* (Washington, DC: Georgetown University Press, 1996).

[26] Zawati, *Is Jihad a Just War?*, 111.

[27] B. Lewis, *The Crisis of Islam* (London: Weidenfeld and Nicholson, 2003), 24–5, emphasis added.

into a position of political power in Medina, the sacred sources of Islam presuppose a situation in which Islam is politically dominant, or in which it will eventually become so. The Islamic empire's expansion until 750 CE, as far as the Indus Valley to the East, and to the western tip of Northern Africa and the Iberian peninsula, gave little reason to revise this perspective.

By the time the Islamic expansion was halted, the connection between divine and political unity (*tawhid*), and thus the assumption of Muslim political authority, was well embedded in Islamic tradition. Hence the world is perceived as divided into *dar al-Islam* ('house of Islam', in which Islam is politically dominant) and *dar al-harb* ('house of war', in which Islamic rule is absent). Between these domains only temporary truce (*dar al-sulh*) ameliorates conflicts. Scholars seeking to challenge this classic division of the world need to argue that it 'was dictated by particular events, and did not necessitate a permanent state of hostility between these territories'.[28] Within the politically controlled territories, subject peoples of recognised religious groups were allowed limited autonomy over their affairs in exchange for payment of a poll tax (*jizya*). Jews and Christians were initially included in this category, which was later extended to Zoroastrians in Persia, and by the Mughals to Hindus in India. This autonomous status generally compares favourably with that of subordinate groups in medieval Christendom, but none the less was an inferior role which does not equate with modern standards of equality or citizen rights.

So, until the modern era, Islamic political history did not involve power sharing between groups of different religious convictions on an equal footing. This in itself is nothing unusual in the history of world religions, since pre-modern political formations tended to resolve religious differences through social stratification, whether by the subordination of Jews in medieval Christendom or of lower castes in the Hindu-dominated Indian caste system. It was only through the division of Western Christendom, brought about by the Reformation (sixteenth century) and the subsequent strife of the wars of religion (seventeenth century), that Europe developed a different way to contain religious difference: through the gradual process of religious belief and practice coming to be seen as a private rather than public matter. This process has not occurred widely in the Muslim world where the connection between political legitimacy and religious orthodoxy (or at least conformity) remains. For example, a survey conducted in 1996–97 in the most populous Muslim countries found that 89 per cent of Egyptians, 84 per cent of Indonesians and 74 per cent of Pakistanis agreed with the proposition that a 'person who says there is no Allah is likely to hold dangerous political views'.[29] Such views raise questions about the role of minorities and the

---

[28] Zawati, *Is Jihad a Just War?*, 5.
[29] Hassan, *Faithlines*, 63.

development of democracy in the Muslim-majority world, an issue to which we shall return in the third section on broader contextual factors shaping prospects for and understandings of reconciliation.

It is fair to say, therefore, that Islam's sacred sources contain an assumption of Islamic political authority, support defensive war, and historically have mostly been understood as legitimising expansive war aimed at extending Islamic political authority. However, this is not the whole story; a number of Muslims have argued that it is necessary to move beyond traditional understandings of relationships with 'others', and that the Islamic tradition has deep resources for doing so.[30] Hence there is also a type of literature, smaller than that on *jihad* but growing, which 'focuses on core Islamic values that provide the basis for articulating the essential premises of active non-violence, such as *'adl* (justice), *ihsan* (benevolence), *rahma* (compassion), and *hikma* (wisdom).[31] To this one may also add *sulh* (reconciliation). It is to these concepts and their contemporary development that I now turn.

Theological Resources for Reconciliation in Islam

> The recompense for an injury is an equal injury thereto (in degree): but if a person forgives and makes reconciliation, his reward is due from Allah.
>
> (Qur'an, Sura 42:40)

> [A]lthough the use of force is prescribed in the Qur'an under specific and strict conditions, nevertheless, Islamic values systematically give higher ground to forgiveness than to revenge or violence.[32]

Scholars who argue that there is a strong warrant in the Qur'an and *hadith* for rooting an Islamic ethic of nonviolence point to the range of virtues extolled in this tradition which supports such an ethos. As well as justice, benevolence and compassion, *'amal* (service), *yakeen* (faith) and *mahabbah* (love) have been highlighted.[33] Supportive values are also found in the Islamic legal tradition, including *shura* (mutual consultation), *ijma* (consensus) and *ijtihad* (independent judgement), and these are particularly relevant to processes of reconciliation because they involve nonviolent methods for settling disputes, or for dealing with post-conflict situations. The scope of both *shura* and *ijma* has been considerably extended by recent commentators. Traditionally, the former has meant consultation amongst elders, but has been extended to all adults, and interpreted as a mandate for democracy. *Ijma* has similarly been extended from consensus amongst scholars to a broader public.

---

[30] Sachidena, 'The Justification of Violence in Islam'.

[31] Abu Nimer, *Nonviolence and Peace Building in Islam*, 37.

[32] Abu Nimer, *Nonviolence and Peace Building in Islam*, 43.

[33] Abu Nimer, *Nonviolence and Peace Building in Islam*, Chapter 2.

Such developments in interpretation depend on the legitimacy of *ijtihad* – literally, 'effort', and from the same root as *jihad* – that is, new interpretation of the Qur'an and *sunna*. Debate on this has been at the heart of controversy between modernist and traditionalist legal commentators for the last 150 years because the consensus among the latter has been that *ijtihad* ended in the tenth century CE. This event, known as the 'closing of the gate of *ijtihad*', has historically exerted a powerful conservative influence on Sunni jurisprudence (*fiqh*), which has persisted to the present. Shi'as, by contrast, never ceased the practice of *ijtihad*, and indeed its use has increased since the mid-nineteenth century.[34] But even amongst Sunnis, since the mid-nineteenth century many reformers have argued for reopening the gate of *ijtihad*,[35] and indeed have challenged the legitimacy of the original 'closing of the gate':

> During the period when Baghdad was under the mercy of the nomadic warriors of central Asia [Moghuls, fourteenth century CE], the jurists in Iraq reached a wrong consensus to close the door of *ijtihad* which they had not practised much anyway since the tenth century AD. No one, in fact, had a right to put a stop to the process of *ijtihad*.[36]

In contemporary Islam, then, there are opportunities for rethinking the tradition in response to new challenges. This is precisely what some scholars argue needs to happen in relation to ideas of nonviolence, so that these should assume a much more central place in the tradition. Hence, where most invocations to reconcile are made to Muslims, and while peacemaking between Muslims and other peoples of the book are advocated, this has been traditionally understood as applying to temporary conditions of truce prior to a future Muslim hegemony, and contemporary conditions challenge this tradition. Hence in a context of global interdependencies, threats of mass destruction, and a geo-political setting in which Muslim-majority states coexist in equality with non-Muslim ones at least formally, some argue that 'past juridical decisions have become irrelevant in the modern system of international relations, and they are thus unable to shed light on the pressing task of recognising religious pluralism as a cornerstone of human relations'.[37]

Hermeneutically, one of the key points underpinning such arguments is that already in the life of the Prophet (especially in the first Meccan period) there is a template for Muslim approaches to living under conditions without political hegemony. In these circumstances, which included persecution, the

---

[34] M. Momen, *An Introduction to Shi'a Islam* (New Haven, CT and London: Yale University Press, 1985).

[35] Exemplars of the practice include Muhammad 'Abduh in Egypt and Muhammad Iqbal in India. See J. Esposito, *Islam: The Straight Path* (Oxford: Oxford University Press, 1994 2nd edn), 116.

[36] A. Rahman, *Shari'ah: The Islamic Law* (London: Ta-Ha, 1984), 69.

[37] A. Sachidena, *The Islamic Roots of Democratic Pluralism* (New York: Oxford University Press, 2000), 49.

nascent Muslim community adopted a nonviolent stance. However, traditionalists may counter such arguments by pointing out that under the Islamic legal principle of *naskh* (abrogation), where there is conflict between earlier and later suras, the later overrides the earlier, thus privileging the Medinan period over the Meccan. Yet many unabrogated verses advocating tolerance from the Meccan period remain.

Furthermore, precedents for nonviolent approaches to dispute resolution – and indeed for a proactive stance by Muslims as mediators and peacemakers – are found in the *sira* (biography) of the Prophet, and stem from the post-*hijra* period. For example, '[I]n the incident of the Aws and Khazraj tribes of Medina, the Prophet acted as mediator according to the Arab tradition and ended their enmity; in arbitration between the Prophet and the Banu Qurayza (a Jewish tribe), both agreed to submit their dispute to a person chosen by the tribes.'[38]

In acting as a third-party mediator in disputes, the Prophet drew on an Arab tradition of conflict resolution that grew out of the pre-Islamic past, and which continues to this day. It is to this tradition, in which Islamic and other cultural elements intertwine, that I now turn.

Traditional and Modern Reconciliation Practices in Contemporary Muslim Societies

> The social and cultural institutions of mediation (*wistahah*), arbitration (*tahkim*), and reconciliation (*sulh*) are integral components of the structure of Muslim communities, traceable to Bedouin traditions, tribal laws, and society, even before the spread of Islam. Many tribes in the Middle East still use these mechanisms in resolving their disputes.[39]

> But indeed if any show patience and forgive, that would truly be an exercise of courageous will and resolution in the conduct of affairs.
>
> (Qur'an, Sura 42:43)

The second quotation here is cited by Abu Nimer as one of three Qur'anic texts recited at the opening of a reconciliation ceremony (*sulha*) between two clans in a Palestinian village in 1998. Hundreds of villagers gathered in the main square to witness the ceremony, which served to reintegrate members of a clan exiled seven years previously, after one of their relatives committed a double murder.[40] The reconciliation ritual represented the culmination of a three-stage process, which began with the victim's family's acceptance of an *atwa*, a sum of money indicating their acceptance of a state of truce (*hudna*) in which the affair would be investigated, and undertaking not to seek revenge

---

[38] Abu Nimer, *Nonviolence and Peace Building in Islam*, 63; referring to M. Kadduri, *War and Peace in the Law of Islam* (Oxford: Oxford University Press, 1955).

[39] Abu Nimer, *Nonviolence and Peace Building in Islam*, 86.

[40] Abu Nimer, *Nonviolence and Peace Building in Islam*, 99.

during this period. After acceptance of the *atwa*, the period of *hudna* can begin.

'Clan' or 'family' in this context is defined as a patronymic extended family of five generations descended from a single grandfather.[41] In this context, honour/shame (*'ird*), which might be understood as a right to treatment as an equal and in which public recognition of this right plays an important role, becomes a central social value.[42] If honour is lost – for example, by the violation (murder or rape) of a relative – the victim's family becomes dishonoured and to restore face must take revenge. But here the Islamic system builds on pre-existing processes within tribal traditions which seek to contain the dangers of spiralling revenge killings through practical and symbolic methods. These include the acceptance of a payment as part compensation, agreement to a process of arbitration, public apology by the perpetrator's family, and waiving of further payments by the victim's family in return.

These traditional practices rely heavily on respect for elders as third-party mediators in disputes. This means that they normally have a rather conservative orientation aimed at restoring rather than changing existing power relations, and hence tend 'to function primarily as a social control mechanism'.[43] This can particularly disadvantage poor families and women – in the latter case a father, brother or elder son may act as a spokesman in dealing with a third party.[44]

In Palestine such tribal processes continue to have influence both in settled rural and urban contexts.[45] In post-civil war Lebanon, the failure of state authority led Hizbullah (*hisb-ul Allah*, 'the party of Allah') to develop such Bedouin practices into a more formalised six-step process in an attempt to reduce revenge killings:[46]

1　Hizbullah is invited to mediate, and presents the victim's family with a choice of taking the dispute to a *sharia* court or entering negotiations.
2　Hizbullah forbids vendettas.
3　Hizbullah prevents vendettas by holding the accused in protective custody.
4　After tensions have subsided, Hizbullah conducts negotiations with both parties seeking agreement over the fate of the accused. The process

---

[41] Abu Nimer, *Nonviolence and Peace Building in Islam*, 98.
[42] F. Henderson Stewart, *Honor* (London: University of Chicago Press, 1994).
[43] Abu Nimer, *Nonviolence and Peace Building in Islam*, 107.
[44] Abu Nimer, *Nonviolence and Peace Building in Islam*, 107.
[45] Abu Nimer, *Nonviolence and Peace Building in Islam*, 97.
[46] N. Hamzeh, 'The Role of Hizbullah in Conflict Management within Lebanon's Shi'a Community' in P. Salem (ed.), *Conflict Resolution in the Arab World* (Beirut: American University of Beirut, 1997).

typically takes one to three years, and the victim's family typically opt for exile for the accused plus compensation (*diya*).

5   All family members are visited to achieve consensus on the outcome.

6   A public ceremony (*musalaha*) is held, including public apology/ acceptance, often the waiving of right to compensation, and a shared meal.[47]

Thus traditional patterns of conflict resolution have been adapted to meet a contemporary need, and in the process been transposed from nomadic to rural to urban contexts.

Modern conflict resolution and peace-building methods – that is, those supported by theories and traditions of practice which generally assume a cultural framework characterised by strong individualism, equality between citizens, and often the presumption of a reasonably effective state – have also increasingly been introduced to Muslim-majority societies, especially since the end of the Cold War.[48] Sometimes responses to these initiatives by Islamic leaders are very positive; Abu Nimer cites the example of a professor from the Islamic University in Gaza, who commented at one such workshop: 'Those values are often repeated in weekly preaching in the mosque. Your training workshop is only a way of systematically operationalizing those skills, so they become accessible to all segments of society.'[49]

However, Abu Nimer also lists a number of frequent obstacles and objections he encountered while running such workshops in North Africa and the Middle East. The first group of obstacles relates to political and organisational cultures: bureaucratic and patronage-based recruitment policies,[50] patriarchal and other hierarchical assumptions which run contrary to the egalitarian ethos of peace-building methods,[51] and a tendency, in imitation of governments, to avoid critical self-examination, focusing instead on blaming external factors for current problems: 'Instead of examining the shortcomings and internal problems of schools, factories, government institutions, and family and tribal structures, the masses, at the prodding of the elites, focus on external factors such as colonialism, imperialism, Zionism, and, more recently, globalization.'[52]

Previous periods of Islamic history may be idealised, deflecting attention from practical and critical analysis of the present.[53] The possibilities for local

---

[47] Hamzeh, 'The Role of Hizbullah', 110–15; also in Abu Nimer, *Nonviolence and Peace Building in Islam*, 94–5.

[48] M. Abu Nimer, 'Conflict Resolution in an Islamic Context', *Peace and Change* 21.1 (2001).

[49] Abu Nimer, *Nonviolence and Peace Building in Islam*, 87.

[50] Abu Nimer, *Nonviolence and Peace Building in Islam*, 113.

[51] Abu Nimer, *Nonviolence and Peace Building in Islam*, 116–17.

[52] Abu Nimer, *Nonviolence and Peace Building in Islam*, 118.

[53] Abu Nimer, *Nonviolence and Peace Building in Islam*, 124.

and small-scale action may be missed because of the apparent hopelessness of political situations, and a focus on elite political action.[54]

A second raft of issues relates to scepticism about the effectiveness, underlying ideologies and cultural appropriateness of peace-building and conflict resolution methods. For example, as the third quotation given at the beginning of the chapter indicates, such methods may be associated with Western countries and agencies, and to be underlain by Western or Christian cultural assumptions. Furthermore, participants may fear that by rejecting violence the individual or community surrender their rights and search for justice, and is thus caving in to Israeli or American pressure.[55] In addition, the relative lack of 'justly resolved political conflicts' in Muslim-majority societies also creates a credibility problem,[56] as well as a belief in the efficacy of violence – the Arabic saying 'what was taken by force can only be returned by force' is often cited in the Palestine/Israel context.[57]

In spite of these difficulties workshops have achieved some successes. Prejudice against nonviolent methods has been overcome by pointing to the example of the Prophet, and by explaining that these methods do not rely on idealisations of a conflict-free society, nor require individuals to abandon their search for rights or justice. Furthermore, the disempowerment participants experience when they find their individual efforts swamped in corruption and politically deadlocked situations can sometimes be countered by focusing on the kinds of helpful actions that are possible. For example, in a workshop in Gaza in 1994, in the wake of deep disillusionment after the failure of the Oslo process to achieve effective progress towards Palestinian autonomy:

> The training team spent one day listening to and identifying problems. After the participants had identified 113 different problem categories, the training team posed these questions: On which of those problems do the Israelis have the least impact? Can those problems be dealt with? In which areas can you as an individual make an immediate impact? After rearranging their priorities, the participants realized their potential range of influence and agreed to act on that basis.[58]

Appropriately facilitated, such workshops can empower participants by enabling them to break out of established patterns of thinking and possibly also behaviour. Activities aimed at encouraging nonviolent methods and constructive engagement in situations of protracted conflict like that in Israel/Palestine can be seen as preparation for possible future reconciliation.

---

[54] Abu Nimer, *Nonviolence and Peace Building in Islam*, 122.
[55] Abu Nimer, *Nonviolence and Peace Building in Islam*, 125.
[56] Abu Nimer, *Nonviolence and Peace Building in Islam*, 121.
[57] Abu Nimer, *Nonviolence and Peace Building in Islam*, 119.
[58] Abu Nimer, *Nonviolence and Peace Building in Islam*, 123.

Abu Nimer and Groves offer an extended discussion of the role of Islam in the Palestinian *intifada* (1987–1993; 2000–) from this perspective, and the account below summarises and develops their account to reflect specifically on issues of reconciliation.[59]

The Palestinian *Intifada*: A Case Study of Islam and Reconciliation

Through the activities of Hamas and Islamic Jihad, Islam's role in the Palestinian *intifada* may be perceived as one of escalating violence rather than promoting reconciliation. Yet it is estimated that no more than 10 per cent of the Palestinian population are active members of these groups; some 49 per cent describe themselves as 'strongly religious' and a further 20 per cent as 'moderately religious', begging the question of the role of religion in the situation for the majority of believers in the Palestinian population.[60] Amongst this group, religious institutions (especially mosques) functioned as a space for organisation, social and practical support, and resistance; religious symbols signified hope and defiance, and a deeply embedded and somewhat religiously encoded culture of hospitality encouraged acts of reconciliation in the face of deepening divisions between Palestinians and Israelis.

Abu Nimer and Groves relate one example from the West Bank city of Hebron in 1989.[61] An Israeli patrol had shot and killed a stone-throwing youth, and a member of the patrol had subsequently become separated and found himself surrounded by an angry mob. Frightened, he beat on the door of the nearest house with his rifle, and was admitted by a woman who served him coffee, and waited until it was safe for him to leave. It was the woman's son that the patrol had killed. The story was recounted to a researcher by a Palestinian man who had been asked about the role of religion in the *intifada*. His initial response had been 'Religion and culture enable us to preserve our humanity', and he told the story when prompted to explain, adding 'We will never become like the Israelis and hate our enemy; we will offer him hospitality. That soldier could come back again, and the woman would offer him coffee again.'[62] The story illustrates the importance of religiously supported practices which witness to a common humanity and the possibility for relationships beyond the military, physical and political barriers separating Palestinians and Israelis.

---

[59] M. Abu Nimer and J. Groves, 'Peace Building and Nonviolent Political Movements in Arab-Muslim Communities: A Case Study of the Palestinian Intifada', in M. Abu Nimer, *Nonviolence and Peace Building in Islam*.

[60] Shadid, *The Legacy of the Prophet*, 662–4, 681–2.

[61] Abu Nimer and Groves, 'Peace Building and Nonviolent Political Movements', 128–9.

[62] Abu Nimer and Groves, 'Peace Building and Nonviolent Political Movements', 128.

Formal interfaith groups which seek to bring deeply hostile parties into some kind of dialogue have also been established, often on Jewish Israeli initiative. Indeed, there is also a tradition of interfaith dialogue that runs back to the British Mandate period.[63] While this was initially restricted to academic circles, contemporary organisations such as the Israel Interfaith Association and Interfaith Encounter Association (IEA) have much wider reach; for example, the IEA has brought settlers from the strongly Jewish nationalist National Religious Party together with Hamas supporters.[64]

Between individual hospitality and formal attempts to create interfaith dialogue lie a range of ways in which religion plays cultural, social and political roles that have the potential to promote reconciliation. The main organisation responsible for the coordination of the *intifada* – the Unified National Leadership of the Uprising (UNLU) – makes considerable efforts to include and represent both Muslims and Christians in its campaign of resistance to the Israeli occupation. Examples include a campaign of fasting led jointly by both Orthodox Christian priests and Muslim *imams*, protest marches led by both religious leaderships, and UNLU publications which use the phrase 'church and mosque' to emphasise unity.[65]

Even for the minority actively involved with Hamas and Islamic Jihad, it is important to recognise that these are not simply organisations dedicated to uncompromising opposition to the Israeli presence. They also provide education, welfare and other social services in the Occupied Territories, for example:

> Hamas runs a network of educational institutions such as kindergartens, schools, libraries, youth and sports clubs, and adult education centers. In addition, like other Muslim Brotherhood associations in neighbouring Arab countries, Hamas provides medical services and runs hospitals as well as charities for the needy. Indeed the Intifada forced Hamas to direct larger portions of its financial resources for the welfare and support of those families whose members had been killed, wounded, or arrested by Israel.[66]

In these roles Islam may be seen as serving reconciling functions amongst Muslims and, to some extent, between Muslims and Christians. However, these forms of reconciliation grow out of an 'Islamicate society', a society in which minorities of Christian and Jews have long been present, but in which it is presupposed that Islam influences the public life of society. Muslims are usually a numerical majority, and there are often restrictions on the role of non-Muslims in public life. Traditions of equality of citizenship regardless of

---

[63] N. Caplan, *Futile Diplomacy* (London: Cass, 1983).

[64] G. Wilkes, *Land of Promise and Conflict*, Module 809 of the Centre for Jewish-Christian Relations MA programme (Cambridge: Centre for Jewish-Christian Relations, 2000), 130. Quoted with permission.

[65] Abu Nimer and Groves, 'Peace Building and Nonviolent Political Movements', 167.

[66] S. Mishal and A. Sela, *The Palestinian Hamas* (New York: Columbia University Press, 2000), viii.

religion, which have grown up in Western democracies, have long been familiar in segments of Muslim-majority societies, but their status is problematic and contested. In this final section, then, I will consider broader questions of the relationship between Muslim cultures, democracy and human rights; given the global influence of these concepts it is Islam's articulation of them that will most likely inspire Islamic understandings of reconciliation.

Broader Contextual Factors: Islam, Civil Society, Democracy and Human Rights

Civil society – a layer of institutions between the individual and the state within which individuals exercise their autonomy by engaging with others in self-chosen association – is seen as important for the development of democratic traditions by Western political scientists and theorists.[67] However, individuation (the development of understandings of the individual as separable from his/her social roles and able to exercise considerable individual agency) and reasonably strong but legally limited state institutions (that effectively and discretely regulate the free market of associational activity) are both important to the concept of civil society, and yet problematic in Muslim-majority societies.

In sociological theory, these processes are both seen as part of a process of social differentiation, and social differentiation has often taken a rather different course in Muslim-majority societies. However, while these differences do present real difficulties – including the problematic reception for concepts perceived as 'Western' in the Muslim-majority world – I shall argue none the less that Islam and civil society are indeed compatible.

Islam is perhaps the prime example of a religious tradition that the West widely considers to be in tension, if not in outright conflict, with the normative tradition of civil society.[68] Contemporary perceptions are now further shaped by the events of 11 September 2001, and subsequent Islamic terrorist attacks. It is therefore extremely important to consider the evidence for these perceptions of incompatibility. In his influential *Conditions of Liberty: Civil Society and its Rivals* the late Ernest Gellner claimed that Islam is fundamentally unsecularisable, and concludes from this that Islam is also incompatible with civil society, both normatively and empirically.[69] Gellner

---

[67] J. Keane, C*ivil Society* (Cambridge: Polity, 1998); J. Habermas, *Between Facts and Norms* (Cambridge: Polity, 1996); J. Cohen and A. Arato, *Civil Society and Political Theory* (Cambridge, MA and London: MIT Press, 1992).

[68] F. Halliday, *Islam and the Myth of Confrontation: Religion and Politics in the Middle East* (London: IB Tauris, 1996).

[69] E. Gellner, *The Conditions of Liberty: Civil Society and its Rivals* (London: Penguin, 1994), 15.

understands secularisation as the declining social significance of religion: 'in industrial or industrializing societies religion loses much of its erstwhile hold over men and society'.[70] While religion remains socially significant, argues Gellner, the development of individual autonomy is constrained. This in turn constrains the development of civil society because, as Özdalga explains: 'Individuals, who are not able to act independently of the community of believers, cannot become the building-stones of the kind of intermediary organizations on which civil society is built.'[71]

This section challenges each stage of Gellner's argument, and hence its polarising consequences. First, I shall argue that Gellner neglects the different ways in which modernity has been mediated to different regions, and hence the consequences of this for modern institutional forms and discourses such as civil society. Second, I shall argue that Muslims have generated a range of responses to the discourses of democracy, civil society and human rights. This contradicts the simplistic integralist position – that Islam insists that all aspects of life should be directly governed by its unchanging precepts – that Gellner attributes to Islam. Third, I shall argue that the historical model on which Gellner bases his argument in fact applies only to a minority of historic Muslim societies, and that the historically predominant model of Muslim society has been characterised by institutional differentiation. Fourth and finally, I shall argue that in practice in many parts of the Muslim world today Islam has proven itself capable of mobilisation as a public discourse by contributing to rather than stifling democratic pluralism.

First, then, the impact of modernity on a region as a whole may be a key factor in shaping the reception and cultural embedding of modern ideas such as civil society. Therborn outlines four routes to modernity. First, the Western and Central European route in which both modernity and anti-modern movements were an internal development.[72] Second, the route of the New Worlds in the Americas and Australia, areas where European settlers came to constitute a majority of the population, and where opposition to modernity was principally perceived to lie in the old European world. Third, the Colonial Zone, where modernity arrived from outside and resistance to modernity was domestic and suppressed, but where those of non-European origin none the less continued to constitute a majority of the population, for

---

[70] Gellner, *The Conditions of Liberty*, 15.

[71] E. Özdalga, 'Civil Society and Its Enemies: Reflections on a Debate in the Light of Recent Developments within the Islamic Student Movement in Turkey', in E. Özdalga and S. Persson (eds), *Civil Society and Democracy in the Muslim World* (Istanbul: Swedish Research Institute, 1997), 74.

[72] G. Therborn, 'Beyond Civil Society: Democratic Experiences and their Relevance to the "Middle East"' in Özdalga and Persson (eds), *Civil Society and Democracy in the Muslim World*, 45–54.

whom 'everyday life ... kept its own laws and customs, though often rigidified by colonial intervention or "indirect rule"'.[73] Fourth, countries characterised by 'Externally Induced Modernization', selectively imported by a ruling elite never over-run but pressured by European and American imperial powers, of which he gives China, Japan, Iran, the Ottoman Empire/Turkey and the North African states most resistant to colonialism as examples.

Most Muslim societies fall into the third or fourth category. In such contexts:

> The key actor [in modernisation] is ... a modernizing part of the ruling body, trying to adapt both the state and society to external challenge and threat. Cleavage patterns tend to run both between modern and anti-modern parts of the elite and between the former and anti-modernists among the people, with the latter sometimes winning, as in Afghanistan and Iran. In this complex pattern of conflicts and alliances ... the meaning of popular rights is ambiguous, not seldom rejected by (large parts) of the people as anti-traditional.[74]

Under these conditions, one might anticipate ambivalent attitudes to modern discourses, including civil society: certainly this has occurred with other modern discourses such as democracy and human rights. Indeed, normatively, Muslims have in fact taken up a full range of positions on the compatibility or incompatibility of the relationship between Islam and both democracy and human rights. Thus Goddard outlines four positions on the relations between Islam and democracy, ranging from the view that democracy is anathema to Islam, to the view that democracy is essential for Islam.[75] Similarly, Halliday outlines five positions that Muslims have taken on human rights, again ranging from full compatibility to outright rejection.[76] Each position within both spectra seeks to justify itself in relation to the Qur'an and Sunna.

This contemporary ideological pluralism corresponds to the diversity of historical forms of Muslim society. For example, Ira Lapidus argues that whereas Gellner, working principally from North African examples, sees just one Islamic blueprint for society, two have in fact been present from a very early stage of Middle Eastern history, with Gellner's model historically the less influential:

> The Middle Eastern Islamic heritage provides not one but two basic constellations of historical society, two golden ages, two paradigms, each of which has generated its own repertoire of political institutions and political theory. The first is the society integrated in

---

[73] Therborn, 'Beyond Civil Society', 50.
[74] Therborn, 'Beyond Civil Society', 51.
[75] H. Goddard, 'Islam and Democracy', paper presented to Politics and Religion Group, Political Studies Association, Sheffield, 24 February 1999.
[76] Halliday, *Islam and the Myth of Confrontation*.

all dimensions, political, social, and moral, under the aegis of Islam. The prototype is the unification of Arabia under the leadership of the Prophet Muhammad in the seventh century ... The second historical paradigm is the imperial Islamic society built not on Arabian or tribal templates but on the differentiated structures of previous Islamic societies ... By the Eleventh century Middle Eastern states and religious communities were highly differentiated ... Thus, despite the common statement that Islam is a total way of life defining political as well as social and family matters, most Muslim societies ... were in fact built around separate institutions of state and religion.[77]

Thus the Western history of social differentiation is not the only one, and historically most Muslim societies have been socially differentiated. Yet Gellner the sociologist does not simply argue that Islam is normatively resistant to differentiation. Rather, he argues that this normative orientation coincides with structural features that render Islam 'secularization-resistant'.[78] Drawing on North African examples, Gellner characterises Muslim history until modernity as a cyclical process driven by relations between two versions of Islam: an urban, scripturalist, 'High' version, and a rural, ritualistic, ecstatic and saint-mediated 'Low' version. The High version is prone to laxity and pragmatic compromise over time: but at just such times it has been reinvigorated by the zeal of discontented followers of the Low version who appropriate the ideals of 'High' Islam, and are powered by *asabiyya* (energy of tribal groups). But modernity broke this cycle:

> Come the modern world however – imposed by extraneous forces rather then produced indigenously – and the new balance of power, favoring the urban centre against rural communities, causes central faith to prevail, and we are left with a successful Ummah at long last. This is the mystery of the secularization-resistant nature of Islam ....[79]

The centralised state, asserting its authority over rural areas and destroying tribal society, is able to sustain the reforming zeal of High Islam. Both versions of High Islam are compatible with instrumental aspects of modernity – such as industrialisation and urbanisation – and hence increasingly displace the popular saint-led Low Islam throughout an increasingly urbanised society, except for Westernised elites. Furthermore, it is the puritanical version of High Islam that triumphs over the lax variant because only the latter has genuine local appeal.[80]

However, while this account helps to explain the popularity of Islam in some, and especially in North African societies, it remains limited. First, it is limited in geographical and cultural scope, because as we have seen

---

[77] I. Lapidus, 'The Golden Age: The Political Concepts of Islam', *Annals of the American Academy*, 524 (1992), 14–15.

[78] Gellner, *The Conditions of Liberty*.

[79] Gellner, *The Conditions of Liberty*, 14.

[80] Gellner, *The Conditions of Liberty*, 23.

(following Lapidus) it does not fit societies where imperial Islam has long predominated and the influence of tribal groups has remained marginal (for example, Ottoman and Mughal lands). Second, it neglects the central historical factors that have shaped the emergence of modern political Islam – namely the crisis in nationalist ideologies and the failure of both socialist and capitalist development models in many parts of the Muslim world.[81] Third, it flies in the face of the fact that where Islamic groups have been permitted to enter the democratic process as political parties, they have shown themselves both willing and able to follow democratic procedures. As Ibrahim comments:

> Beyond the Arab world, Islamists have regularly run for elections in Pakistan, Bangladesh and Turkey since the 1980s. In Indonesia, Malaysia and the Islamic republics of the former Soviet Union, Islamists have peacefully been engaging in local and municipal politics ... It is important to note that in three of the biggest Muslim countries (Pakistan, Bangladesh and Turkey) women have recently been elected to the top executive office in the land ... The important thing in all these cases is that Islamic parties have accepted the rules of the democratic game and are playing it peaceably and in an orderly manner.[82]

Furthermore, other discourses dependent on strong individuation – such as human rights – have also taken firm root in many Muslim societies, such that, in spite of the ambivalence associated with them, they now form part of the terms of public debate. This is illustrated by Dwyer's conversations with intellectuals about human rights in Tunisia, Morocco (precisely the societies Gellner characterises as dominated by an integralist version of Islam) and Egypt, many of whom were active in human rights organisations. Indeed the range and persistence of such organisations, in spite of the difficult conditions in which they operate, is itself refutation of Gellner's thesis. But more than this, Dwyer shows the extent to which human rights discourse, contested and polysemous as it is, has penetrated contemporary Middle Eastern societies. As he concludes, 'Few Middle Easterners I spoke to seem ready to dismiss the idea from their cultural repertoire: they may challenge its foundations, or its provenance, or the content given it by specific groups, but the concept itself has come to constitute a symbol of great power.'[83]

Thus Gellner essentialises connections between Islam, civil society and democratisation which are in fact contingent. Islam is not necessarily incompatible, normatively or practically, with structural differentiation, and many Muslim societies in practice support both diverse civil societies and democracy, even though, and unsurprisingly given the manner of their reception of modernity, these discourses are contested and viewed with

---

[81] N. Ayubi, *Political Islam* (London: Routledge 1990).

[82] S. Ibrahim, 'From Taliban to Erbakan: The Case of Islam, Civil Society and Democracy', in E. Özdalga and S. Persson (eds), *Civil Society and Democracy in the Muslim World*, 41.

[83] Dwyer, *Arab Voices*, 192.

ambivalence. Furthermore, it is important that the problematic reception of these discourses in the Muslim world is not viewed against their presumed-to-be unproblematic acceptance in the West. Here too the articulation of these concepts is problematic;[84] yet both in the West and Muslim-majority societies there are many resources for reconciliation that give grounds for optimism.

Conclusion

From perspectives influenced by assumptions of secularisation, Islam has shown itself to be surprisingly capable of rearticulating itself in conditions of structural modernisation, such as global communications systems, social differentiation and urbanisation. Sometimes this articulation has taken integralist ideological forms hostile to democracy and human rights: yet forms of Islamism that engage positively with discourses of democracy and human rights have also developed across many parts of the Muslim-majority world (Egypt, Turkey, Indonesia), and are arguably on the ascendant.[85] Considering these political developments alongside the textual traditions and local practices of reconciliation we have examined, it seems that there are some good reasons to hope for the development of reconciliation between Muslims and non-Muslims both within the Muslim-majority world and in the West, in spite of the formidable antagonisms that have developed.

---

[84] H. Lanham and D. Forsythe, 'Human Rights in the New Europe: A Balance Sheet', in D. Forsythe (ed.), *Human Rights in the New Europe: Problems and Progress* (Lincoln: University of Nebraska Press, 1994).

[85] C. Murphy, *Passion for Islam: Shaping the Modern Middle East: the Egyptian Experience* (London: Scribner, 2002); G. Abdo, *No God But God: Egypt and the Triumph of Islam* (Oxford: Oxford University Press, 2000).

PART II

THE DYNAMICS OF RECONCILIATION AND CHRISTIAN THEOLOGY

CHAPTER 4

Putting Forgiveness in its Place:
The Dynamics of Reconciliation

Joseph Liechty

In Northern Ireland, work towards reconciliation long preceded careful reflection on the meaning and dynamics of reconciliation. As reflection began to emerge, it revealed shared themes and understandings, but considerable confusion as well. As I explore the broader international literature on reconciliation, I find much the same. Even work of real value can betray less than careful understandings of the elements of reconciliation and the relationship between them, if not outright confusion.

Wherever reconciliation is addressed, a jumble of terms is likely to emerge, with forgiveness, repentance, apology, justice, truth, peace and, of course, reconciliation itself being among the most common ingredients of the reconciliation stew. Unfortunately, these and related terms are too often undefined, ill-defined, or idiosyncratically defined, and they are linked in varied and sometimes bewildering fashion. I take as a typical example a recent book, *Forgiveness and Reconciliation: Religion, Public Policy and Conflict Transformation*. I choose this book not because it is weak but because it is excellent and therefore suggests how pervasive is the problem. That title, *Forgiveness and Reconciliation*: why have these two concepts alone been plucked from the reconciliation stew? Are they the same thing? Complementary qualities? What is the relation between them? Is one part of the other? Are they sufficient to account for the whole of the reconciliation process? Apparently not, because early in their introduction, the authors announce that this book is 'a study in political penitence'.[1] Then why is 'penitence' not included in the title? Is this another synonym and therefore needless? Is it part of reconciliation or part of forgiveness? In this book as in many others, I do not find clear answers to such questions.

Neither good understanding of reconciliation nor still less good practice will be entirely stymied by weak conceptualisation, of course. But sometimes confusion does distort practice, and both understanding and

---

[1] Raymond G. Helmick and Rodney L. Petersen (eds), *Forgiveness and Reconciliation: Religion, Public Policy and Conflict Transformation* (Philadelphia, PA and London: Templeton Foundation Press, 2001), xvii.

practice would be enhanced by a better grasp of the whole network of actions and qualities that make up reconciliation. Towards that end, I focus here on sketching a brief account of reconciliation as a set of interlocking dynamics, with a particular emphasis on placing forgiveness within that framework.[2]

Repenting and Forgiving

At its most basic, reconciling involves the complementary dynamics of repenting and forgiving, the first a way of dealing with having done wrong, the second with having suffered wrong. Thus reconciliation is achieved when perpetrators have repented and victims have forgiven. While the picture is much complicated in a situation of long-term conflict like Northern Ireland, where determining which parties are perpetrators and which victims, and in what proportion and combinations, becomes itself a cause of contention, repentance and forgiveness remain underlying requirements for reconciliation.

Given the necessity of both repenting and forgiving for reconciliation and their complementarity, it is worth noting that the Christian tradition, and with it the broader Western tradition, is heavily weighted towards forgiving rather than repenting. That these traditions are weighted towards forgiving I base on impressions to which I can recall just one significant counter, the recent and remarkable attention to apology in Australia. A useful measure of the bias towards forgiveness at the expense of repentance comes from the online bookseller, Amazon. In preparing a lecture, I had occasion to search the Amazon.com website for books on forgiveness and repentance. 'Forgiveness' turned up 387 titles, a mixture of pop psychology, pop religion and serious scholarship, with only a tiny minority written from perspectives other than Christian or secular. 'Repentance', on the other hand, yielded just 72 titles, and what had been a tiny minority of Jewish authors under 'forgiveness' became a large minority under 'repentance'. Furthermore, the 22nd best-selling book on repentance was already designated 'out of print/limited availability', while the 93rd best-selling book on forgiveness was the first to be out of print.[3] Virtually every reading of mainstream Western culture I can think of points towards the same conclusion: that the Western imagination is captivated by forgiveness in a way that repentance cannot match.

---

[2] What I cannot develop within the confines of this essay is how the dynamics of reconciliation differ depending on the level of social or political organisation to which they are applied. My contention in such an account would be that the understanding of the dynamics of reconciliation that I develop here has significant applications to all kinds of human relationships and conflicts, whether those be interpersonal, intercommunal, or interstate.

[3] These figures were taken from the Amazon.com website on 29 September 2004.

Whatever the reason for the imbalance, it is unhealthy. However difficult, forgiving involves dealing with how we have been wronged, while repenting involves what most of us find more difficult, dealing with what we have done wrong. Moral maturity requires both. Healing of relationships, that is, reconciliation, whether personal or political, requires both.

While the dynamics of repenting can be named in various ways, five stages typically emerge when working with groups in Northern Ireland: acknowledging a wrong done, accepting responsibility, expressing remorse, changing attitudes and behaviour, and making restitution. These stages are in a logical order, with the exception of 'expressing remorse' and 'changing attitudes and behaviour', either of which might come before the other. Minimally, we might label a process as repenting if it yields changed behaviour, especially if that change is willing, the three previous stages can be taken as implicitly accomplished or the change would not have occurred. Restitution, though, is the capstone, too rarely applied, that completes and fulfils the repenting process; restitution is also the element most likely to persuade the party wronged that repentance has been genuine.

The idea of apology, with its overtones of verbal expression of regret, corresponds closely to 'expressing remorse'. As such, apology occupies an ambiguous position in repentance and therefore in reconciliation. On the one hand, it is not strictly necessary, since effective change may itself function as a non-verbal but powerful expression of remorse. On the other hand, apology can play a critical role in repentance. The right words of apology at the right time can be as decisive as restitution in persuading the other party that repentance has been authentic. In fact, where complete and literal restitution is not possible (and in situations of endemic conflict, full restitution rarely is possible), then apology – verbal expressions of regret – may also become part of symbolic restitution. Furthermore, apologising marks a crucial development in the repenting process. Apologising is the first of these five stages that requires the repenting party to turn what could have been up to that point a private and internal process into one that recognises that this is about restoring a relationship and therefore takes the difficult step of turning outward to address the offended party.

Forgiving, like repenting, might be defined in terms of stages in a process. Because I want to identify some problems around the way the concept of forgiveness is used, however, I will instead work with two main strands of meaning. Forgiveness is a broad and rich concept. Ironically, in that very breadth lies the possibility, too often realised, of intellectual confusion that can limit the potency of forgiving in practice.

The first strand is forgiving as 'letting-go'. This feels familiar, because letting-go has become the conventional meaning of forgiveness in modern therapeutic terms. But the roots run much deeper. However one assesses Hannah Arendt's claim that '[t]he discoverer of the role of forgiveness in the realm of human affairs was Jesus of Nazareth',[4] it was clearly a central theme of his teaching and of the New Testament, and thus hugely influential in the Western tradition. Forgiving as letting-go may well derive from this source, as this is the apparent root meaning of the New Testament Greek word, *aphiemi*, which is usually the word translated as 'forgive'. If 'forgive' is almost always a translation of *aphiemi*, the reverse is certainly not the case. In fact, *aphiemi* is translated as 'forgive' in less than half of its 146 occurrences. It is more often translated as 'leave' and beyond that in an apparently bewildering variety of ways, including 'consent', 'divorce', 'give', 'neglect', 'yield', 'abandon' and 'desert'. 'To let go' is one way of naming the common meaning behind all the translations.

That variety of translations suggests one of the key conceptual and practical problems around forgiveness: in letting go, exactly what are we letting go of? The answer will vary from case to case, but if it is to fit under the heading of forgiveness it will always involve letting go of at least three things: vengeance, punishment of the wrongdoer in exact proportion to the wrong done,[5] and, in so far as possible, those feelings, especially hatred, that will damage, immediately or eventually, the wronged party. Whatever else may need to be let go of in *particular* circumstances, nothing else need be let go of in *all* circumstances. And if the practice and pursuit of forgiveness is to be meaningful, one thing *may not* be let go of: that is, the justice claim that occasioned the need for forgiveness. As suggested by the ideas of 'letting go of vengeance' and 'exactly proportionate punishment', forgiving is a way of dealing with a justice claim. True, it is sometimes radically different than other ways of dealing with justice, but it is not the abandonment of a justice claim. In fact forgiving has little meaning other than as a way of dealing with a justice claim.

A second strand of the meaning of forgiveness is 'love given before',[6] 'love' being understood in this case in the entirely unsentimental sense of willing, seeking and extending oneself for the good of another. As such it is the perfect complement to forgiving as letting-go, indicating what is embraced in place of what has been let go of. It is worth noting that love-

---

[4] Hannah Arendt, *The Human Condition* (Chicago, IL and London: University of Chicago Press, 2nd edn 1998 [1958]), 238.

[5] Here and elsewhere through this section, I am closely following the work of Donald Shriver, especially *Forgiveness and Politics: The Case of the American Black Civil Rights Movement* (London: New World Publications, 1987), 20. See also his later work: Donald Shriver, *An Ethic for Enemies: Forgiveness in Politics* (New York: Oxford University Press, 1995).

[6] I had been labouring for some years under the impression that the prefix 'for' in forgiven was equivalent to 'fore' and thus 'before'. However, my Goshen College colleague Paul Keim, a linguist, has pointed out to me that in this case the meaning of the prefix 'for' has nothing to do with 'fore' or 'before', so it is simply an interesting and unlikely linguistic accident that the strand of forgiveness being discussed here can be described as 'love given before'.

given-before, although a major New Testament theme, is not described there as 'forgiving', which is largely confined to the letting-go function. Incorporating love-given-before into forgiveness seems to be an addition in the English language, and perhaps others. Thus in a Christian context, stories like Jesus' encounter with Zacchaeus the tax collector or the parable of the prodigal son are commonly understood to be about forgiveness, because they exemplify love given before and apart from whether the other person has in any way earned or deserved it, although the Bible never uses the word 'forgive' about these situations.

The letting-go strand of forgiveness is in fact a continuum, running from a minimalist end that might be described as forbearance of vengeance to a full and final letting-go that can be called absolution.[7] If both forgiving as letting-go generally and as love-given-before generate some problems, they are as nothing compared with the confusion arising from forgiveness as absolution. In some ways, absolution fits poorly with the meanings of forgiveness that we have been discussing. Forgiving as letting-go and as love-given-before are initiating, risk-taking, pre-emptive strategies for change. Forgiveness as absolution follows rather than initiates, it is a response to change more than a strategy for change. After conflicting parties engaged in repenting and forgiving as letting-go and love-given-before have done all the hard work of being reconciled, absolution is little more than the recognition that reconciliation has occurred.

Two examples will suggest the confusion that can arise because of the radical difference between forgiveness as absolution and forgiveness in its other functions. Theologian Rodney Petersen's account of the terminology and rhetoric surrounding forgiveness shows the kind of conceptual confusion that can arise when discussions of forgiveness slip without acknowledgement between forgiveness as absolution and forgiving in its other capacities. I cite three references from a single page: 'This [self-justification] blocks the process of forgiveness and, consequently, the possibility of restored relationships or reconciliation'.[8] Here forgiveness is part of reconciliation and precedes the possibility of reconciliation. A couple of paragraphs later, however, Petersen writes:

> Reconciliation, a restoration or even a transformation toward an intended wholeness that comes with transcendent or human grace, expresses the result of a restored relation in behavior. Forgiveness expresses the acknowledgment and practice of this result. In this sense, *forgiveness* is not so much a middle term as one that includes both justification and reconciliation.[9]

---

[7]   I am grateful to my co-editor, David Tombs, for the long conversations that have helped me to clarify the relationship between love-given-before, letting-go, and absolution.

[8]   Rodney L. Petersen, 'A Theology of Forgiveness: Terminology, Rhetoric, and the Dialectic of Interfaith Relationships', *Forgiveness and Reconciliation*, 13.

[9]   Peterson, 'A Theology of Forgiveness', 13, original emphasis.

These words only make sense if he is talking about forgiveness as absolution, and he correctly points out that in this absolving sense, forgiveness is not so much part of reconciliation, it is a broader term that includes reconciliation. Just three sentences later, however, he goes on to say, 'Reconciliation not only draws upon forgiveness, but also elicits the qualities of truth and justice in the recovery of harmony or peace.'[10] And again he has returned to talking about forgiveness as part of reconciliation. This sliding back and forth, unacknowledged, between forgiveness as absolution and forgiving in its other functions makes a coherent account impossible.

When the legal scholar Martha Minow seeks a way *Between Vengeance and Forgiveness* in the aftermath of mass violence, it is primarily forgiveness as premature or unwarranted absolution that she wishes to avoid.[11] Forgiving in its other senses is not without problems, but it can contribute significantly to seeking a way forward in the aftermath of violence. Although in most ways sophisticated and generally satisfying, Minow's argument would be stronger if it explicitly recognised the different meanings of forgiveness – specifically the stark difference between absolution and the initiative-taking forms of forgiveness. Should it become a commonplace that recovery from mass violence requires a way between vengeance and forgiveness, it would be most damaging if all strands of forgiving were carelessly conflated into one, and this one reduced to absolution.

Confusion between forgiveness as absolution and in its other meanings also lies behind the frequent but rarely fruitful debate about whether repentance must precede forgiveness. Once the differences between these aspects of forgiving are recognised, the issue all but resolves itself. Forgiving as letting-go and love-given-before generally precede repentance. They are in their essence initiatives and would be deprived of their possibilities as a form of power for change in the hands of wounded parties were they confined to responding to repentance. Absolution generally follows repentance. It can, of course, precede repentance, and this may in some instances be necessary or wise. But absolution is most naturally a response to repentance. If it easily or frequently precedes repentance, it will soon require the kind of critique represented by Dietrich Bonhoeffer's stinging attack on cheap grace, including 'the preaching of forgiveness without requiring repentance'.[12] Of course Bonhoeffer's target here was forgiveness as absolution, not as risk-taking initiative.

In Northern Ireland, this issue of the relationship of forgiveness and repentance causes real existential pain, as wounded parties cry out, 'I would

---

[10] Peterson, 'A Theology of Forgiveness', 13.

[11] Martha Minow, *Between Vengeance and Forgiveness: Facing History after Genocide and Mass Violence* (Boston, MA: Beacon Press, 1998), 14–24.

[12] Dietrich Bonhoeffer, *The Cost of Discipleship* (New York: Macmillan, rev. edn 1963 [ET 1948]), 36.

like to forgive him, but I can't, because he hasn't repented.' As with Bonhoeffer, it is forgiveness as absolution they have in mind, but the conflation of all forms of forgiving into one is likely to deprive them of the opportunities for change offered by other forms of forgiveness. Thus in Northern Ireland it is vital to affirm on the basis of empirical observation (that is, listening to a lot of stories) that forgiving and repenting do not relate to each other in any particular order. Either can come first and inspire the other. Forgiving as letting-go and as love-given-before can be undertaken before the other party has repented, if the forgiving party is able, wants to do so, and is willing to risk getting no response in hopes that forgiveness might inspire a response. What cannot be accomplished until the other party has repented is reconciliation; what is likely to be inappropriate until the end of the process is absolution. I suspect that the confusion around this topic is directly related to the tendency to use inflated definitions of forgiveness that make it a synonym for reconciliation and to give too much prominence to forgiveness as absolution.

Conceptual clarity would certainly be served by regarding absolution not as part of forgiveness but as a separate action. That is not going to happen. First, absolution is well entrenched as one of the popular meanings of forgiveness. Second, and conclusively, in one fundamental sense absolution does belong as an integral part of forgiveness, because it is nothing if not a form of letting-go.

Since absolution will remain part of forgiveness, two things are necessary to avoid the kind of confusion that limits the power of forgiveness. One, as suggested, is to distinguish clearly between the various forms of forgiveness. The other is to be quite clear about what absolution should and should not mean in terms of human relations. In a Christian context, this would begin by recognising at least four levels of absolution: God's absolution, the church's absolution as a representative of God, the state's absolution of wrongdoers, and the absolution offered by wronged individuals or groups to other individuals or groups. One implication of absolution shared by all levels is the determination that past wrongdoing will be in some way set aside so that the relationship between the offended party and the perpetrator may be restored. In terms of the last level, human relations, that is the only legitimate meaning of absolution. The absolution offered by God and the church, however, is also a kind of metaphysical transaction that alters the ultimate standing of the sin committed by the sinning party; the state, as a quasi-transcendent entity, might also be seen to offer a parallel quasi-metaphysical absolution. This is absolution offered by the sinless to the sinning, and thus irrelevant to and inappropriate in the realm of ordinary human relationships. The kind of absolution offered here has nothing to do with the ultimate standing of the sinner's sin; its only appropriate concern is the relationship between estranged parties. None the less, in some reluctance to offer forgiveness as absolution, I see traces or even clear evidence of an arrogant assumption of a God-like status: being parsimonious with forgiveness lest ultimate standards be offended. At least in this one sense, some Jews are right to recoil, I believe, at the Christian assumption of the power to forgive, because in terms of this kind of absolution, truly only God can forgive sins.

Justice and Truth

In practice, repenting and forgiving need justice-seeking and truth-seeking to keep them honest. Were repenting and forgiving practised with full integrity, we might need to add nothing more to this account of the dynamics of reconciliation, because justice and truth are already built in to these concepts. For repenting, this is obvious: it involves acknowledging and dealing with an injustice; repenting has no meaning outside the concept of justice. But forgiving too is integrally, necessarily connected to justice. Forgiving is always a way of responding to an injustice, and it can also be a stance from which to pursue justice without being overcome by bitterness when that justice is long delayed. This relationship should be a given. In reality, however, when forgiving and repenting go wrong, it is often because justice-seeking and truth-seeking have been neglected or distorted in some way, so these things need to be named. Without justice and truth, forgiveness and repentance will be insipid, partial and cheap.

But neither are justice and truth independent sentinels that stand alone. 'Any justice which is only justice', wrote Reinhold Niebuhr, 'soon degenerates into something that is less than justice. It must be saved by something which is more than justice.'[13] What a justice which is only justice can degenerate into is a polite pseudonym for mere retribution or revenge. What justice requires for its salvation, I propose, is that it be pursued in the larger context of seeking reconciliation. As for truth-seeking, one need not accept all of Michel Foucault's critique of 'regimes of truth'[14] to recognise that truth can be debased to serve as a means of domination, so its health too requires that it be understood in the context of seeking reconciliation.

What I have suggested thus far about the relationship of these four actions – forgiving, repenting, justice-seeking and truth-seeking – might be caught up in the metaphor of a web. To function at its greatest strength, each action must be connected to every other, and the resulting criss-crossing strands have collective strength and possibilities that none would have on its own. It may

---

[13] Reinhold Niebuhr, *Moral Man and Immoral Society* (New York: Scribner, 1960 [1932]), 258.

[14] Michel Foucault, *Power/Knowledge: Selected Interviews and Other Writings, 1972–1977*, trans. Colin Gordon et al. (New York: Pantheon Books, 1980), 131.

be possible to move towards reconciliation with one or more of these actions weak or absent (the work of the South African Truth and Reconciliation Commission was predicated on such a gamble, repenting and even more so justice being the comparatively weak elements) but they work best and most powerfully when working together.

Trust, Hope and Confidence

What follows requires a shift from the organic metaphor of a web to a mechanical one, in which each of these four actions is a meshing cog in a machine. If this reconciliation machine is to run smoothly, it will require a lubricant and fuel. The lubrication comes in the form of certain personal and social virtues, certain characteristics of disposition. In the first instance, these will include at least trust, hope and confidence. People simply cannot choose meaningful, uncoerced change without a certain level of confidence, and they will not change without trust and hope. Thus no reconciling process, whether personal or political, can go anywhere without these qualities, although a well-constructed process might make do with less confidence, trust and hope, or even inspire them. The protracted endgame in the Northern Ireland peace process might fruitfully be analysed in terms of these three categories: why they are so weak, and what is required to nurture them.

A fourth characteristic of inner disposition is harder to name, but still more crucial, and functions as the fuel for reconciliation. In terms of the dynamics of personal reconciliation it is easily named: it is love, in the entirely unsentimental sense of concern and care for another and a willingness to extend oneself for that other. The same applies to social and political reconciliation, but love is not a usable term for such purposes, so I borrow a phrase from Byron Bland, director of the Stanford Center for Conflict and Negotiation. Bland describes reconciliation as driven by the sense that somehow 'we belong together': 'reconciliation', he says, 'involves a profound rediscovery that those who have been deeply divided in the past do indeed belong together in the future'.[15] This profound sense may be the result of high idealism or of a kind of revelation or of social analysis or even of grudging realism – that is, unless we have a future together, however distasteful and distressing that notion, we have no future. But whatever the reasons for it, without this sense that 'we belong together', reconciliation will not happen.

This simple sketch of the place of forgiveness in the reconciliation process has only opened up some of the main areas that need to be addressed. None

---

[15] Byron Bland, unpublished and untitled essay on reconciliation, from the Stanford Center on Conflict and Negotiation Working Papers, 1999.

the less, I hope that it can serve as a pointer towards the kind of account of the dynamics of reconciliation that scholars might develop in order to undergird both sound thinking and sound practice in the pursuit of reconciliation.

CHAPTER 5

Reconciliation: An Intrinsic Element of Justice

Ada María Isasi-Díaz

'That they all may be one so that the world may believe' are words placed on the lips of Jesus by John the evangelist (John 17:21). The context of these words is important: Jesus wants the world to believe that he is one with God and that God has sent him. Jesus knows that his mission, to reveal and begin to establish the kin-dom[1] of God, will be fruitful only if the world believes in him. Furthermore, Jesus knows that whether the world does or does not believe in him and his mission depends on his followers living according to what he has taught them. The world will not believe unless his followers live according to the truths Jesus has taught: unless Christians are indeed one in body and soul, in mind and heart. Matthew 25:31–46 has the clearest explanation of what Jesus meant by being 'one'. In this parable one finds a stark picture of reality: some are hungry, some have food; some are homeless while others have shelter; some are naked, some have clothing; some are prisoners while others are free; some are sick and others are healthy. There is a rift between different groups in the community. The teaching of the parable is that the rift has to be healed and that only those who work to heal it will belong to the family of God. The healing of what splits humanity, of what separates one from the other, is the true meaning of reconciliation. If what separates us is not bridged, justice will not be able to triumph and the kin-dom of God will not become a reality in our midst.

At the beginning of the twenty-first century the many divisions that exist in our world make it obvious that a central element of the Christian understanding of justice and of work on behalf of justice is reconciliation. Justice is not only 'a constitutive dimension of the preaching of the Gospel',[2] but it is essential to the meaning and mission of the church today. The Bible, as well as a great variety of documents produced by different Christian

---

[1] The use of 'kin-dom' instead 'kingdom' or 'reign' stems from the desire to use a metaphor that is much more relevant to our world today. From my perspective as a *mujerista* theologian, the point of reference for kin-dom of God is the concept of family and community that is so central to my Latina culture. There is also the need to move away from 'kingdom' and 'reign' that are sexist and hierarchical metaphors.

[2] 1971 Synod of Bishops, 'Justice in the World,' in Joseph Gremillion, *The Gospel of Peace and Justice* (Maryknoll, NY: Orbis Books, 1975), 514.

churches in the last forty years, makes it clear that the work of justice is a religious practice. By extension, then, since reconciliation is an element of justice, the work of reconciliation is a religious obligation for all Christians: 'All Christians can agree in saying that reconciliation is an essential mission of the Church, that is, that one cannot be a true Christian if one is not motivated permanently by a preoccupation for reconciliation.'[3]

Very simply said, it is not possible to conceptualise reconciliation apart from justice, and one cannot be a justice-seeking person without an ongoing practice of reconciliation. This is the belief and understanding on which this article is built. In it I seek to articulate an understanding of reconciliation as a social, political and theological virtue within the parameters of justice. My intention is to present a theo-ethics of reconciliation that will contribute to make justice a reality since without justice the kin-dom of God cannot flourish; there can be no fullness of life, no peace.[4]

Reconciliation as an Element of Justice

The mode of divine revelation set forth in the Bible provides the basis for understanding justice as a process. The Bible does not set definitions. It does not offer theories but presents rich narratives about the lived experiences of its people. It is in the midst of their lives that God's revelation happens, that the people of Israel and the followers of Jesus come to understand who God is and the demands God makes on humans. Following this biblical tradition, many systems of Christian ethics and moral theologies today eschew a theoretical approach to justice that focuses on universals apart from any social context or on rational reflections that attempt to demonstrate their validity by being self-enclosed systems. Instead justice is embraced as a process that starts with the experience of those who suffer injustice, and who, therefore, seek to change present oppressive structures. As a process justice does not avoid rationality but rather proposes normative reflections that are historic and contextual. To understand justice as a process is to embrace the fact that all 'normative reflection must begin from historically specific

---

[3] René David Roset, 'Para Una Teología y Pastoral de Reconciliación desde Cuba' (unpublished article), (November 1981, revised in 1982), 3. Professor David is an elderly Roman Catholic theologian who has taught for many years at the Catholic seminary in Havana, Cuba with whom I have visited. Originally he is from Canada.

[4] This echoes the well-known quotation of Martin Luther King, 'Without justice, there can be no peace'; see Martin Luther King Jr, *Stride Towards Freedom*. This also echoes the thinking of Pope Paul VI that 'If You Want Peace, Work for Justice'; see 'Message of His Holiness Pope Paul VI for the Celebration of the "World Day of Peace"' (1 January 1972). http://www.vatican.va/holy_father/paul_vi/messages/peace/documents/hf_p-vi_mes_19711208_v-world-day-for-peace_en.html; accessed 19 July 2004.

circumstances because there is nothing but what is, the given, the situated interest in justice from which to start'.[5]

Acknowledging justice as a process, however, does not mean that it is only a matter of describing what is. Justice aims to evaluate the actual experience of people as well as their hopes and expectations. This evaluation is also 'rooted in experience of and reflection on that very society'.[6] It is not a matter of importing from other societies and cultures ideas of 'the good' and 'the just' to evaluate what is. It is a matter, rather, of listening to the cries of the poor and the oppressed in our midst so as to discover how individually and as a society we fail to make it possible for all to become the persons God created us to be. The norms and ideals used to evaluate the presence of justice in any given situation arise, then, from the yearnings of those who suffer oppression and poverty. They arise from those with whom individually and as a community we have not established right-relationships. The desire for right-relationships is not a foreign or an imposed idea but rather arises out of the desire of the people to have in their lives that love of neighbour that the gospel of Jesus turned into a commandment for Christians. This understanding of the basis for and meaning of justice makes it clear that different elements of justice will need to be emphasised at different times. However, no matter what element of justice is being discussed, justice, like any other norm or principle, requires exploration of its various meanings and implications.

In the twenty-first century our considerations about justice must start with the fact that two-thirds of the world lives in poverty and/or is oppressed, lacking what is needed to develop fully. In examining oppression and poverty one discovers some fundamental reasons for these adversities: personal and systemic violence, exploitation, powerlessness, marginalisation and prejudice. These are not only causes but also mechanisms that operate at many different levels in our world. As mechanisms they are interconnected and create personal and societal modes of being and doing that maintain a *status quo* where less than one-third of the world controls, consumes and enjoys most of the natural and humanly developed resources of our world. Justice requires an in-depth examination of the various causes of oppression so that effective strategies can be developed. One of the main reasons for the few positive results of the struggles for justice, despite the goodwill and untiring commitment of many around the world, has been the lack of serious analysis of the causes of oppression and poverty.

How is power understood and used? Who has it and whom does it benefit? An analysis of power is urgently needed if we are to understand the dynamics of oppression in our world. A second area that needs thorough examination is

---

[5] Iris Marion Young, *Justice and the Politics of Difference* (Princeton, NJ: Princeton University Press, 1990), 5.

[6] Young, *Justice and the Politics of Difference*.

the distribution of goods, both material goods and other goods such as rights, opportunities, self-respect, participation in decision making and the power to 'define' the symbols, images, meanings, behaviours and myths that give character to the different societies. A third area in which much work is needed concerns our notions of diversity and differences. It is precisely our present understanding of differences as what separates, excludes and places persons in opposition to each other that is at the core of all modes of oppression,[7] causing divisions and brokenness. Such an understanding leads to conceptualising those who are different as outsiders, with those who have power deciding what is normative – themselves – and what is deviant – others. As long as this is the prevalent understanding there is no possibility of having right-relationships, and it will be impossible to create just societal structures that are inclusive instead of exclusive.

Identifying similarity and difference seems to be one way people make sense of their 'perceptions, experiences, identities, and human obligations'.[8] However, this does not necessarily have to lead one to assign consequences to differences and to positioning one group in relation to another. In other words, usually the way differences are understood and dealt with includes making moral judgements about them, deciding without much reflection that because some are different they are better or worse, never just different. Society has capitalised on 'categories of difference that manifest social prejudice and misunderstanding',[9] and has ignored ongoing relationships among people that are based on similarities. Society understands boundaries as keeping people away from each other instead of highlighting that 'the whole concept of a boundary depends on relationships: relationships between the two sides drawn by the boundary, and relationships among the people who recognize and affirm the boundary'.[10] This means that because boundaries do not exist outside connections among people, if we are to bring about a paradigm shift in how we understand differences, we need to emphasise the role of differences in relationships rather than relating them only to what separates.

How can this be done and, more importantly, why should it be done? The fact is that unless one recognises differences and deals with them in a way contrary to the present mode, there is no possibility to heal the rifts that exist – there is no real possibility of solidarity among people. True solidarity insists on genuine mutuality which can be reached only by recognising the common interests that bind humanity. Unless we embrace differences and diversity as constituents of relationships instead of seeing them as separating and opposing elements, we will not be able to heal what divides us. We will not be

---

[7] Young, *Justice and the Politics of Difference*, 169.
[8] Young, *Justice and the Politics of Difference*, 7.
[9] Young, *Justice and the Politics of Difference*, 9.
[10] Young, *Justice and the Politics of Difference*, 10.

able to be reconcilers. In other words, the work of reconciliation is intrinsic to changing the paradigms that have governed the understanding of differences. The work of reconciliation is a key process in the struggle to create communities of solidarity committed to building a future together. Therefore, reconciliation and solidarity are key elements in our work for justice, for a just future, one where no one is excluded.

Reconciliation as a Moral Choice

The work of reconciliation is a humble process, a road to be travelled together, one step at a time, by those seeking to be reconciled. Reconciliation does not consist in unveiling preconceived answers to a given situation. Instead, the work of reconciliation projects itself into the future, opening up and concentrating on possibilities. It is not a matter of repeating or of limiting oneself to the past. Reconciliation understands that there is a plurality of truths and that this plurality is precisely what creates possibilities, what roots human freedom and makes choices possible. These rich possibilities propose and demand options that make reconciliation a moral virtue, a way of being and acting that requires responsible choice. Responsible choice is not about working to control situations. It is not a matter of being absolutely certain, before any steps are taken, that what one chooses is the most effective possible choice or one that guarantees success. Responsible choice recognises that what one chooses is but one way to proceed, that it is the best possible way to proceed given the present situation and the understanding one has.

Reconciliation makes it all the more obvious that moral responsibility has to focus on responding to others and establishing and maintaining mutuality and that this in turn redefines the concepts of autonomy, self-reliance and self-definition. The work of reconciliation focuses on responsibility as

> participation in a communal work, laying the groundwork for the creative response of people in the present and the future. Responsible action means changing what can be altered in the present even though a problem is not completely resolved. Responsible action focuses on and respects partial resolutions and the inspiration and conditions for further partial resolutions ... [by ourselves] and by others.[11]

The work of reconciliation must recognise that those who have been apart and opposed to each other need to move together, one step at a time, willing to accept that risk, ambiguity and uncertainty are part of the process. The work of reconciliation asks above all for a commitment to mutuality, to opening possibilities together even if one might never see them become a reality – this

---

[11] Sharon Welch, *A Feminist Ethics of Risk* (Minneapolis, MN: Fortress Press, 1990), 68.

over and above a desire for tangible changes. Reconciliation must be guided by a sense that the results of much work and commitment may be only a list of shared desires and possibilities, but even such a minimal outcome is the result of mature ethical commitment and work that allows and obliges one to sustain a reconciling attitude and behaviour.

Reconciliation is a moral choice because it makes one remember that all persons have themselves been, at some point in their lives, oppressors and exploiters. This makes one understand that good intentions are not enough. Moral action requires the risk of taking steps together, of being accountable to each other, of participating in a process that concentrates on the future precisely by working to alter the present. Reconciliation as moral action makes it clear that healing the rifts that divide people cannot be incidental to one's life. Reconciliation is essential to being a human being, a responsible person, a person fully alive.

Reconciliation for any community that is divided – and as long as there is injustice divisions among people will exist – is the only just way to proceed. It is the only way to embrace the responsibility we all have for our communities and for the country in which we live. The only way to participate effectively, to contribute effectively to the future of our world, is to be reconciling people willing to suggest and explore possibilities together with those we have oppressed or who have oppressed us. Reconciliation is the only way to proceed with all sides recognising that reality always transcends what is and that the future cannot be a slavish repetition of the present or of the past. Reconciliation is the only way we will all come together to create possibilities for a common, inclusive future that is life-giving for all. Such is the moral responsibility of all those who call themselves Christians. Such is our vocation as a religious people who, while acknowledging our potential for self-deception,[12] believe in eternal possibilities because we believe in an ever-abiding divine presence among us.

Reconciliation: Biblical Basis

The way reconciliation is understood is greatly influenced by the process and elements the churches have historically considered necessary for what some earlier called 'the sacrament of penance' or 'confession', and is now called 'the sacrament of reconciliation'. For many, from a religious perspective, reconciliation requires interior repentance, an attitude that rejects wrongs freely done in the past and at the same time accepts responsibility for them. Interior repentance also requires a firm purpose of amendment: in other

---

[12] Stanley Hauerwas, *Truthfulness and Tragedy* (Notre Dame, IN: University of Notre Dame, 1977), 82–98.

words, a staunch resolution not to repeat the errors of the past. The sacrament of reconciliation also entails confessing one's sins to God or to a priest as well as offering satisfaction or reparation for the wrong done. This satisfaction or reparation is not made only to God, whom the sinner has offended, but also to the persons who have been 'injured by sin, for example, as reparation for injured love, for damage to reputation or property'.[13] Only once all these requirements are fulfilled is forgiveness granted.[14]

If we begin to conceive reconciliation, however, as an intrinsic element of justice and ground it in the biblical understanding of the absolute need to heal divisions as described in the parable in Matthew 25, reconciliation becomes different from how it has been traditionally conceived. Reconciliation as an element of justice is an essential way of knowing and healing brokenness in the world. Three requisites need to be fulfilled before one can come to know the reality of brokenness. First, to know brokenness one must be in the midst of brokenness, one has to be touched by it and have one's life impacted by it; second, one must take responsibility for it, understanding one's role in it; third, one must do something to heal it.[15] To heal brokenness – the work of reconciliation – begins the minute one enters into this threefold process of knowing its reality. To take responsibility for and start to work to heal the divisions that exist in any one given situation is already to become involved in the process of reconciliation. We simply cannot defer healing. Reconciliation begins to unfold even though only one side is willing to start working to make it happen. It cannot be postponed until those on the other side of the rift are willing to enter into this process. It cannot be postponed until reparation and restitution are made. Reconciliation should not be withheld or postponed for any reason whatsoever.

Perhaps this is nowhere clearer than in the early church's understanding of reconciliation reflected in the epistles of Colossians, in 2 Corinthians and in 1 John. The early followers of Jesus understood God's love and reconciliation to be something freely given, something that invited them to respond but was not conditioned by or dependent upon an expected response. The author

---

[13] Karl Rahner and Herbert Vorgrimler, 'Satisfaction', in *Dictionary of Theology* (New York: Crossroad, 1990), 462. See also articles on 'Penance', 'Penance, Sacrament of', 'Contrition', 'Metanoia', and 'Penalties of Sin'.

[14] The way these different elements are embodied depends of the different church traditions. For example, in the Roman Catholic tradition, confession of one's sins is to a priest while in the Protestant traditions, confession is to God.

[15] I am applying here Ignacio Ellacuría's understanding of the process of knowing reality to knowing the reality of brokenness and the need for reconciliation. There is a fuller explanation of this process in the article, '*Lo Cotidiano*: A Key Element of *Mujerista* Theology', in Ada María Isasi-Díaz, *La Lucha Continues: Mujerista Theology* (Maryknoll, NY: Orbis Books, 2004), 92–106. See Ignacio Ellacuría, 'Hacia una fundamentación del método teológico latinoamericano', *Estudios centroamericanos* 30, Nos 322–3 (agosto–septiembre, 1975), 419.

of 1 John says it succinctly: 'We are to love, then, because God loved us first' (I John 4:19). God loves first and unconditionally and we should respond by loving others in the same manner and not setting conditions to our love. In Colossians the author talks about Christ's reconciling act which does not depend on who is being reconciled or demands reparations but which indeed calls for a response. Reconciliation is presented as a one-sided process on God's part. God knows the reality of brokenness because the rift between God and those created to share in the divine 'affects' God, if in no other way than by disrupting God's plans. In 2 Corinthians two ideas about reconciliation become all the more clear. First, 'It is all God's work' (2 Cor. 5:18). Second, reconciliation happens because God does not hold the faults of humanity against us (v. 19). Nowhere in this text does it say that humanity must change for reconciliation to happen. It says precisely the contrary: humanity changes because of the reconciliation God freely bestows.

Reconciliation was for the early church an intrinsic part of its mission, and mission was considered a constitutive element of the church. The church was to appeal to all to be reconciled to God but this reconciliation was only a second step. The first step has already been given by God: God already has carried out the work of reconciliation. God's love comes first. The church knew that it could not preach what it did not live so it had to be a reconciling church, offering reconciliation freely, placing no conditions on it. The church knew that God appealed to all through the church's preaching and, particularly, through its behaviour. That appeal was precisely an appeal to reconciliation (2 Cor. 5:20).

Based on these gleanings from Scripture, reconciliation must be considered an element in the justice-seeking process that focuses on the future – a future that starts with the present and takes into consideration the past. In this sense reconciliation is a prophetic action: it has to do with healing people who suffer brokenness and divisions, and it looks for ways to make their hopes and expectations a reality in our world. Reconciliation is a prophetic action because it is about a preferred future of justice for all.

Reconciliation as a Religious, Social and Civic Virtue

From an ethical perspective reconciliation is a virtue. As such, reconciliation is not only a value but also a praxis: a way of acting in a conscious and reflective way. One has to work at it in order to become a good practitioner of reconciliation. Virtues are not themes to be elaborated in eloquent speeches but rather a way of living. To be good at the virtue of reconciliation one has not only to understand what it is but also to practice it. Virtues involve the disposition and actual competence to accomplish moral good: the virtue of reconciliation leads to actual reconciling behaviour. From an ethical perspective, to practise the virtue of reconciliation one must work in a concrete and effective way to build bridges over the rifts created by prejudices or by diversity of experiences, world-views or values. The virtue of reconciliation, like any other virtue, requires working at it so it can become a habit, the regular way of relating to others. In turn, because reconciliation becomes a regular way of relating, it also becomes a stable disposition of the person. This means that one cannot say one is in favour of reconciliation and at the same time believe it is enough to work at developing formulas for reconciliation so complex that they are not achievable, or think, for whatever reason, of whole groups of people that are to be excluded from the process of reconciliation. One has to find effective ways of working at reconciliation even if the results are only limited, even if it involves only a few people, even if all it accomplishes is to strengthen one's resolve and provide new perspectives regarding the work of reconciliation. It is obvious, then, that reconciliation does not exist unless one is in the process of reconciling oneself to others, unless one is working to reconcile oneself and others with those from whom we are estranged.

Reconciliation is a religious virtue because, for Christians, the main motive for it is precisely the Gospel message. It is a religious virtue because Christians believe that this is the kind of behaviour that Jesus demands from his followers. The biblical passages presented above make it clear that reconciliation is an important element in the manner the God of Jesus 'behaves', a behaviour self-communicated by God in a way that makes it possible for human beings to embrace it. As a religious virtue, then, reconciliation is a specific form of love. It is a specific form of grace. This means that reconciliation is one of the means God uses to enable human beings not only to relate to the God-self but to participate in divine nature itself.[16] Finally, from a religious perspective, reconciliation, as mentioned above, is not only a matter of personal behaviour but is a matter of the mission and very nature of the church.[17]

Reconciliation is also a social virtue. Human beings are social beings called to be in relationship and called to live as members of various communities – family, workplace, neighbourhood – that come together to form societies. Unfortunately, if it is true that human beings are social beings, it is also true that we fail repeatedly to be in right-relationships, that mistakes are made, that enmities are created. In this sense human beings live in tension between depending on others and being responsible to them while at the same

---

[16] Though the language I use here is the traditional Roman Catholic theological language, this understanding is also embraced by the Protestant tradition, though different terminology is used. See Rahner and Vorgrimler, 'Grace', in *Dictionary of Theology*, 196–200.

[17] This point is clear in 2 Corinthians 5:18–20. This is also one of the points René David makes so clear in his 1981 article.

time wanting to be self-sufficient even to the point of becoming selfish and turning against others. Reconciliation as a social virtue imposes the duty to overcome what separates human beings, what turns one against another, in order to be able to live the sociability that is an intrinsic characteristic of humanity. Not to do so, not to work at overcoming what creates rifts among human beings, is a betrayal of what is a fundamental human characteristic. To create or maintain divisions among persons and peoples is detrimental to all of humanity. This is precisely why reconciliation is a much-needed social virtue.

Finally, in the specific case of the United States at the beginning of the twenty-first century, when this country has waged wars or armed conflict as the aggressor, reconciliation is a civic virtue. It is a disposition and a practice that committed and faithful citizens of the US must embrace if they believe in the absolute need for justice in order for this country to flourish. A true commitment to reconciliation will bring about a revival or the creation of a moral commitment on the part of this country to respect differences. The 'American way of life' – that is, the way the US is politically, economically and socially organised, its mores and core values, both secular and religious that constitute the organising principle of the nation – may be the preferred way for the US but it is not the only way of life that is good. It is not, therefore, the way of life that must be chosen by other nations and other peoples in our world. Reconciliation as a civic virtue in the US at the beginning of the twenty-first century must necessarily start with sobering humility. The US must recognise that it needs the rest of the world. It must search its soul and candidly disclose that it needs others, that it must build common interests with nations and peoples around the world. This country must recognize that without authentic mutual solidarity with other nations the 'American way of life' is condemned to disappear. Reconciliation as a civic virtue obliges the people of the US to recognize that the richness and privileges they enjoy have been obtained and are maintained, to a great extent, at the expense of others. The exploitation that makes possible the riches and privileges enjoyed in the US is what has created the rift between the US and other countries and peoples. The need to heal that rift for the sake of the future of the world – that is what reconciliation as a civic virtue aims to accomplish.

Reconciliation: Building a Common Future for All

Reconciliation necessitates that people come together and agree on the future of our world. True reconciliation necessarily will arouse shared feelings and lead to joint action. Reconciliation involves building a common programmatic vision about our world, and this cannot be done outside a process of dialogue. In authentic dialogue the parties involved seek not to convince one another or to move the other to one's own perspective. They seek instead to move all those involved to a point of view and a programme of action that has been forged together. For the kind of dialogue needed for reconciliation to happen, we must embrace a way of understanding differences, as explained above, that does not focus on what separates, excludes and sets us in opposition, but rather recognises that differences presume boundaries that enable people to make connections and come together. Dialogue cannot happen unless we recognise differences and diversity not necessarily as what separates us but as what we each bring to the table, as the resources from which each of us involved in the process of reconciliation can draw to conceptualise the future and begin to create it.

Such an understanding raises a question: what about our values? A call to true dialogue and reconciliation is not a call to betray one's values. However, all those who engage in dialogue need to understand there are different values and/or that the same values can be actualised differently in diverse circumstances. Sometimes through the process of dialogue one comes to know that what originally were thought to be values contrary to ours are simply values different from ours, not necessarily values opposed to ours. It often happens that personal insecurity makes us incapable of seeing what we could well consider positive in the values held by others. Of course there are values and counter-values. Some values directly oppose or work to diminish the ones we hold. This is important and should not be minimised. However, there are more areas of similarities than of dissimilarities among the values that people hold. Commitment to dialogue makes us become experts in finding these similarities, these areas of agreement, joint understandings, common visions about the future of our world, our future as a people and a nation.

Understanding, appreciating and learning from realities, experiences and world-views of people who might be quite different from us is essential to the process of dialogue and reconciliation. We are linked to others no matter how dissimilar we might be, for in our world today no country can consider itself isolated, apart from others, not interconnected with others. Common interests exist in our world. We do not need to invent them. We do need, however, to recognise consciously those common interests, to embrace the infinite number of ways in which we are interconnected with people who live far away as much as with people who are nearby.

The first realisation in this part of dialogue is indeed the acceptance that we all, out of our experiences, have something to contribute to a common future. Secondly, we are called to learn to see reality from the point of view of others. We are called to decentralise ourselves and not only understand the perspective of others but also learn to see what is positive in their understandings, how their understandings can enrich us. Of course this is not an easy process. We are talking about building a programmatic world-view that uses a shared understanding of history, the experiences of the everyday life of people who live in very different circumstances, and our own dreams and expectations about our world. A programmatic world-view must remain open to developments because it is not about an absolute future but about a historical future. It must remain open to developments for it must not impose an ideology but rather respond to the needs of the people and be intentional about being open to different possibilities.[18] Therefore, no matter where we live, we need to realise that getting to know each other and learning about the many interconnections that exist among people all over the world is a viable and important first step in the process of reconciliation. We are all the poorer when we forget how we need each other, how we are related to each other. When we do not understand that who we are and what we are about is closely linked to the rest of the world, we are dehumanised because life becomes poorer when it is deprived of what gives all human beings meaning: friendship, love, relationships.[19] Without a strong sense of interdependence we lose in part what is precisely characteristic of the human species: sociability.

This will not happen easily. Often it seems almost impossible even to get those with whom we seek to be reconciled to come to the table. And, though the gratuitousness of God's reconciliation demands of us to be reconciling persons, the process of reconciliation involves more than one party. This means that those with whom we are trying to be reconciled must recognise that reconciliation is needed. Perhaps the key is to make those we need to be reconciled with understand that what one seeks is not to convince them that they are wrong or to win them to one's side. What we seek is true dialogue that will move us jointly to a place we have created together. What all involved need to understand is that reconciliation is a process and that the dialogue that is central to this process must start as soon as possible, at whatever level is possible, in whatever circumstances exist. Dialogue in this situation becomes a practice of reconciliation which needs to be sustained and enriched by the common experiences of coming together, of getting to know each other and understanding each other for the sake of a common future.

Reconciliation: Dealing with the Past, Rooted in the Present, in View of the Future

The process of becoming acquainted in new and better ways and of building together a programmatic world-view is but one of the elements of

---

[18] Aloysius Pieris, *An Asian Theology of Liberation* (Maryknoll, NY: Orbis Books, 1988), 24–31.

[19] See Antjie Krog, *Country of My Skull* (Johannesburg: Random House, 1998), particularly Chapter 10.

reconciliation. Undoubtedly and necessarily we also must deal with the wrongs that have been committed on all sides causing pain and suffering to many. This makes the process of reconciliation all the more taxing and difficult, all the more demanding and urgent. Suffering is not the prerogative of any one side. There has been and there is suffering on all sides. There is no easy way through this rough and dangerous part of the path to reconciliation. However, even when it comes to wrongs committed and suffering inflicted we have to keep in mind that reconciliation is first of all about the future, and not about the past. We always have to keep in mind, when looking at the past, that the passing of time makes retrieving it impossible, that who we are today is different from who we were in the past, who we were even in the recent past, even yesterday. This is why 'any return is not a return: it is coming into a new place.'[20] This is why looking at the past only makes sense if it is part of constructing the future.

The second thing to keep in mind is that, in the process of reconciliation, dealing with the past, dealing with the wrongs we have done and the pain we have caused each other, cannot be in any way related to a sense of revenge.[21] Revenge is a destructive force that becomes a never-ending and widening spiral of violence. Revenge is a stagnating force that makes future-oriented movement impossible. It is antithetical to reconciliation because it capitalises on what separates us; it insists on payment for what simply cannot be paid for.[22] Revenge refuses to recognise that wrongs have been committed and suffering has been caused on all sides. Revenge does not make right what was wrong or restore the value of what was lost. Most often revenge stems from attempts to assuage guilt for what we did or allowed to happen, guilt we feel but will not admit. Revenge promotes a self-centredness that makes any attempt to build common interests and actions impossible.[23]

---

[20] Robert J. Schreiter, *Reconciliation – Mission and Ministry in a Changing Social Order* (Maryknoll, NY: Orbis Books, 1992), 11.

[21] The violence between the Israelis and the Palestinians rages on while I write this article. Yesterday a Palestinian woman who lives in a border town in Gaza spoke in her broken English with a US television reporter. 'The people who want revenge have a little heart,' she said gesturing with her hand to show the tiniest of space between her two fingers. Behind her one could see her children playing with their little friends.

[22] The importance of giving up any desire for revenge is striking in the following event. In 1996 the Cuban Air Force shot down two small civilian airplanes belonging to a Cuban exile group, 'Brothers to the Rescue'. Though the families of the four men killed have pursued action against the Cuban government in the US courts, one of the families has taken the position of not asking for nor accepting any monetary compensation for the death of their son. In part their reason might be not to 'put a price' on the life of their dead relative. But part has also to do with the desire not to seek revenge.

[23] In the history of my own country, Cuba, there is an important example of the need not to seek revenge. The 'Manifiesto de Montecristi', Cuba's declaration of independence from Spain, written by José Martí, 'the father of the country', on 25 March 1895, twice speaks against vengeance. The document insists that those declaring war have been cleansed of hatred

   In dealing with the past we often talk about restitution and retribution. When we claim retribution for those who suffered and are no longer with us, is it not our own needs and expectations that motivate us? Just as we say that the dead demand restitution and retribution, we could say that they pardon those who harmed them and that their memory pleads for reconciliation. Those of us living now are the ones who decide how to appropriate and use what has happened in the past. We do indeed choose how to read into the present and future the sufferings of the past. Those who are alive today, not those who have died, are the ones who will benefit from any restitution and retribution. Therefore, those who are alive today can also move beyond restitution and retribution that focuses on the past and embrace reconciliation with their eyes fixed in the future.[24]

   What can we say about those who are still alive who have been personally wronged, who have endured pain and suffering, who can point to specific individuals who have exploited and abused them? This is a most delicate and personal matter but not a private one. Personal forgiveness or non-forgiveness is something in which we all are involved. Any attempt to hide or to ignore the pain and suffering inflicted on some will be devastating for the creation of a common future. But how we deal with that pain and suffering cannot be left in the hands of individuals, for what they do becomes part of how we all make possible or impede reconciliation. Though we need to acknowledge and give a public hearing to the voices of those who have suffered, reconciliation must prevail instead of the demand for retribution or the decision not to forgive.[25]

   We must recognise that if we do not make public the memories of those who suffered personally, individual and national healing will not be possible. However, we also must embrace the fact that without reconciliation we cannot move on to build together the future.[26] As a people we must understand that those who have suffered need to tell their stories, to have others witness to the horror that has been inflicted on them, in order to have their memories respected, to find a way of dealing with what they have endured, to regain their dignity and wholeness as human beings. Unless those who have suffered can be healed, the nation will suffer by not being able to

---

and have a sense of indulgence regarding Cubans who are timid or who are mistaken. It also mentions that during the war and once it is over they will be merciful with those who repent. See Carlos Ripoll, *José Martí – Antología Mayor* (New York: Editorial Dos Ríos, 1995), 59–61.

[24] Desmond Tutu, *No Future Without Forgiveness* (New York: Doubleday, 1999), 257–82.

[25] I heard Sister Helen Prejean, a nun who works with persons on Death Row and who opposes capital punishment, make this point in a public lecture a few years ago. See, Helen Prejean, *Dead Man Walking – An Eyewitness Account of the Death Penalty in the USA* (New York: Random House, Vintage Books, 1994).

[26] This is the understanding of Archbishop Tutu which has become entrenched in large areas of South African society and which has guided the work of the South African Truth and Reconciliation Commission.

benefit from what they can contribute to the building of our common future. Yet the process of personal healing must happen within the national process of reconciliation and in no way can it militate against it.[27] Those who for many reasons find it difficult to embrace reconciliation, given what they have personally suffered, might do well to take seriously the many who have been at each other's throat, who have been enemies, and yet have chosen to struggle to live together in peace.[28]

A Spirituality, a Culture, a Mystique of Reconciliation

At the beginning of the twenty-first century I believe the future of the US as a nation and of the whole world depends on our ability to develop a spirituality, a culture and a mystique of reconciliation that will make it possible for us to practice reconciliation as a religious, social and civic virtue. To embrace a spirituality of reconciliation is to understand that for Christians there can be no possibility of relating to God unless we have a reconciling attitude and a reconciling practice towards each other. Because our relationship with God is intrinsically linked to the way we relate to each other, a reconciling God cannot but ask of those who believe to have a reconciling attitude towards each other. To relate to God is not something apart from how we live our daily lives. Therefore, our response to a reconciling God has to be a reconciling day-to-day living without exception and without conditions.

Culture includes all that we humans have cultivated and dreamed, all that we have created to deal with the world: tools, customs, societal structures,

---

[27] The *Sunday Times* of Capetown, South Africa (6 December 1998) carried an article entitled, 'Forgive the torturer, not the torture', written by Wilhelm Verwoerd, lecturer in political philosophy and applied ethics at Stellenbosch University. The article talks about Ashley Forbes, a black South African, tortured by Jeffrey Benzien, who before the Truth and Reconciliation Commission of that country had 'publicly demonstrated his notorious "wet-bag" torture technique'. The article says that it was 'Forbes's choice to put aside legitimate feelings of anger and humiliation and thus, "get on with the rest of my life"'. The article goes on: 'Sometimes victims are asked to forgive for the sake of perpetrators, to release the wrongdoers from their burden of guilt. That is an important part of forgiveness, but not the whole story ... Forbes shows that forgiveness should be encouraged, perhaps in the first place, as an antidote to the poison of unresolved bitterness and repressed resentment, as a call to those violated to liberate themselves from the prison of victimhood – for the sake of themselves, their children and the rest of society ... A powerful emotional reason for resisting forgiveness is because it is seen as diminishing the seriousness of violations. Forgiveness becomes a sign of disrespect to those who have been violated ... Archbishop Desmond Tutu ... is requesting nobody to forgive the gross human-rights violations of the past. It is a call to recognise the humanity of "perpetrators" even if their humanity is hidden behind a wet-bag ... Those who suffered and continue to suffer are given the moral first place they deserve. The truth commission process flows from that commitment.'

[28] See Antjie Krog, *Country of My Skull*, 23–5.

ideas about reality, and representations of ideas. A culture of reconciliation, therefore, requires us not only to counter in every way possible enmity, opposition and alienation, but actually to nurture and foster openness, dialogue and a dynamic understanding of differences not based on exclusion and confrontation. A culture of reconciliation is key in this whole process because all nations have a cultural origin before they have a political one. A culture of reconciliation is important for the US because the way it has dealt and still deals with many nations and peoples around the globe has resulted in deep-seated mistrust, enmity, war. Given the primacy of culture in all national identification, reconciliation has to be an option that those of us who live in the US make for ourselves, a practice that we implement in every aspect of our lives.

Finally, we need a mystique of reconciliation. A mystique is an intangible force that enables those who embrace it to face all reality. It refers to an understanding that provides a social cohesion, enabling participants to do what they have not been able to do alone but what becomes possible when one participates in a shared experience.[29] A mystique of reconciliation, therefore, makes it possible for us, even in the most adverse of circumstances, to practise the virtue of reconciliation as a way – the most needed way – to be truly Christian, to be truly patriotic. A mystique of reconciliation provides the strength that we might not have individually to struggle against the conviction that we have nothing to repent about, that as a country our motives always are liberty, freedom and democracy. A mystique of reconciliation will make it possible for us to be open to the dreams and the hopes of people all over the world, particularly the poor and oppressed. It will allow us to welcome other ways of understanding reality and of organising societies, economies, governments different from those in the US. Only then will we have a solid base on which to build peace and justice. Only a mystique of reconciliation will help us create a world in which the main preoccupation is how to stand together as one, how to recognise the common interests that bind us, how to be inclusive societies that take into consideration the well-being of all peoples.

---

[29] Renny Golden, *The Hour of the Poor, the Hour of the Women* (New York: Crossroad, 1991), 17.

CHAPTER 6

The Theology of Reconciliation and the Recovery of Memory Project in Guatemala

David Tombs

Political theology emerges out of a readiness to see God's presence in the political world, and a willingness to think through the implications of this from a faith perspective and for a faith perspective. As such, political theology requires a two-way engagement with political issues. As a first step, it means learning about politics and the realities of the political world. As a second step, it involves an openness to rethinking theological doctrines in ways that will sustain Christian concern for peace, justice and reconciliation. It is the willingness to rethink theology in the light of concrete political experience that gives political theology much of its creativity and relevance. It reformulates the understanding of Christian doctrines in the light of practical experience.

In this way, a theological perspective can help to deepen an understanding of the thorny issues raised in the processes of political reconciliation, including transitional justice, truth-recovery, political forgiveness, social healing, apologies and reparations.[1] At the same time, the theological challenges raised by these reconciliation processes – like the relationship between truth and freedom, reconciliation and healing, forgiveness and apology, and amnesty and amnesia – can be important resources for understanding and critiquing how these dynamics operate in Christian doctrines.

For this reason, the South African Truth and Reconciliation Commission (1995–98) has been the focus of particular theological interest. The involvement of prominent church leaders in the commission, and the implicit

---

[1] For good overviews on the dynamics of political reconciliation, see especially David Bloomfield et al., *Reconciliation After Violent Conflict: A Handbook* (Stockholm: Institute for Democracy and Electoral Assistance, 2003); Neil J. Kritz (ed.), *Transitional Justice* (3 vols; Washington, DC: United States Institute of Peace Press, 1995); Ruti G. Teitel, *Transitional Justice* (Oxford: Oxford University Press, 2000); Andrew Rigby, *Justice and Reconciliation: After the Violence* (Boulder, CO: Lynne Rienner, 2001); Martha Minow, *Between Vengeance and Forgiveness: Facing History after Genocide and Mass Violence* (Boston, MA: Beacon Press, 1998); Nigel Biggar (ed.), *Burying the Past: Making Peace and Doing Justice After Civil Conflict* Georgetown, SC: Georgetown University Press, rev. edn 2003 [2001]; on truth commissions, see especially Priscilla Hayner, *Unspeakable Truths: Confronting State Terror and Atrocity* (New York and London: Routledge, 2000).

– and at times quite explicit – Christian 'theology of reconciliation' that developed in the commission's work, give it an obvious theological significance.[2]

Desmond Tutu repeatedly emphasised his faith in the healing power of truth-telling, captured in the banners 'Revealing is Healing' at commission hearings, and personally urged those involved to forgive in a spirit of reconciliation.[3] Tutu was a charismatic and inspiring example for many South Africans, but some critics questioned whether it was legitimate to include prayers and hymns at public hearings and orientate the commission so much around confessional convictions. It seemed that Christian morality had too prominent a place and Christian notions of forgiveness were being giving precedence over the victims' rights to justice.[4]

In comparison with South Africa, the religious elements in Latin American truth-recovery processes have had a much lower profile. Yet the Latin American commission are still important resources for grounding a theology of reconciliation.[5] It is unfortunate that so little has been written about them from a theological perspective.[6]

---

[2] The commission's final report has been published as Truth and Reconciliation Commission of South Africa (TRCSA), *Truth and Reconciliation Commission of South Africa Report* (5 vols; Cape Town: Juta and Co., 1998; London: Macmillan, 1999), hereafter *TRC Report*. On the work of the commission, see Alex Boraine, *A Country Unmasked: Inside South Africa's Truth and Reconciliation Commission* (Oxford: Oxford University Press, 2000); Piet Meiring, *Chronicle of the Truth Commission: A Journey Through the Past and Present into the Future of South Africa* (Vanderjipark, SA: Carpe Diem Books, 1999); Antjie Krog, *Country of My Skull* (Johannesburg: Random House, 1998; New York: Times Books, 1999); Kader Asmal, Louise Asmal and R. Suresh Roberts, *Reconciliation Through Truth: A Reckoning of Apartheid's Criminal Governance* (New York: St Martin's Press, rev. edn 1997 [1996]); Charles Villa-Vicencio and Wilhelm Verwoerd (eds), *Looking Back and Reaching Forward: Reflections on the Truth and Reconciliation Commission of South Africa* (Cape Town: University of Cape Town Press; London: Zed Books, 2000). For some of the theological issues arising in relation to the commission, see H. Russel Botman and Robin M. Petersen (eds), *To Remember and to Heal: Theological and Psychological Reflections on Truth and Reconciliation* (Cape Town: Human and Rousseau, 1996).

[3] See especially Desmond Tutu, 'Foreword by Chairperson', in *TRC Report*, Vol. 1, 1–23. For his own autobiographical account of the experience, see Desmond Tutu, *No Future without Forgiveness* (New York: Doubleday; London: Rider, 1999). On the theology of ubuntu underlying Tutu's calls for forgiveness and reconciliation, see Michal Battle, *Reconciliation: The Ubuntu Theology of Desmond Tutu* (Cleveland, OH: Pilgrim Press, 1997); John De Gruchy, *Reconciliation* (London: SCM Press, 2002).

[4] See, for example, Richard Wilson, *The Politics of Truth and Reconciliation in South Africa: Legitimizing the Post-Apartheid State* (Cambridge: Cambridge University Press, 2001).

[5] This is even more notable in view of the fact that the South African commission was in many ways an innovative experiment and its adoption of 'selective amnesty' makes it the exception rather than the rule.

[6] A partial exception to this is Walter Wink, *When the Powers Fail: Reconciliation in the Healing of the Nation* (Minneapolis, MN: Augsburg Fortress, 1988), 33–48.

For those interested in how the debates might look rather different when related to the Latin American context, the recent Guatemalan truth commissions, which deal with roughly the same period as the South African commission, offer an interesting comparison. In terms of Christian involvement in the issues, the Guatemalan experience is also particularly relevant because the official UN commission 'Guatemala: Memory of Silence' (1997–99) was accompanied by a church initiative entitled 'The Recovery of Memory Project' (1995–98) motivated by an explicitly theological concern.[7]

The church initiative (usually known by its Spanish acronym as the REMHI project) illustrates how the church can be practically involved in a positive way in the truth-seeking process, and demonstrates the significance this has for reconciliation. REMHI is an inspiring testimony to the social ministry of the Catholic Church in Guatemala. Its commitment to truth as a path of reconciliation deserves much wider public awareness and recognition. However, despite the success of the REMHI project as a truth-recovery process, the Guatemalan experience is also a clear illustration of the wider problems that often remain. Nowhere is this more clear than in Guatemala's weak judicial system and the high levels of impunity that the Guatemalan military continues to enjoy.

The elusiveness of justice in Guatemala highlights the limitations of any reconciliation initiative when perpetrators remain unrepentant and unaccountable. For those committed to peace-building and reconciliation this poses an unavoidable dilemma. On the one hand there is an ethical and theological requirement that justice and reconciliation should always go together; yet on the other hand in many situations this seems to be an impossible hope. Those who work for reconciliation do not want to accept that in such situations nothing can be done; but nor can they accept that justice be left out of the discussion. Ways have to be found for the integrity of the reconciliation process to be preserved even when external constraints seem to undermine the foundation of justice on which it should be built. This is not just a political challenge; it is also an ethical and theological issue that goes to the heart of the credibility of a political theology of reconciliation.

Truth and Memory in the REMHI Project

Guatemala has experienced high levels of political repression ever since the Spanish conquest (1524–34). However, its recent history has included three

---

[7] This is also significant because much of the theological debate around truth commissions has centred around the South African Truth and Reconciliation Commission, and been influenced to a greater or lesser degree by a Protestant outlook. The REMHI project offers an opportunity for engagement with a distinctively Catholic theological perspective.

particularly brutal periods of political violence: first in 1954, after the US-sponsored coup against the reformist government; then again in 1967–71, when organised right-wing paramilitaries first emerged and death squads started to kill and 'disappear' people; and finally in 1978–85, the period which is often referred to simply as *'La Violencia'*.[8]

The UN Historical Clarification Commission had been agreed in 1994 as part of the peace negotiations and began its work in 1997 after the final peace agreements in 1996.[9] It was to study the period 1962–94 and recommend measures to promote peace and reconciliation.[10] The Recovery of Historical Memory project (known as the REMHI project) was an interdiocesan initiative of the Catholic Church established in 1995 to support and supplement the UN commission in dealing with this painful chapter in Guatemalan history.[11] The REMHI project compiled 5465 testimonies documenting 52,467 victims of human rights violations.[12] It identified the Guatemalan military and associated paramilitaries as responsible for nearly 90 per cent of the abuses, whilst attributing less than 5 per cent to the guerrillas.[13] The worst of the violence took place between 1980 and 1983 – under the military regimes of General Lucas García (1978–82),

---

[8] Of the extensive literature on the Guatemalan conflict, see especially Susanne Jonas, *The Battle for Guatemala: Rebels, Death Squads and U.S. Power* (Boulder, CO: Westview Press, 1991); for an extensive bibliography, see Ralph L. Woodward, *Guatemala* (Oxford: Clio, rev. edn 1992 [1981]).

[9] The commission is usually known by its Spanish acronym as the CEH (*Comisión de Esclarecimiento Histórico*). Whilst it is commonly referred to as a 'truth commission', the Guatemalan military insisted that the commission did not have the word 'truth' in its official title, which was 'The Commission to Clarify Past Human Rights Violations and Acts of Violence that have caused the Guatemalan Population to Suffer'. The final twelve-volume report was presented in February 1999, and published four months later as CEH, *Guatemala: Memoria del Silencio* (Guatemala: United Nations, 1999) available on CD-ROM (published April 2000), or at <http://shr.aaas.org/guatemala/ceh>. An English translation of the Prologue, Conclusions (including statistical appendices) and Recommendations, has been published as: United Nations Commission for Historical Memory, *Guatemala Memory of Silence: Summary* (New York: United Nations, 1999), and is available at <http://shr.aaas.org/guatemala/ceh/report/english>. On similarities and differences between the CEH and the South African TRC, see Joanna R. Quinn, 'Lessons Learned: Practical Lessons Gleaned from Inside the Truth Commissions of Guatemala and South Africa', *Human Rights Quarterly* 25.4 (November 2003), 1117–49.

[10] Most commentators refer to the 'thirty-six-year war', dating this period as 1960–96. For background to the REMHI report and its objectives, see M. López Levy, 'Recovery: The Uses of Memory and History in the Guatemalan Church's REMHI Project' in M.A. Hayes and D. Tombs (eds), *Truth and Memory: The Church and Human Rights in El Salvador and Guatemala* (Leominster: Gracewing, 2001), 103–17; Kathy Ogle, 'Guatemala's REMHI Project: Memory from Below', *NACLA* 32.2 (1998), 33–4.

[11] REMHI is the Spanish acronym for 'Recuperación de la memoria histórica'.

[12] REMHI, *Guatemala: Never Again!*, 289.

[13] REMHI, *Guatemala: Never Again!*, 290.

General Efraín Ríos Montt (1982–83), and General Oscar Mejía Víctores – which accounted for nearly 80 per cent of the victims recorded by REMHI.[14]

Drawing on the REMHI statistics and combining them with its own investigations and other sources, the UN CEH report estimated that in total 200,000 people had been killed or disappeared, as well as 200,000 children orphaned and 40,000 women widowed during the conflict.[15]

The conviction that documenting the truth of what happened in these years would make an important contribution to long-term healing at both an individual and a political level guided the REMHI project from start to finish. Chaired by Bishop Juan Gerardi, who was Auxiliary Bishop for Guatemala City and Head of the Archdiocesan Human Rights Office (ODHAG), the REMHI organisers made a careful study of how their work might be of most help to the victims and survivors of the violence.[16] This makes the project one of the most significant and creative examples of the work of the church in Latin America for human rights.[17] After three years of work the four-volume report *Guatemala: Nunca Mas!* was presented on 24 April 1998.[18] The

---

[14] REMHI, *Guatemala: Never Again!*, 290.

[15] The CEH registered a total of 42,275 victims (including men, women and children) and noted that 83 per cent of identified victims were members of indigenous communities; CEH, *Guatemala: Memory of Silence: Conclusions*, §1. It also confirmed REMHI's verdict that the Guatemalan military were responsible for the overwhelming majority of these, estimating that state forces and associated paramilitaries were responsible for 93 per cent of the violations, *Conclusions*, §80. Furthermore, after a careful study, the CEH confirmed that the military's scorched-earth offensive in the highlands (1981–83), should be classified as an act of genocide; *Conclusions*, §§108–23. On the statistics relating to the conflict, see especially Patrick Ball, Paul Kobrak and Herbert F. Spirer, *State Violence in Guatemala: 1960–1996: A Quantitative Reflection* (Washington, DC: American Association for the Advancement of Science, 1999); Patrick Ball, 'Exploring the Implications of Source Selection in the the Case of Gautemalan State Terror, 1977–1995', *Journal of Conflict Resolution* 46.3 (June 2002), 427–50.

[16] On Gerardi's life, work and untimely death, see especially Scott Wright, 'Oscar Romero and Juan Gerardi: Truth, Memory and Hope' in M.A. Hayes and D. Tombs (eds), *Truth and Memory*, 11–43.

[17] As a ground-breaking church initative in human rights work, REMHI stands in continuity with the remarkable *Nunca Mais* report compiled by the Archdiocese of São Paulo in the previous decade; *Torture in Brazil: A Shocking Report on the Pervasive Use of Military Torture by the Brazilian Governments 1964–79, Secretly Prepared by the Archdiocese of São Paulo* (trans. Jaime Wright; ed. Joan Dassin; New York: Vintage Books, 1986 [Portuguese orig. 1985]). On the compilation of the *Nunca Mais* report, see Lawrence Weschler, *A Miracle, A Universe: Settling Accounts with Torturers* (Chicago, IL and London: University of Chicago Press, rev. edn 1998 [1990]).

[18] REMHI, *Guatemala Nunca Más* (Informe proyecto interdiocesano de recuperación de la memoria histórica; 4 vols; Guatemala: and Oficina del Derechos Humanos del Arzobispado de Guatemala [ODHAG], 1998), it is available online via <http://www.odhag.org.gt>.

following year an abridged version was published in English as *Guatemala: Never Again!*[19]

As Thomas Quigley of the US Catholic Conference notes in his Foreword to the English edition, *Guatemala: Never Again!* is more than a truth commission report: it should also be considered as a theological work and part of the church's pastoral mission for reconciliation and healing.[20] Christians are called to this work in the faith that this mission is not just ethical but truly 'theological'; it deepens the understanding of God's painful love for the world.

From a Christian perspective, there is an important biblical principle behind the truth-seeking of investigative commissions. Bishop Gerardi made this explicit in his REMHI presentation speech in the Cathedral in Guatemala City, when he pointed to the promise made in John 8:32: 'For you will know the truth and the truth will set you free'. As Gerardi observed, REMHI sought to give practical expression to Christian faith in the power of truth:

> The essential objective behind the REMHI project during its three years of work has been to know the truth that will make us all free (John 8.32). Reflecting on the Historical Clarification Accord, we, as people of faith, discovered a call from God for our mission as church – that truth should be the vocation of all humanity.[21]

Picking up on the words of the preceding verse, 'If you continue in my work, you are truly my disciples' (John 8:31), Gerardi explained:

> If we orient ourselves according to the Word of God, we cannot hide or cover up reality. We cannot distort history, nor should we silence the truth … To open ourselves to truth and to face our personal and collective reality are not options that can be accepted or rejected. They are indispensable requirements for all people and societies that seek to humanize themselves and to be free. They make us face our most essential human condition: that we are sons and daughters of God, called to participate in our Father's freedom.[22]

The Greek word for truth – *aletheia* – which literally means 'uncovered' (*a-letheia*), is an apt expression for truth-telling as 'dis-covery'. To discover what has hitherto been hidden and bring it out into the open may involve new pain, but it can also help society and individuals to deal with the past and discover new paths for the future.

---

[19] REMHI/ODHAG, *Guatemala: Never Again!* (The Official Report of the Human Rights Office, Archdiocese of Guatemala; trans. G. Tovar Siebentritt; Maryknoll, NY: Orbis Books; London: Catholic Institute for International Relations and Latin America Bureau, 1999).

[20] Thomas Quigley, 'Foreword to the English Edition' in *Guatemala: Never Again!*, xv.

[21] Juan Gerardi, 'Speech on Presentation of the REMHI Report', in REMHI, *Guatemala: Never Again!*, xxiii–xxv (xxiv).

[22] Gerardi, 'Speech on Presentation of the REMHI Report', xxiv–xxv.

As Gerardi commented:

> It is a liberating and humanizing truth that makes it possible for all men and women to come to terms with themselves and their life stories. It is a truth that challenges each one of us to recognise our individual and collective responsibility and to commit ourselves to action so that those abominable acts never happen again ... Discovering the truth is painful, but it is without doubt a healthy and liberating action.[23]

Gerardi therefore explicitly linked the REMHI project's search for truth with the church's pastoral ministry of reconciliation, saying that 'We are called to reconciliation. Christ's mission is one of reconciliation. His presence calls us to be agents of reconciliation in this broken society and to try and to place the victims and perpetrators within the framework of justice.'[24]

In some cases, the actual process of investigation and testimony can be as important as the publication of the findings. In testifying to a commission, survivors document their story. Sometimes this is the first time that they have been able to record it officially. To have their testimony formally acknowledged in this way often provides a strong sense of vindication, especially if it follows years of systematic denial by the authorities and wider society, and even their own self-denial. In presenting the REMHI report, Gerardi recognised that recovering the memory of past abuses would create new pain for many of the survivors. He was aware that 'It is a painful truth, full of memories of the country's deep and bloody wounds.'[25] For some victims, testifying to the truth about atrocities might at first seem to be an additional punishment rather than an affirmation of their dignity. None the less, the REMHI project was founded on the belief that despite the pain, for many people facing up to the memory of past atrocities was an essential step in the healing process. As Gerardi put it: 'To open ourselves to truth and to face our personal and collective reality are not options that can be accepted or rejected. They are indispensable requirements for all people and societies that seek to humanize themselves and to be free.'[26]

Many interviewees testified to the significance of breaking the silence as the starting point for healing. For those able to face it, recalling the abuse and re-experiencing its pain ultimately had positive consequences. One testimony affirmed: 'To make things bearable we have to bring them to light. That's the only way the wounds will be healed.'[27]

Opening the scars in order to help wounds that never properly healed is the central principle behind therapeutic work for a wide range of traumas. As trauma expert Judith Herman puts it: 'Atrocities ... refuse to be buried.

---

[23] Gerardi, 'Speech on Presentation of the REMHI Report', xxv.

[24] Gerardi, 'Speech on Presentation of the REMHI Report', xxiii.

[25] Gerardi, 'Speech on Presentation of the REMHI Report', xxv.

[26] Gerardi, 'Speech on Presentation of the REMHI Report', xxiv–xxv.

[27] Case 0569 Cobán (September 1981); cited Carlos M. Beristain, 'Guatemala: Nunca Más', *Forced Migration Review*, 3 (December 1998), 23–6 (25).

Equally as powerful as the desire to deny atrocities is the conviction that denial does not work ... Remembering and telling the truth about terrible events are prerequisites both for the restoration of the social order and for the healing of individual victims.'[28]

The experience of many torture victims shows that it is naïve to think that healing can occur in some magical way as soon as the truth becomes known. State terror is likely to leave deep scars.[29] The scale of the violence, the different ways in which it is experienced (often in combination), its continuance over time, its communal element and the fact that it is legitimated by the state multiplies the experience of trauma. Survivors often need long-term help and support in rebuilding their personal identities and their social confidence. Yet therapists who have worked with Latin American torture victims support the view that the past usually needs to be confronted in order to make new futures possible. One group of therapists who have specialised in this work in Chile comment:

> ... the more victims try to forget and leave their terrible experience in the past, the more they tend to reproduce it in the present in the form of emotional illness. But once they begin to confront the past directly, the past, present, and future can be adequately discriminated. To achieve this, we have found that the person or the family needs to recount the traumatic experience in detail, and express the emotions it produced.[30]

The South African Commission also cautioned against over-optimistic visions of storytelling as healing. They note that the dynamics involved are often much more complex than simple formulas suggest.[31] Whilst there were a number of well-publicised examples of victims finding healing, and other cases in which victims and perpetrators experienced meaningful reconciliation, there were also cases which seemed to be made worse rather than better. In some cases victims were retraumatised by the very experience of giving testimony, in others they felt an initial sense of healing but then suffered anti-climax and frustration.[32] Alongside the cases of reconciliation there were many cases where victims and perpetrators remained estranged.

------

[28] Judith Herman, *Trauma and Recovery: From Domestic Abuse to Political Terror* (London: Pandora, rev. edn 2001 [orig. 1992]).

[29] See Dianna Ortiz, *The Blindfold's Eye: My Journey from Torture to Truth* (Maryknoll, NY: Orbis Books, 2002).

[30] D. Becker et al., 'Therapy with the Victims of Political Repression in Chile: The Challenge of Social Reparation', *Journal of Social Issues* 46.3 (1990), 133–49 (142); see also Nancy C. Hollander, *Love in a Time of Hate: Liberation Psychology in Latin America* (Rutgers, NJ: Rutgers University Press, 1998).

[31] For a careful discussion, see B. Hamber, 'Does the Truth Heal? A Psychological Perspective on Political Strategies for Dealing with the Legacy of Political Violence', in N. Biggar (ed.), *Burying the Past: Making Peace and Doing Justice after Civil Conflict* (Washington, DC: Georgetown University Press, 2001), 131–48 (esp. 133–8).

[32] Feelings of frustration were exacerbated by the long delay over remuneration, especially in contrast to the relatively quick progress on amnesties.

Truth-recovery processes will not affect everyone the same way. Each individual is different and will react in his or her own individual way. Thus whilst there are good arguments in support of individual and political healing through truth, there are obvious problems with any simplistic 'formula approach' to truth-telling as healing.[33] A universal expectation of healing through truth is unrealistic. Equally unrealistic is a belief that truth on its own can heal every social injustice or transform political power. Other structural and social changes are needed alongside the recovery of the truth if political and economic institutions are to be changed for the better. 'Healing through truth' is not a universal law, nor is it a simple mechanical process. Likewise, truth-recovery is not a sufficient condition or a guaranteed means of political reconciliation. None the less, the recovery and official acknowledgment of truth will often be a critical early step in the complex process of individual healing, political reconciliation and social justice.[34]

Aware of the complexity of truth-telling and memory-recovery, the organizers of the REMHI project deliberately sought to reconstruct their history as a process of healing. To gather this history REMHI interviewers went out to the communities rather than expecting the communities to come to them. Carlos Beristain, a coordinator of the project, notes that when interviewers were asked why reconstructing this history was so important, they would answer, 'to understand the truth, to dignify the dead, to recover the power of speech and of social initiative, and to instil the value of memory in future generations'.[35] To be sensitive to local needs, REMHI trained more than 800 local interviewers who would be aware of local customs. The interviews did more than ask for the bare facts; they sought to get to the heart of the experience. They explored people's subjective experience, examined the social impact that the violence had, and asked about how it was interpreted by those who suffered it most.[36] The seven questions used in collecting testimonies were: What happened? When? Where? Who were the people responsible? What effect did this have on people's lives? What did they do to face up to the situation? Why did they think it happened?[37]

In this way, the project was important for the process as well as for the product. For many Guatemalans it was the first chance for their painful experiences to be acknowledged and their stories to be shared with others.

---

[33] As the South African Commission points out, the context in which truth-telling takes place is very important. The healing potential of storytelling is much likelier when it is for an official body and in front of a respectful audience; *TRC Report*, Vol. V, 351.

[34] See Victoria Sanford, *Buried Secrets: Truth and Human Rights in Guatemala* (New York: Palgrave, 2003).

[35] Carlos M. Beristain, 'The Value of Memory', *Forced Migration Review* 2 (August 1998), 24–6 (25).

[36] Beristain, 'The Value of Memory', 25.

[37] Beristain, 'The Value of Memory', 24–5.

Alongside the gathering of information, the project also helped to organise follow-up activities, including community discussions and celebrations.

When Gerardi presented the findings of this work to the people of Guatemala at a special ceremony at the Cathedral on 24 April 1996 he spoke in a moving way of why the project was so important. He warned, 'We are collecting the people's memories because we want to contribute to the construction of a different country. This path was and continues to be full of risks, but the construction of the Kingdom of God entails risks, and only those who have strength to confront those risks can be its builders.'[38]

The truth of this warning was illustrated two days later when Gerardi was bludgeoned to death in the garage of his house on 26 April 1998.[39] In a callous reference to Gerardi's comments in his address two days earlier, when he mentioned the Suffering Servant disfigured beyond human semblance (Is. 52.13–53.4), the assassins used a concrete block to beat Gerardi's face beyond recognition.[40]

Gerardi's murder was both a savage reprisal against someone who had dared to make the truth known, and a warning to others that Guatemala had not changed so much. It sent the clear message that the violence did not just belong in the past and remained an ominous threat in the presence. Gerardi's standing as a bishop gave him as much informal protection as any individual might have in Guatemala and his murder showed that that nobody was safe from the violence. It reminded others that thinking and speaking for justice in Guatemala could be a matter of life and death. This was seen as an assertion of military impunity. It was intended as a symbolic message that little in the country had changed. That even with truth there would not be justice.

The Struggle for Justice in Guatemala

Many critics of truth commissions have pointed to the difficulties in achieving justice as one of the most significant limitations of truth commissions. A Christian theology of reconciliation needs to take these concerns seriously.[41] An important legacy from liberation theologies in Latin America and

---

[38] Gerardi, 'Speech on Presentation of the REMHI Report', xxiii–xxiv.

[39] On the bizarre intrigues of the investigation into his murder, see Francisco Goldman, 'Murder Comes for the Bishop', in *The New Yorker* (15 March 1999), 60–77; Judith Escribano, 'The Cook, the Dog, the Priest and His Lover: The Murder of Bishop Gerardi', in Hayes and Tombs (eds), *Truth and Memory*, 59–80.

[40] This may also have been a reference to the cover of the REMHI report, which has four panels showing an indigenous figure. First with his mouth covered, then with his eyes covered, then with his ears covered and only in the last panel with his mouth, eyes and ears open and finally shouting out a message.

[41] On the Latin American challenges, see Iain Maclean (ed.), *Reconciliation: Nations and Churches in Latin America* (Aldershot: Ashgate, forthcoming).

elsewhere is the recognition that in any situation where the power relations between oppressors and the oppressed are not addressed then calls to peace will ring hollow.[42] There is a need to see beyond pious language to look at concrete realities. Reconciliation means nothing if it means ignoring justice; without justice, neither true peace nor real reconciliation are possible.[43]

This is one of the most important practical challenges for any Christian theology of reconciliation. In many situations, the political constraints on justice are so intractable that calls for perpetrators to be held accountable seem doomed to frustration. Most of the major Latin American transitions, including Brazil, Chile, El Salvador and Guatemala, involved *de jure* blanket amnesties. Even when there was no formal amnesty law there was rarely the political commitment to prosecute, and political opposition to prosecutions usually amounted to a *de facto* amnesty. Even in rare cases like Argentina, where the commission's investigations were able to support prosecutions, the political difficulties of actually accomplishing this made it very hard. The top military leadership was successfully prosecuted but it was much harder to pursue cases against other military perpetrators and even the earlier convictions were eventually undermined by the early release of those convicted.

In Guatemala, investigation and prosecution of Gerardi's murderers was beset by the endemic problems of a weak criminal justice system. On 8 June 2001, after a protracted period of investigation and many delays in the trial, three officers from the Military High Command (Colonel Lima Estrada, his son Captain Lima Oliva, and former military adviser Sergeant Obdulio Villanueva) were convicted for Gerardi's murder.[44] Mario Orantes, a priest who shared the house with Gerardi, was also convicted as their accomplice.[45] Yet on 8 October 2002 an appeal court overruled the sentences and ordered a retrial on the pretext of unreliable evidence. After further appeals, the Supreme Court reinstated the sentences on 12 February 2003. However, on

---

[42] For this reason progressive and politically orientated theologians in Latin America have tended to focus on liberation rather than reconciliation in their work. Although there is no reason in principle that concern for reconciliation should mean a lack of regard for justice, in Latin America this has invariably been the case. For a Latin American approach to reconciliation that seeks to take justice seriously, see José Comblin, 'The Theme of Reconciliation and Theology in Latin America', in Iain Maclean (ed.), *Reconciliation: Nations and Churches in Latin America*. Originally published in *Revista Eclesiástica Brasileira*, 46 (June 1986), 272–314.

[43] Paul F. Seils, 'Reconciliation in Guatemala: The Role of Intelligent Justice', *Race and Class* 44.1 (2002), 33–60.

[44] The first judge appointed to the case resigned after accusations of incompetence; the second resigned when he received death threats; the third resigned after over accusations of bias in favour of the accused; see Escribano, 'The Cook, the Dog, the Priest and His Lover', 80.

[45] Margarita López (the housekeeper who was also charged with being an accomplice) was acquitted.

the same day, Obdulio Villanueva was decapitated during a violent riot at the prison where he was being held.[46]

The Gerardi case is only the tip of the iceberg for the inadequacies of Guatemala's judicial system. Whilst the REMHI project and CEH commission have successfully documented and acknowledged much of what happened, few perpetrators are ever likely to be brought to justice. As elsewhere in Latin America, the high level of impunity that the guilty enjoy severely limits meaningful social reconciliation.

The South African approach to a selective amnesty in exchange for full disclosure of crimes to the South African Truth and Reconciliation Commission raises a different but equally difficult set of questions. Some form of amnesty was required under the political agreement reached between the African National Congress and the National Party to allow the transition from apartheid to democracy without widespread bloodshed. Without the amnesty arrangement the transition would have been much more difficult. However, because the commission took on the amnesty process as part of its official work, some have argued that it compromised its own ethical foundations from the start.

Assessment of this aspect of the South African commission needs to recognise both the moral principles and the practical issues involved. At the level of moral principles, concessions over criminal justice need to be addressed in terms of other equally important moral principles.[47] They cannot be morally justified simply by an appeal to practical circumstances. It is therefore helpful to distinguish different types of justice, including restorative justice, so that this debate is between genuinely moral principles and not between morality and pragmatism. At a practical level, part of the issue is whether a truth and reconciliation commission (which integrates the work of reconciliation with truth-recovery) is preferable to a truth commission (which sees these as two separate and usually sequential processes). In terms of truth, integrating the amnesty process into the commission's work opened up a new way for the commissioners to work at uncovering the truth. In terms of reconciliation, the amnesty hearings also produced some memorable moments when victims were reconciled with perpetrators in public. However, these dramatic reconciliations could also have their drawbacks. Well-

---

[46] The circumstances around Villanueva's death remain unclear, but his murder meant that he could not try to plea bargain any further information he had on the involvement of others in exchange for a reduction in the newly enforced sentence. However, church lawyers remained suspicious that former president Alvaro Arzu was involved in the murder in some way. See Sergio De Leon, 'Six Killed in Guatemala Prison Riot', *Associated Press* (13 February 2003); Escribano, 'The Cook, the Dog, the Priest and His Lover', 80.

[47] See especially Amy Gutmann and Dennis Thompson, 'The Moral Foundations of Truth Commissions', in Robert I. Rotberg and Dennis Thompson (eds), *Truth V. Justice: The Morality of Truth Commissions* (Princeton, NJ: Princeton University Press, 2000), 22–44.

publicised examples of reconciliation between perpetrator and victims in public hearings put unfair pressure on others who felt unable to do this and distorted the wider political objectives of the commission into individual transactions.

The issues are always more complicated than a simple polarity of 'truth versus justice' allows. There are different types of justice that a society needs. Alongside retributive justice there is often a need for restorative justice.[48] If the challenges of reconciliation are to be adequately conceptualised in Christian theology, and properly engaged with, then its relationship to both truth and justice will be priority tasks. Despite the strengths of the REMHI report in terms of reconciliation and truth, it has done relatively little to link these to justice, repentance and forgiveness. Unpacking the complexity of the issues in terms of the Latin American transitions remains an avenue to be explored.

For this to happen, attention needs to go beyond the personal and sacramental focus found in most official Catholic teaching on reconciliation, such as John Paul II's *Reconciliation and Penance* (2 December 1984). The personal and sacramental dimensions of reconciliation need to be integrated into an approach that opens new avenues for a more holistic theology of reconciliation.[49] The political, existential and theological levels of reconciliation need to be held together. There is much to learn here from liberation theology, and especially from Gustavo Gutiérrez's insistence in his foundational work, *A Theology of Liberation*, that these three levels all be held together in any adequate account of liberation as salvation.[50] These same three levels – and possibly others as well – also need to be held together in any holistic theology of reconciliation. Furthermore, the distinctive methodology developed by liberation theologians in Latin America is well suited to taking this work forward, through careful reflection on political praxis in the light of the word of God.[51] Yet thus far, Latin American liberation theologians have given little attention to elaborating the different dimensions of reconciliation. During the 1970s and 1980s, when the liberation theology movement enjoyed its heyday in Latin America, many liberationists saw reconciliation as a compromise that distracted from true liberation.

---

[48] The Truth and Reconciliation Commission was much better as an exercise in restorative justice than critics of the selective amnesty usually acknowledge.

[49] See especially Robert Schreiter, *Reconciliation: Mission and Ministry in a Changing Social Order* (Maryknoll, NY: Orbis Books, 1992); *idem, The Ministry of Reconciliation: Spirituality and Strategies* (Maryknoll, NY: Orbis Books, 1998).

[50] See Gustavo Gutiérrez, *A Theology of Liberation: History, Politics and Salvation* (trans. and ed. C. Inda and J. Eagleson; Maryknoll, NY: Orbis Books; London: SCM Press, 2nd edn, 1988 [English trans., 1973; Spanish orig. 1971]), 24–5.

[51] For more on the historical and theological development of liberation theology in Latin America, see David Tombs, *Latin American Liberation Theology* (Boston, MA and Leiden: Brill, 2002).

A similar debate also arose around black theology in the US. The emphasis on liberation in the work of James Cone and others stressed the importance of justice, and led to a suspicion of any talk of reconciliation. At the time, there was good reason for both black and liberation theologians to put the emphasis on liberation and justice. Yet as James Deotis Roberts noted, liberation and reconciliation are not alternatives, they are integrally related: 'We must be liberated – Christ is the liberator. But the liberating Christ is also the reconciling Christ. The one who liberates reconciles, and the one who reconciles liberates.'[52] Liberation and reconciliation are interdependent on each other, and must both be underpinned by justice.

Conclusion

Guatemala's Recovery of Memory project was a practical exercise in the political theology of reconciliation undertaken in courageous hope. It showed the importance of breaking a culture of denial, the need to confront the truth as honestly as possible, and the importance of acknowledging the suffering of victims if there is to be real healing for those who have suffered and for society as a whole. As part of the social ministry of the church, it shows how the gospel can be incarnated into a contemporary and prophetic mission. Yet the brutal murder of Gerardi just two days after presenting the final report is also a stark reminder of the limitations that projects of this type face in situations where justice is routinely set aside.

For Christian theologians and ethicists, the REMHI project is an inspiring example of a commitment to truth and truth-recovery and how this can contribute to reconciliation. Yet at the same time, REMHI highlights both the need for justice and the seemingly insurmountable barriers there can be to this.

For political theologians influenced by the emphasis on social justice during the last third of the twentieth century – especially in the prophetic witness of Latin American, black and feminist liberation theologies – this is likely to give a serious sense of unease. How can a truth-recovery process be meaningful if it does not lead to justice? Reconciliation is not an alternative to justice; it must be built on justice. Where justice is denied, full reconciliation will not be possible.

A theology that is to be of use for the real world – and in the real world – cannot ignore this dilemma and the challenges that it creates. Theologians will need to grapple with how political reconciliation can have political, ethical and theological integrity that recognises both the demands of justice

---

[52] J. Deotis Roberts, *Liberation and Reconciliation: A Black Theology* (Maryknoll, NY: Orbis, rev. edn 1994 [1971]), 20.

and the constraints to justice. This is a crucial task for political theology. A richer and more complex understanding of reconciliation and its relationship to truth and justice is required if further progress is to be made. There will be no easy answers, but exploring this challenge in conversation with the REMHI project and similar bodies in Latin America and elsewhere will keep such explorations grounded in the real world.

PART III
THE ONGOING CHALLENGES OF RECONCILIATION

Towards Inclusive Remembrance after the 'Troubles': A Philosophical Perspective from within the South African Truth and Reconciliation Commission[1]

Wilhelm Verwoerd

It was a few years ago on a cold, windy midsummer's evening in Cork city, Ireland, at the junction of Grand Parade and South Mall, when I stumbled upon these chilling words: 'If I could grasp the fires of hell in my hands, I would hurl them in the face of my country's enemies.'

This embittered cry for the wrath of hell to be visited on his beloved country's enemies came from a Mr John Mitchell, one of the 'gallant men of 1798, 1803, 1848 and 1867 who fought and died in the wars of Ireland to recover her sovereign independence'.

I could identify with the desire for political freedom underlying Mitchell's vengeful curse: as a young, white Afrikaner nationalist in South Africa during the 1960s and 1970s my political consciousness was deeply influenced by the thousands of women and children who died in British concentration camps during the 'Anglo Boer War' (1899–1902), as well as the subsequent struggle of 'my people' to overcome English political and economic domination. During the 1970s and early 1980s my political and moral vision was further blinkered by the tragically successful systematic separation of different racial groups, universally known as the system of apartheid: a separation that was deepened by a pervasive cultivation of fear that our Afrikaners' hard-won freedom would be lost if the 'Communist-inspired' black liberation movement achieved its goal.[2]

To some extent I could also relate to Mitchell's call for vengeance. My recent work with the South African Truth and Reconciliation Commission

---

[1] Revised from material originally presented as John Whyte Memorial Lecture, University College Dublin (20 November 2003).

[2] For a more detailed account of my personal struggle to overcome a blinkered apartheid upbringing, see Wilhelm Verwoerd, *My Winds of Change* (Johannesburg: Ravan Press, 1997). See also David Goodman, 'The Odyssey of the Verwoerds', in *idem*, *Fault Lines: Journeys into the new South Africa* (Berkeley: University of California Press, 1999).

(TRC)[3] has taught me to respect the legitimate demand for vindication behind (some) victims' desire for vengeance.[4]

Still, I was deeply disturbed. I was alarmed by the fact that Mitchell's statement was inscribed on a 'National Monument' erected through the efforts of the Cork Young Ireland Society, not only to 'perpetuate the memory' of past heroes but also 'to inspire the youth of our country to follow in their patriotic footsteps'. How deep must the anger, the sense of historical injustice be when an image of utter destruction of 'the enemy' is used to inspire the youth? How can 'the youth of our country' gather the fires of hell without burning their own hands to the bone? And will these young warriors *and* their children be able to put out the fires that continue to smoulder underground, long after the wars of liberation are over, if they have forgotten to see the face of their former enemies?

As I struggled to sleep that night, these questions mingled with vivid memories of 'enemies of the people' being 'necklaced' during the dark days of the anti-apartheid struggle in South Africa. I saw again the nauseating images of another *impimpi* (suspected informer) or black policeman dying a horrible, slow death, with a burning tyre around his neck and a group of young people cheering as the ring of fire consumed his face.[5] And I was haunted again by the testimony of former security police captain Dirk Coetzee before the TRC amnesty committee. He confessed how he and his colleagues in the security police would burn the body of an activist they had killed, and while they waited for the fire to destroy 'the enemy', would drink beer and have a barbecue.[6]

Implicit in all these violent images of the fiery destruction of political enemies is a disturbing forgetfulness, a moral forgetfulness which undermines

---

[3] The Promotion of National Unity and Reconciliation Act, no. 34 of 1995, mandated the TRC to (a) get as 'complete a picture as possible' of the 'nature, causes and extent' of politically motivated gross human rights violations (that is, acts of torture, killing, abduction and severe ill-treatment) which occurred during the period of 1 March 1960 to 10 May 1994, (b) help restore the human and civil dignity of victims by granting them an opportunity to relate their own accounts of the violations of which they are victims, (c) grant amnesty to those individuals giving 'full disclosure' of politically motivated crimes during this period of resistance to and defence of the apartheid system, and (d) make recommendations to the President and Parliament on reparation and rehabilitation measures to be taken, including measures in order to prevent the future commission of human rights violations. Under the chairpersonship of Archbishop Desmond Tutu, these tasks included making findings on more than 36,000 alleged gross violations of human rights contained in 20,300 statements taken from victims or survivors of these violations. A comprehensive report was handed to the President on 28 October 1998; see *The Truth and Reconciliation Commission of South Africa Report* (Cape Town: Juta, 1998). The above tasks were divided between three statutory committees, the Human Rights Violations, Amnesty, and Reparation and Rehabilitation Committees, which, in turn, were supported by an Investigation Unit and a Research Department. The amnesty part of the process was only completed in late 2001, with two additional volumes added to the TRC Report in April 2003.

[4] See Trudy Govier, *Forgiveness and Revenge* (London: Routledge, 2001).

[5] See *TRC Report*, Vol. II, 387–9.

[6] See Antjie Krog, *Country of My Skull* (Johannesburg: Random House, 1998), 60–61.

individual or collective efforts to respond constructively to gross injustices or being deeply harmed. To appreciate the destructive potential of this moral forgetfulness and to highlight the creative potential of its opposite, which might be termed inclusive moral remembrance, I want to reflect here on an underlying moral dynamic of the South African Truth and Reconciliation Commission (TRC). While my emphasis will be on the South African TRC process, I do believe that a clarification of the moral 'genre'[7] of this process will be of some relevance to current debates in Northern Ireland on these islands about appropriate, creative responses to the hurt and harming associated with the 'troubles'.

Towards Remembering the Hurt and Harming on all Sides[8]

To appreciate the kind of moral remembrance promoted by the TRC I find it very useful to compare this process with the life and legacy of what has been described as the 'first Truth and Reconciliation Commission'[9] on South African soil. In 1998, as I completed my time in the TRC, preparations were under way to commemorate the hundredth anniversary of the outbreak of the 'Anglo Boer War' in 1899, a war which saw 26,000 Afrikaner women and children (amongst others) die in British concentration camps.

Many people remember Emily Hobhouse for her passionate condemnation of the British government for abuses committed during the 'Anglo Boer War', especially against Boer women. She is widely respected for the selfless relief work she undertook in the concentration camps. It is a less well-known fact that after this war she organised food, clothing, ploughing and harvesting for the Boer families returning to their farms, which had been devastated by Kitchener's scorched-earth policy. Hobhouse went further than these concrete reparation measures and thus,

> on her own started the first Truth and Reconciliation Commission in South Africa. She collected sworn statements by survivors, and had them published, first in *The Brunt of the War and Where It Fell* in 1902, and then again in *War Without Glamour, or Women's War Experiences Written by Themselves, 1899–1902* in 1924. Her aim was to impress on the British public the need for some form of requital or at least some compensation for the survivors and a public condemnation of the colonial officials and military officers who were responsible for these transgressions.[10]

---

[7] On the importance of this kind of clarification, see Wilhelm Verwoerd, 'Towards the Recognition of Our Injustices', in Charles Villa-Vicencio and Wilhelm Verwoerd (eds), *Looking Back, Reaching Forward: Reflections on the South African Truth and Reconciliation Commission* (London: Zed Books, 2000), 156–7.

[8] In this section I am drawing on Verwoerd, 'Towards the Recognition of Our Injustices'.

[9] Johan Snyman, 'Interpretation and the Politics of Memory', *Acta Jurudica* (1998), 327.

[10] Snyman, 'Interpretation and the Politics of Memory', 327–8, 334.

The vital point highlighted by Snyman is that for Hobhouse the human suffering of these Boer women had a universal significance beyond narrow ethnic borders. Her speech at the 1913 inauguration ceremony of the Women's Memorial in Bloemfontein contained these words:

> Your visible monument will serve to this great end – becoming an inspiration to all South Africans and to the women in particular ... For remember, these dead women were not great as the world count greatness; some of them were quite poor women who had laboured much. Yet they have become a moral force in your land ... And their influence will travel further. They have shown the world that never again can it be said that women deserves no rights as Citizen because she takes no part in war. This statue stands as a denial of that assertion ... .[11]

For Hobhouse the suffering of these Boer women formed part of a world-wide struggle for recognition; their sacrifices contributed 'towards a greater solidarity of humankind against the indifference to suffering'. It is this message – speaking across the political divides between Boer and British and between white and black – that gave the suffering of the Boer women and children such moral force. It was this message that was literally censored in subsequent decades as Afrikaner nationalists increasingly monopolised the meaning of the suffering of the 'Boer War' for themselves. This selective remembrance is vividly illustrated by the following omissions from Hobhouse's prophetic speech in later commemorative issues (censored passages are in italics):

> In your hands and those of your children lie the power and freedom won; you must not merely maintain but increase the sacred gift. Be merciful towards the weak, the downtrodden, the stranger. Do not open your gates to the worst foes of freedom – tyranny and selfishness. *Are not these the withholding from others in your control, the very liberties and rights which you have valued and won for yourselves?...*
>
> *We in England are ourselves still but dunces in the great world-school, our leaders still struggling with the unlearned lesson, that liberty is the equal right and heritage of man, without distinction of race, class or sex. A community that lacks the courage to found its citizenship on this broad base becomes a 'city divided against itself, which cannot stand'.*
>
> *... Does not justice bid us remember today how many thousands of the dark race perished also in the Concentration Camps in a quarrel which was not theirs? Did they not thus redeem the past? Was it not an instance of that community of interest, which binding all in one, roots out all animosity?*[12]

It was, of course, not only Emily Hobhouse's speech that was censored. None of the many Afrikaans books on the war I read as a child, nor any of my history books at school contained any reference to the 13,315 Africans that,

---

[11] Emily Hobhouse, *Boer War Letters* (ed. Rykie Van Reenen; Cape Town: Human & Rousseau, 1984), 406–7; quoted in Snyman, 329.

[12] Hobhouse, *Boer War Letters*, 406–7; quoted in Snyman, 'Interpretation and the Politics of Memory', 329.

according to official figures, also died in concentration camps.[13] Never did I learn about atrocities committed by the Boers themselves. I grew up with a perception of myself as a member of a minority 'victimised' by 'British imperialism'. I was only reminded of the horror done *to* people I saw as 'my people'. Infused with this narrow, exclusivist remembrance it became more difficult to see the many horrors done *by* 'my people' – during what is more appropriately known as the South African War (1899–1902), but especially during the apartheid years.

This moral forgetfulness of Afrikaners, induced by a selective, ethnic remembrance of past suffering, highlights the nature and significance of the TRC process. This institution was the outcome of an extensive, democratic process, receiving its mandate from the legislative arm of the new state, representing in a real sense the 'people of South Africa'. This highly public and transparent TRC was not the lonely effort of a single woman, struggling to get her government's attention. Furthermore, given the remarkable inclusivity of this TRC process, it has a much better chance of getting the kind of message across advocated long ago by Emily Hobhouse. Anyone who attended a victim hearing, or read transcripts of these hearings, or read the report, will attest to the fact that the violated from all sides of the conflicts of the past were included in the process, with more than 20,000 of them making use of the opportunity 'to relate their own accounts of the violations of which they are the victims'.[14] Similarly, the amnesty part of the process has succeeded in drawing out those directly involved from all parties to the conflict. The violent actions of white agents of the apartheid state, and racist AWB supporters, as well as the suffering of those who bore the brunt of the brutality of the 'Boers', indeed featured prominently in the TRC process. But the actions of many MK operatives, SDU and SPU members, APLA cadres, Askaris, IFP activists, UDF supporters, homeland security forces, and black policemen also came under the spotlight.[15]

In addition, the series of special hearings – looking specifically at, for example, the experiences of women, children and white male conscripts – as well as sector or institutional hearings which focused, amongst other things,

---

[13] S.B. Spies, *Methods of Barbarism? Roberts and Kitchener and Civilians in the Boer Republics, January 1900–May 1902* (Cape Town: Human & Rousseau, 1977).

[14] TRC Act, 3(1)(c); see *TRC Report*, Vol. I.

[15] See *TRC Report*, Vols II and III. The following are descriptions for the series of acronyms used in this paragraph: AWB – *Afrikaner Weerstandsbeweging* (Afrikaner Resistance Movement); MK – *mKhonto we Siswe*, military wing of the African National Congress (ANC); SDU – Self Defence Units, ANC-aligned youth vigilantes; SPU – Self Protection Units, Inkatha Freedom Party (IFP)-aligned youth vigilantes; APLA – Azanian People's Liberation Army, military wing of the Pan African Congress (PAC); Askaris – members of liberation movements turned state informers; UDF – United Democratic Front.

on the mostly indirect contributions to past violations by the media, the health and business sectors, faith communities, the judiciary, all allowed the commission to throw its net of remembrance wider than any previous truth commission in other parts of the world.[16]

Of course, there remains much to be criticised about these aspects of the TRC process, and the relative inclusivity is no guarantee that the temptation to, or existence of, selective remembering has been entirely overcome or will be avoided in future. The point is that this TRC has been a vast improvement on the 'first TRC' nearly a hundred years ago. It will now, and in future, be much more difficult for certain groups to monopolise the meaning of past suffering to the detriment of all the people in South Africa.

Towards Remembering the Horrible, the Human and the Heroic

There is a further, less obvious layer to the inclusivity of the moral remembrance promoted by the TRC. To help me articulate this layer I want to focus briefly on one of the most painful and inspiring amnesty hearings during my time in the TRC.

On 25 August 1993, Amy Biehl, an American exchange student who was deeply committed to the struggle against apartheid, was dropping off a friend in Gugulethu township. She was seen by a group of young men who were returning from a political rally, during a time of intense political unrest, where they had been encouraged to see all whites as settlers who took away their land and who deserved to be killed. She was wrongfully identified as a settler and became the tragic victim of a mob attack. Four of her killers were convicted of murder and imprisoned during 1994. In June 1998 they were granted amnesty by the TRC.

Amy's political commitment and her South African friends helped her parents to understand the context within which their daughter was killed. They decided not to oppose amnesty being granted and managed to transform their sadness and deep loss into a whole range of grass-roots projects in Gugulethu and other townships, sponsored and facilitated by the Amy Biehl Foundation.

'I never personalised Amy's so-called killers. As the information came to me in the beginning it was a mob,' said Linda Biehl in a recent interview.[17] 'A mob without faces.' During the trial she struggled 'to put faces to their deeds ... I didn't feel anything ...'.

---

[16] See *TRC Report*, Vol. IV.

[17] Interviewed by Paul Haupt, Institute for Justice and Reconciliation, Cape Town, 27 March 2001.

In May 1999, almost a year after the four applicants were granted amnesty, Peter Biehl was contacted – through a trusted intermediary – by two of them: Ntobeko Penni and Easy Nofemela. They wanted to set up a youth group in the name of Amy Biehl.

This was the start of a gradual process of reconciliation that involved Ntobeko and Easy first joining a training programme in making bricks and construction, run by the Amy Biehl Foundation. They then became deeply involved in the bakery started by the Foundation.

According to the late Peter Biehl it was

> ... very gratifying to see Easy and Ntimbeko really serving in our bakery business in important ways. They have pride in what they bring to the party and what they bring is very, very significant. It is great to see them be able to be aspiring, natural human beings. And yet we know that what they carry with them is more than any of us can know because none of us has been involved in the taking of life. That has got to be very, very difficult. They are still tormented about how they are perceived in the community. But somehow they seem able to rise above all this.

Peter believed 'they can do it because they feel purposeful, because they feel that they are serving their community and because we seem to relate to one another on a very human level'.[18]

Personally, I still find it impossible to forget the horrifying detail of her merciless killing that was vividly recalled on that day in the amnesty hearing room in Cape Town: 'She was running across the street, blood streaming from her face. Stones were thrown and then Manqina tripped her. I had a knife and with seven or eight others we stabbed at Amy.' But mixed with this disturbing memory, is a growing wonder at what a newspaper heading described as the 'amazing grace of Amy's parents'.[19] And I feel a sense of hope inspired by a racist, brutal murder's legacy of reconciliation.

What is one to make of this heady, uneasy mixture of the horrific and humanness?[20] To start with I find it useful to recall the following statement by Paul Ricoeur:

> We have learned from the Greek storytellers and historians that the admirable deeds of the heroes needed to be remembered and thus called for narration. We learn from a Jewish storyteller like [Elie] Wiesel that the horrible – the inverted image of the admirable – needs to be rescued still more from forgetfulness by the means of memory and narration.[21]

It seems to me that the Biehl amnesty hearing provides us with a story in which both these lessons are contained. We are reminded of the horrible, but

---

[18] Interviewed by Paul Haupt.

[19] *Sunday Independent* (30 August 1998).

[20] Many of the recent South African discussions of humanity have recognised the value of the Xhosa word 'ubuntu' (humanity) for emphasising the significance of social relations.

[21] Paul Ricoeur, *Figuring the Sacred* (Minneapolis, MI: Fortress Press 1995), 290.

also of truly admirable deeds; we are prompted to recognise the human potential to commit horrific deeds, but while doing so, to hold on to our potential to transcend the horrible.

It is this kind of inclusive moral remembrance that the TRC also promoted with its facilitation of the telling, translation and recording of many stories – accounts by those termed 'perpetrators' and 'victims' of gross violations of human rights, but also testimonies by those who can better be described as victors over these violations.

Remembering the Horrible

To explain more fully this layer of inclusive remembrance, in which the horrible *and* the heroic is remembered, let us begin by taking a closer look at the TRC's attempt to help rescue the horrible from forgetfulness. This rescue attempt was described as follows by Antjie Krog: 'For me the Truth Commission microphone with its little red light was the ultimate symbol of the whole process: here the marginalized voice speaks to the public ear, the unspeakable is spoken – and translated – the personal story brought from the innermost of the individual bind us anew to the collective.'[22]

Krog referred to the so-called victim hearings where the trauma of survivors of specified categories of gross human rights violations were given centre stage. But her description can also be applied to the public hearings of the Amnesty Committee, where the little red light continued to flicker much longer and probably more loudly, where often the unspeakable was spoken, translated and recorded, as was the case on that day in Cape Town at the hearing of 'Amy's killers'. By providing a table, chairs, a microphone and a translator to, for example, Mongesi Manqina, Vuzumzi Ntamo, Easy Nofemela and Ntobeko Penni, the TRC contributed to 'establishing as complete a picture as possible of the causes, nature and extent of the gross violations of human rights' that occurred within the mandate period.[23]

There were obvious and important historical, legal and psychological dimensions to this truth-seeking activity. Some of the facts and the findings emerging from these 'victim' and 'perpetrator' hearings have already and will continue to be challenged by lawyers and historians. Given the higher standards of evidence they should work with (under fewer time and resource constraints), one would expect some of these criticisms to help us move closer to more reliable factual and historical truth about particular aspects of the period covered by the TRC mandate.

---

[22] Krog, *Country of My Skull*, 237.
[23] See TRC Act, 3(1)(a).

However, the limitations of the TRC's search for factual truth should not obscure the vital moral truths gathered by this process – truths about past injustices, about gross human rights violations. If evil is roughly understood as 'denying someone his or her right to be fully human',[24] then the TRC's facilitation of thousands of oral and written testimonies of those whose dignity was grossly violated can also be interpreted as a remembrance of many individual and institutionalised expressions of evil.

Why was it important that the TRC thus helped to rescue some of the horrible aspects of the recent South African past from forgetfulness? I share the position of Ricoeur, Wiesel, Todorov and others that this kind of moral remembering is not about a macabre fascination with 'the horrible', *per se*. An important way to remember moral evil is to allow those who were dehumanised to tell their stories, or if the victims are no longer alive, to continue to tell and retell what happened to them. In doing so, we prevent forgetfulness from killing the victims twice; in a 'tiny way' we thus 'repay the debt we owe to the victims';[25] we help to 'restore the human and civil dignity of such victims by granting them an opportunity to relate their own accounts of the violations of which they are the victims'.[26]

But rescuing the horrible from forgetfulness is not only about helping to restore the dignity of those against whom the horrible was committed; this respectful remembrance of evil is not only about ensuring that at least the memory of *past* victims live on. This remembrance is also of potential significance for *future* victims.

For by highlighting the plight of those who were killed, abducted, tortured and severely ill-treated, the TRC process promoted a 'morality of the depths', a sensitivity to 'the line beneath which no one is [should be] allowed to sink'.[27] Through a sustained public focus on gross violations of human rights the TRC process stressed minimum protections for human dignity and underscored minimum standards of decency.[28] By giving a prominent public space to what happens if human rights are not respected, the TRC process thus gave South Africans, amongst others, some of the tools to build probably the most effective bulwark against future violations.[29] That is, the TRC

---

[24] Tzvetan Todorov, *Facing the Extreme: Moral Life in the Concentration Camps* (London: Weidenfeld and Nicholson, 1999), 289.

[25] Ricoeur, *Figuring the Sacred*, 290.

[26] TRC Act, 3(1)(c).

[27] Henry Shue, *Basic Rights* (Princeton, NJ: Princeton University Press, 1980), 18–19.

[28] Rajeev Bhargava, 'The Moral Justification of Truth Commissions', in Villa-Vicencio and Verwoerd (eds), *Looking Back, Reaching Forward*, 60–67.

[29] I concur with Susan Mendus' interpretation of human rights as primarily 'bulwarks against evil' and not 'harbingers of goods', and agree that 'the political impetus for human rights comes from the recognition of evil as a permanent threat in the world'; Susan Mendus, 'Human Rights in Political Theory', in David Beecham (ed.), *Politics and Human Rights* (Oxford: Blackwell, 1995), 23–4.

window on some grievous wrongs of the past provided us with invaluable raw material for nurturing a culture of human rights.[30]

An important component of this raw material is the humility that accompanies an honest facing of the horrible, a humble recognition of the ongoing need to counter the forces of dehumanisation, given the potential for inhumanity inside all of us. As former president Mandela put it in a response to the work of the TRC: 'All of us, as a nation that has newly found itself, share in the shame at the capacity of human beings of any race or language group to be inhumane to other human beings. We should all share in the commitment to a South Africa in which that will never happen again.'[31]

Remembering the Human

However, for this commitment against inhumanity to be realised, for the TRC's rescue attempt to fulfil its potential, it is important to be aware of the tensions that accompanied its remembering of the horrible.

One of these tensions is graphically alluded to in the following cartoon by South Africa's most famous political cartoonist, Zapiro.[32] This cartoon powerfully portrays a tension between moral remembering and forgetting: when one is engaged in rescuing the horrible from forgetfulness, it is tempting to refrain from remembering the humanity of those responsible for the horrible; when faced with the gravity of the inhumane, it becomes rather difficult to rise above a sea of victims' skulls. If a heavenly parent seems to be in two minds whether the culprits retain their status as God's 'children', how are ordinary mortals suppose to remember their shared parentage with 'the people who did this'?

In this regard, the TRC Report expressed a concern about the apparent inability of 'ordinary South Africans' to follow Mandela's lead in recognising

---

[30] See Jonathan Allen, 'Balancing Justice and Social Unity: Political Theory and the Idea of a Truth and Reconciliation Commission', *University of Toronto Law Journal* 49 (1999), 315–53.

[31] Quoted in *TRC Report*, Vol. I, 134. In other words, an important *goal* of rescuing the horrible from forgetfulness is to help restore the dignity of past victims, but remembering the stories of past victims' suffering is also a *means* of public education, awareness raising and human rights training. Using past victims' stories as a means is consistent with the goal of dignity restoration because (a) survivors of past violations and the loved ones of those who did not survive are included in the category of (potential) future victims, and (b) to the extent that past victims' suffering contributes to the prevention of future violations, their suffering was not in vain, that is, highlighting a connection between remembrance and prevention can be a source of healing for past victims and their loved ones, and may assist the restoration of their dignity.

[32] Zapiro, *Mail & Guardian*; reprinted Wilhelm Verwoerd and Mahlubi 'Chief' Mabizela (eds), *Truths Drawn in Jest: Commentary on the Truth and Reconciliation Commission through Cartoons* (Claremont, SA: David Philip, 2000), 12.

those who committed inhuman acts as 'one of us', as fellow human beings. The Report acknowledged that

> ... the greater part of the Commission's focus has been on what could be regarded as the exceptional – on gross violations of human rights rather than the more mundane but nonetheless traumatising dimensions of apartheid life that effected every single black South African. The killers of Vlakplaas have horrified the nation.[33] The stories of a chain of shallow graves across the country, containing the remains of abducted activists who were brutalised, tortured and ultimately killed, have left many South Africans deeply shocked. The media has understandably focussed on these events – labelling Eugene de Kock, the Vlakplaas commander, 'Prime Evil'.[34]

It then went on to state:

> This focus on the outrageous has drawn the nation's attention away from the more commonplace violations. The result is that ordinary South Africans do not see themselves as represented by those the Commission defines as perpetrators, failing to recognise the 'little perpetrator' in each one of us. To understand the source of evil is not to condone it. It is only by recognising the potential for evil in each one of us that we can take full responsibility for ensuring that such evil will never be repeated.[35]

---

[33] 'Vlakplaas' – the name of a farm outside Pretoria, used as a covert base and torture centre by the security police.

[34] *TRC Report,* Vol. I, 133.

[35] *TRC Report,* Vol. I, 133.

The Report suggests that this inclusive recognition of the potential for evil, and the hoped-for, accompanying sense of shared responsibility, can be enhanced by giving more attention to the 'mundane but nonetheless traumatising dimensions of apartheid life', to, in the words of Hannah Arendt, the 'banality of evil' beyond the actions of a 'Prime Evil'.[36] I agree that this wider focus provides a promising route to bridging the moral gap between ordinary South Africans and those who 'horrified the nation', between those who became publicly known as perpetrators and the often elusive 'little perpetrator in each one of us'. The TRC itself attempted to counter a focus on the outrageous through its wide range of institutional/sector hearings.[37] By highlighting the various ways in which faith communities, the media, the judiciary, the health sector, the business sector – through acts of commission and omission – contributed to a climate in which violations took place, the TRC process challenged a convenient criminalisation of those engaged in political violence: it exposed the temptation to shirk various levels of shared responsibility by scapegoating those who directly bloodied their hands in the course of political conflict. In this regard it is also worth stressing the rather disconcerting message of an important chapter on the social psychology of gross human rights violations in the TRC Report. The main thrust of this chapter is that we should move away from individual pathology as the explanation for why people commit these gross violations, and give much more weight to social identity and 'situationalism', thus appreciating the power of various binding and blinding forces that enable an ordinary person to kill or torture another human being.[38]

Inclusive moral remembrance thus involves the recognition of a certain moral equality, a constant guarding against the denial of the potential for evil in each one of us. Despite the Report's shortcomings, I agree with the following assessment of its promotion of this difficult, painful kind of remembrance:

> The final report could be described as the founding document of the new South Africa ... The term 'founding document' is more commonly used to describe a country's Constitution. And there are grounds for pride in the South African Constitution ... But, for all that, the Constitution is a theoretical exercise, in large part the product of intellectual effort in the ivory towers of academia. The final report, in a very real and immediate way, defines us. With all its horrors, it is the earthly product of the blood and tears attendant on a difficult birth. It is a testament to the equality of man, if more in the disregard for the tenets of humanity than the observance of them.[39]

---

[36] See Hannah Arendt, *Eichman in Jerusalem: A Report on the Banality of Evil* (New York: Viking Press, 1963).

[37] See *TRC Report*, Vol. IV.

[38] See *TRC Report*, Vol. V, 259–303.

[39] *Mail & Guardian* (6–12 November 1998).

Remembering the Heroic

With all this talk about remembering evil and 'the horrible', one may well ask: what about the inspiring human potential for goodness? What about remembering 'the admirable deeds of the heroes'? Indeed, for some critics there was not enough room for Greek-style storytelling within the TRC process. For example, appearing under the heading 'Tutu's Report Tells the Truth but not the Whole Truth', anti-apartheid veteran Jeremy Cronin criticised the report for focusing too much on 'the little perpetrator' inside each of us. He is concerned that not enough room was given to celebrate the struggle, the '"little freedom fighter", the collective self-emancipator that we all could be'.[40]

It is true that neither the Report, nor, more broadly, the TRC process, allowed much space for a conventional, Greek-style celebration of 'the struggle', in the sense of allowing heroes to tell stories of bravery and victory, of risking life and liberty on the battlefields of past conflicts. But given the limitations imposed by its mandate, I am not sure that the TRC can fairly be criticised for this omission. Furthermore, there are obvious risks involved in the insensitive glorification of military (masculine?) heroism which might downplay the human costs of these actions.

In this regard it is significant that Cronin expanded on his concern about the TRC Report's apparent over-emphasis on 'the potential for evil in each one of us', by asking why the Report did not give more attention to 'the "humanist", ubuntu-filled ways of crossing the bridge' from past injustices to a truly democratic South Africa.

While there is some truth in Cronin's criticism as far as the Report is concerned – most of it is indeed devoted to a historical and statistical overview of violations within different regions, by different parties – his question in fact draws attention to a further aspect of the inclusive moral remembrance within the TRC process, namely its emphasis on the potential for goodness in each of us. It is important, however, to be clear about which way(s) the TRC process exhibited this potential and/or encouraged its realisation.

A lengthy chapter in the Report (V:350–435), highlights some of the many examples from the TRC process where individuals and communities provided concrete evidence of the human potential for goodness. One might see this chapter, entitled 'Reconciliation', as a celebration of admirable deeds – showing the potential of those harmed to move beyond victim-hood, and even survivor-hood, to becoming victors over evil. The above-mentioned chapter also includes a range of examples where individuals and institutions were brave enough to acknowledge responsibility for wrongdoing or harm

---

[40] *Sunday Independent* (15 November 1998).

and to express remorse or moral sensitivity towards those they violated – thus demonstrating the human potential for moral transformation.

But do these examples really provide evidence of the potential for goodness inside each of us? The Biehls and many others might not be conventional military heroes, but are they not exceptional moral heroes? After all, how many of us 'ordinary people' would be able to embody an 'amazing grace' which helped parents to treat as grandchildren some of those who mercilessly murdered their daughter? Unless this concern about the representative quality of the examples mentioned above is addressed, the TRC and I myself remain open to the criticism that, by using these examples to promote inclusive moral remembrance, we are exerting unrealistic and inappropriate moral pressure on, amongst others, ordinary South Africans.

I would concede that the examples of understanding, mercy, forgiveness and reconciliation highlighted by the TRC process have an extraordinary quality to them. However, this extraordinariness is compatible with the promotion of inclusive remembrance of the admirable for the following reasons. First, though the Biehls' grace was 'amazing', they and many others were 'ordinary people', unlike say a Nelson Mandela. Very few of them are the kind of people that would be expected to adorn the front pages of newspapers or make headline news; they are moderately successful businesspeople like the Biehls, a junior officer in the prison service like Irene Crouse, an administrative officer at a gold mine like Zenam Papiyana, a university teacher like Ginn Fourie, or a political activist turned administrator like Ashley Forbes.

It is true that some of these people received more media attention than others, the Biehls being the obvious example. The fact that they are Californians, coupled with the dramatic, archetypical features of the tragedy that befell their activist daughter – an attractive, young, white woman being brutally murdered by a group of black men – certainly encouraged a lot of media interest and even sensationalism. These factors also influenced my interest in the case. However, I do not accept that because the Biehls come from a white, middle-class, liberal, American background, that their mercy towards and friendship with some of those who killed their daughter therefore have little to say to other people. Lyndi Fourie, a beautiful, young, white woman was also killed by a group of black men, and her mother, a middle-class, English-speaking South African woman, was willing to engage in a unilateral forgiveness initiative. Irene Crouse, a white, working-class, conservative, Afrikaner woman also showed mercy, and the examples in the Report represent a range of people from different racial, cultural, class and gender backgrounds. All these people exhibited an ability and willingness to forgive and/or show mercy. The point is that there is not a simplistic causal relationship between background and a propensity towards creative, healing responses towards profound hurt. I therefore see no reason, apart from a media-induced false sense of exceptionality, why the American background of the Biehls should disqualify their admirable actions from being interpreted, carefully, as pointers to a widespread human potential to show mercy or to forgive, even when faced with an extremely difficult situation.

The difficulties of the situations confronted by the people mentioned above draws attention to a second reason why their extraordinary deeds may legitimately be used to articulate and promote inclusive remembrance of the admirable post-apartheid South Africa. This reason emerges from the extraordinary moral challenges posed by this transitional context to all citizens: a time for the establishment and consolidation of a stable, sustainable democracy after many years of apartheid.

Tzvetan Todorov formulated the moral challenge I have in mind as follows:

> While it is true that ordinary virtue can be found everywhere and that we must rejoice in this fact and speak it loud for all to hear, there can come a time in the life of a society, as in that of the individual, when ordinary virtue is not enough. In such moments of anguish and despair … the heroic virtues, courage and generosity, become as necessary as the ordinary ones.[41]

Todorov drew this conclusion from his reflections on the moral behaviour of people faced with the extreme conditions of concentration camps. While people like the Biehls were not faced with the desperate conditions of concentration camp inmates, they were certainly confronted with a time of deep anguish when faced with the brutal death of a beloved child. With the Report, I rejoice in their display of courage in not succumbing to anguish or bitterness, and their generosity in showing mercy. And given the deep wounds we as a South African society carried over from the past, and the vulnerability of trust in goodness after the 1994 election, I would argue that it was indeed an urgent necessity for the TRC process and Report to name out loud, for all to hear, some of the examples where ordinary people displayed those 'heroic virtues'.

The TRC's facilitation of the telling, recording and remembering of admirable deeds by ordinary people thus needs to be located in its extraordinary context: a transitional time which demanded and still requires the courageous and generous kind of deed, which the Biehls and others demonstrated to be possible.

This emphasis on the courage and generosity that helped to make those acts of forgiveness and mercy possible draws attention to a third way in which one may bridge the apparent gap between extraordinary examples and inclusive remembrance of the admirable. In explaining what he means by these heroic virtues in less extreme conditions than the camps, Todorov acknowledges with sadness that 'the just, those righteous men and

---

[41] Todorov, *Facing the Extreme*, 295.

women who combine' courage and generosity with ordinary kindness 'are few in number', but he continues to hope that people can at least, when the moment comes, take the risk to 'meet the gaze' of the stranger in need.[42] A number of ordinary heroes within the TRC process were willing to take the considerable risk of 'meeting the gaze' of a stranger who was not only in need, but who also killed a loved one; many of them went further and were prepared to forgive, or show mercy; some even engaged in a process of deep, interpersonal reconciliation. But the point is that the willingness to look beyond the boundaries of family and tribe and, in effect, remember that strangers (former political enemies) are fellow human beings, lies at the root of what these heroes did. Even if the rest of what they did is too much to swallow, at least the minimal 'meeting' advocated by Todorov could and should be pursued by all those that need to learn to live together, peacefully. Put differently, admiring the actions of the Biehls does not imply that everyone should blindly follow in all their steps. But it does mean that everyone should at least follow them in their sensitive seeing of 'strangers'.

War-thinking Versus Tension-filled Balancing Acts

The preceding discussion of the inclusive moral remembrance underlying the TRC process demonstrates that while trying to 'rescue the horrific from forgetfulness',[43] we dare not forget the humanity of those responsible for the horrible. For if we do not rescue this moral remembering from forgetfulness, we may well be accused of joining their deeds in the moral gutter. If we demonise or animalise 'perpetrators', then we also become guilty of a dehumanisation, which typically was a crucial step in making it possible for them to commit the horrible against faceless victims. If the horrible, and the suffering arising from the horrible, blind us to the faces of the 'perpetrators', then we fail to promote that respect for human life and dignity which is so desperately needed after decades, if not centuries, of systematic dehumanisation in South Africa.

Instead of contributing to a spiral of dehumanisation, the TRC process challenges us, in the words of Cynthia Ngewu, another mother who lost a child, 'to demonstrate a humanness [ubuntu] towards [perpetrators], so that [it] in turn may restore their own humanity'.[44] The potential of this humanising dialectic is illuminated by Ntobeko Penni's response to the Biehls' mercy – their respect for his humanity has not only helped to restore

---

[42] Todorov, *Facing the Extreme*, 295–6.
[43] Ricoeur, *Figuring the Sacred*.
[44] *TRC Report*, Vol. V, 366.

his own humanity, he has also embarked on a process of seeing Amy Biehl's humanity. On that fateful day in 1993 she was a faceless white 'settler'. Now 'he wants to know more about her,' related Linda Biehl. 'Amy's spirit really has a grip on him. Recently he spent an hour just chatting with Amy's older sister, Kim. At the end of that Kim came in the office and she just grabbed me and started to cry. It was as if Ntobeko was planning Amy's week this year on his own and he wanted to know who Amy was.'[45]

The preceding discussion furthermore makes it clear that promoting inclusive moral remembrance should not be confused with striving after tension-free unity, with a romantic hankering after heavenly harmony. The TRC process included many difficult balancing acts – between moral accountability and equitable amnesty, between the rights of victims and the well-being of perpetrators, between respect for past victims and the protection of future victims.

The focus here has been on the further challenge of balancing 'shame at the capacity of human beings of any race or language group to be inhumane to other human beings'[46] with pride in the potential we all have to be humane to other human beings.

If there is too much remembering of the horrible, individuals and/or communities run the risk of getting bogged down in badness; if the encouragement of mercy and forgiveness receives too much attention, this promotion may easily come across as insensitivity to the consequences of dehumanisation. Looking the reality of evil in the eye may blind one to the faces of those behind the evil, thus continuing the cycle of dehumanisation; making too much room for the humanity of perpetrators downplays the horrific and may undermine the restoration of victims' dignity through vindication.

Recognising the various tension-filled balancing acts that are involved in the TRC process not only militates against a monistic desire to absolve all tensions and conflicts in a dangerous conception of 'unity'.[47] The moral inclusivity that underlies the remembrance promoted by the TRC also stands in opposition to a Manichean attraction to moral 'apartheid' and the accompanying discomfort with ambiguity. Within an apartheid mindset, to put it crudely, 'blacks' were typically seen as bad, and 'whites' as wonderful, while within an anti-apartheid mindset it sometimes became tempting to just reverse the roles – black became beautiful and whites were often branded as 'Boers'. The lure of adopting a sharp dichotomy between pure black 'victims' and polluted white 'perpetrators' seems to be particularly strong in a

---

[45] Haupt interview.

[46] Mandela, quoted in *TRC Report*, Vol. I, 134.

[47] On the dangers associated with illiberal 'monism', see Isaiah Berlin, 'Two Concepts of Liberty', in *idem, Four Essays on Liberty* (Oxford: Oxford University Press, 1969), 167–72.

post-apartheid context, as demonstrated by the relative neglect of equity regarding amnesty applicants. In this regard I am reminded of Paul Russell's vital insight: 'If truth is the main casualty in war, then ambiguity is another ... One of the legacies of war is a habit of simple distinction, simplification and opposition ... which continues to do much of our thinking for us.'[48]

Through its promotion of inclusive moral remembrance the TRC process provided us with invaluable raw material and role models for the formidable, ongoing task of challenging 'war-thinking', of uprooting the seductive 'habit of simple distinction, simplification and opposition'. A striking feature of, for example, the Biehl amnesty hearing was that 'Amy's killers' did not 'conform to the familiar plot-lines of Hollywood films such as Richard Attenborough's *Dry White Season* [or *Cry Freedom*], where the police figure as evil-looking Nazis with thick Afrikaans accents'.[49] Neither was the person killed a black victim of those 'Boers'.

By recognising the victimhood of (many) perpetrators, amongst other mitigating factors, a commitment to equity helps to paint a more complex picture of those granted amnesty within the TRC process. By acknowledging the '"little perpetrator" in each one of us', and recognising how interchangeable the roles of 'victim' and 'perpetrator' often are, it becomes more difficult to adopt an exclusive, morally superior, counter-productive position of victimhood. Thus, mutuality in terms of mercy and forgiveness and understanding are encouraged.[50]

More generally, the notion of inclusive moral remembrance gives a deeper meaning to the official language of 'Truth and Reconciliation' – with 'truth' standing also for the need to remember the horrible, while the linkage with 'reconciliation' beckoning us to move creatively beyond evil. And in thinking about 'national unity and reconciliation', the tensions between 'truth' and 'reconciliation' brought to the fore by the TRC process prepare one not to expect easy, warm embraces, but an ongoing, difficult series of balancing acts. The Truth and Reconciliation Commission might not have been very successful in bringing large numbers of individual 'victims' and 'perpetrators' closer together, but at least a careful reading of the process

---

[48] Krog, *Country of My Skull*, 99.

[49] *Cape Times* (6–7 August 1997).

[50] See Trudy Govier and Wilhelm Verwoerd, 'Taking Wrongs Seriously: A Qualified Defence of Public Apologies', *Saskatchewan Law Review* 65 (2002), 153–5, on some of the pitfalls of mutuality/mutual forgiveness. In particular it should be stressed that the mutuality and humility arising from a more complex picture of hurt and harming in apartheid South Africa does not amount to a moral equation of those who fought against and those who defended a crime against humanity. See the chapter on 'Amnesty and Equity' in Wilhelm Verwoerd, 'Equity, Forgiveness, Mercy: Interpreting Amnesty within the SA TRC' (PhD diss., Johannesburg, 2003).

allows one to better appreciate the nature of the challenge described as 'promoting national unity and reconciliation'.

An important part of this challenge is coming to terms with the painful truth that not only amnesty within the TRC process, but 'national reconciliation' itself involve an ongoing series of difficult balancing acts. It is, however, important not to overstate the unavoidability of tensions associated with inclusive moral remembrance and national reconciliation.

Take, for example, the difficult balancing act between the rights of victims and the well-being of perpetrators, or, put differently, between justice and mercy. With the benefit of hindsight it is clear that much of the agony could have been taken out of this balancing act by a different institutional design of the TRC, such as giving the Reparation and Rehabilitation Committee more power to implement tangible reparation, giving the Human Rights Violations Committee more resources for immediate therapeutic support, or by timing the release from prison of those granted amnesty to coincide better with tangible recognition of victims' suffering.

Or take the general tension between the two arms of inclusive moral remembrance – between remembering the horrible and remembering the admirable, between 'truth' and 'reconciliation'. If a separate committee, or even subcommittee, was given the time and resources to promote the kind of actions brought together in the Reconciliation chapter, then the Commission would better have lived up to its name of being a Truth and Reconciliation Commission, instead of mostly being described as the Truth Commission. Furthermore, I know from personal experience that many admirable actions that took place within the TRC process failed to be recorded due to a lack of time and resources. If more than one researcher was given the opportunity and support to focus on recording creative responses to evil within the TRC, we could easily have ended up with a full volume, instead of one chapter, devoted to Reconciliation, thus providing a better balance in the Report between remembering our potential for evil and celebrating, carefully, our potential for goodness.

Conclusion: Towards Humanising Remembrance

The destructive consequences of the moral forgetfulness encouraged by and supporting the system of apartheid loudly proclaim the vital importance of a remembering that looks beyond the skulls of those harmed, without overlooking the gravity of the harm; an ability to see the inherent dignity of the harmers, despite what they have done; a willingness to recognise the humanity of the bystanders and beneficiaries, despite what they have not done, and the courage and generosity to resist the reduction of fellow human beings to 'enemies' that deserve to be burnt to ashes.

Nurturing this kind of remembrance is central to the sustainability of peace in post-apartheid South Africa.[51] Although it might not be my place to say this, I therefore wish that Archbishop Tutu's prayer in the Zapiro cartoon, Linda Biehl and her now-deceased husband's vision, as well as the moral sensitivity of a Ntobeko Penni, could be added to a different kind of national monument than the one standing at the junction of Grand Parade and South Mall in Cork City. I hope that soon there will be a national monument – in an agreed island of Ireland, in South Africa and in other societies struggling to overcome deep divisions – that will inspire our youth to honour their often neglected moral heroes from the past, and to acknowledge respectfully the suffering of survivors, including those victims on the 'other side'. And last but not least, may this monument also help us and our children to remember that our enemies are also 'children of God'. A 'God' who lives in the clouds might have the luxury to doubt the need for this inclusive remembrance. Few of us sharing the same island or planet have this choice – we simply must learn, at least figuratively, to see our 'enemies' face to face.

---

[51] I am, of course, not suggesting that inclusive, humanising moral remembrance will provide a sufficient basis for sustainable peace. Elsewhere I have addressed additional requirements, such as more tangible, practical reparations and creative socio-economic redistribution – see Trudy Govier and Wilhelm Verwoerd, 'The Promise and Pitfalls of Apology', *Journal of Social Philosophy* 33.1 (2002), 67–82; Wilhelm Verwoerd, 'Individual and/or Social Justice after Apartheid? The South African Truth and Reconciliation Commission', *European Journal of Development Research* 11.2 (1999), 115–40.

CHAPTER 8

Between Embrace and Exclusion[1]

Cecelia Clegg

Introduction

In what follows I put forward three interrelated theses. The first is that Christian churches and faith communities have largely left out of account the social dimension of a theology of reconciliation, preferring to concentrate on the personal dimension.[2] This has had two effects. First, it renders the concept of limited use in situations of intergroup conflict or division. Secondly, and more importantly, it denies to the Christian community a vision of creation and salvation, and a description of the mission of the church, which speaks directly to the fragmented state of societies and of the world.

My second thesis is that the personal and social dimensions of a theology of reconciliation entail a holistic understanding of human being as both conscious and unconscious. Such an understanding is significantly lacking in Christian theology, which tends to be dominated by a vision of human personhood as largely conscious and rational. In consequence, Christian churches struggle and often fail to educate both clergy and church members in ways that will promote and help them to sustain the peaceful, life-giving relationships, at the heart of any process of reconciliation.

My third thesis is that processes of ecumenical engagement, at all levels, over the last ninety-plus years, whilst achieving some laudable positive movements in relationships and in reflection, are seriously flawed. They have in many ways failed to equip and inspire Christian churches to live more

---

[1] This chapter is an edited version of a paper that was presented first in the *Margaret Beaufort Lecture Series*, Cambridge University, England, November 2002, and subsequently published as 'Between Embrace and Exclusion', *New Blackfriars* 85 (January 2004), 83–96.

[2] In this chapter I talk about 'churches', 'Christian groups' and 'Christian faith communities'. I do so to acknowledge the many different ways of living out Christian faith commitment in community, which are growing up alongside traditional church denominations, and whose members would not consider themselves as forming a 'church'. We have a significant number of these faith communities in Northern Ireland. When I use the word 'church', then, I am referring primarily to the four larger denominations in Ireland: Roman Catholic, Methodist, Church of Ireland and Presbyterian. I make no apology for the Northern Irish orientation of this chapter, it is the context of my ministry, and it is one part of these islands which both desperately needs the gift of reconciliation and has, I believe, much to teach others about processes of surviving and healing deeply antagonised religious and political divisions.

congruently the mission of the church as reconciliation in their relationships with one another, and as a counter-witness to increasing religious-ethnic conflicts around the globe. The balance of this chapter explores a more psychosocial vision of reconciliation and its implications for church renewal and ecumenical relationships.

I begin with some semi-biographical reflections that describe practical reconciliation work in Northern Ireland, which has shaped my thought. In the second section, I will look at a psychosocial view of a theology of reconciliation through the lens of 'embrace', a category which I have borrowed from the Croatian theologian Miroslav Volf, whose writings have significantly influenced my work in recent years.[3] The final part of this chapter will reflect on the relationships of the churches, issues of exclusion and some of the questions these pose.

Theory Meets Practice

It is a scary experience for any theologian who, fresh from the exertion of completing doctoral work on the theme of human development and reconciliation, is offered a job in which she is asked to test out her theories in practice, especially in the cauldron that was Northern Ireland in the mid-1990s. Such was my situation when the Irish School of Ecumenics employed me, along with my colleague, Dr Joseph Liechty, on a six-year research project called 'Moving Beyond Sectarianism'.[4] We were tasked with what the late Dr Eric Gallagher termed 'speaking the truth in love to the churches',[5] about their responsibility for creating, for maintaining, and their resources for moving beyond sectarianism. So within weeks of defending my thesis, I found myself living in Belfast, spending a lot of time sitting in parish halls, libraries and community centres around Belfast, Derry/Londonderry, Armagh and Omagh listening to stories: stories of unspeakable pain, of terrifying hatred, and of breathtaking courage, faith and resilience.

My work within the project was to bring together groups of church-affiliated Catholics and Protestants, of various denominations, in areas marked by violence to discuss, sometimes for the first time in an inter-tradition setting, issues of identity and sectarianism. The conversations were seldom dull, often humorous and illuminating, sometimes heart-breaking and

---

[3] Miroslav Volf, *Exclusion and Embrace: A Theological Exploration of Identity, Otherness and Reconciliation* (Nashville, TN: Abingdon Press, 1996).

[4] The project ran from January 1995 to June 2000. The report of the research is available in Joseph Liechty and Cecelia Clegg, *Moving Beyond Sectarianism: Religion, Conflict, and Reconciliation in Ireland* (Dublin: Columba Press, 2001).

[5] From the unpublished address with which the late Revd Dr Eric Gallagher launched the Moving Beyond Sectarianism project in Belfast on 3 April 1995.

occasionally so heated that I had to step between male members as they 'squared up' to one another across a room. The people who took part in those groups, at times under physical threat as they made their way to and from meetings, and the many others I encountered in different ways, taught me slowly but surely about the harsh social realities facing any cosy religious notion of reconciliation I might have entertained. I was given the privilege of experiencing the depth of their pain, of realising the enormity of the tasks of both forgiveness and repentance, the delicacy of achieving any kind of justice, especially where lives have been taken or irrevocably destroyed, and perhaps most of all the complexity of understanding the 'truth' about any event or process. It was a truly de-centring experience for me personally.

Gradually, as I regained my balance, I found myself replaying parts of group conversations and wondering what it would take to bring people even close to a state of sustainable, positive relationship, let alone to a state of reconciliation, such was the gulf between them. A gulf that lurked not in the conversation itself, which was often conducted with candour and flashes of Northern humour, but in the silences and in the inevitable retreat into myths, fear, prejudice or well-worn patterns of antagonised division almost every time an external event, such as a bombing or shooting, occurred. My questioning arose partly because the people who attended the group work were not extremists; they were not, on the whole, bigots; they were not young, or indeed not so young, hotheads, though they did express themselves passionately. They were, largely, committed, church-going, middle-aged to older members of various denominations. These were the people who cared enough and were open enough to be engaged in a process that they hoped would help to develop peaceful relationships in their neighbourhood. These are people who believe in peace and reconciliation and pray for it earnestly.

I want to let two of their voices give you a flavour of the conversations and the issues concerning reconciliation and ecumenism that they raised for me. The first voice is Bill, a Protestant man, middle-aged, professional, who when he heard the story of sectarian abuse suffered by one of his own congregation said, 'I have worshipped with you for thirty years in this church and I never knew that had happened to your family.' Such ignorance is not uncommon in Northern Ireland. Its roots are many. It could be a defence mechanism which leads to studied avoidance of what is under people's noses because to admit it would be too traumatic or might impel a person to risky action. It could be the silence of victims, who until the last few years did not feel that they had the right to speak or that anyone would listen to them if they did voice their stories. Or it could be a combination of those factors. What was most sobering for me in this example was the fact that these men could live, worship and socialise in a small Christian community, which is in a flashpoint area of Belfast, and after thirty years still not have shared some of the dominant events of their lives. Seamus Heaney's famous line 'whatever you say, say nothing',[6] echoes through this whole conversation and through the lives of people who have lived terrible suffering whilst locked into stifling silence even within the Christian community.

The second voice is that of a Roman Catholic woman, Catherine, in North Belfast. This woman is a grandmother, active in her parish, and committed to inter-church work. She was a faithful and active member of one of my groups through a terrible period in North Belfast, when young Roman Catholic men were being shot almost daily in reprisal for the murder of Loyalist Volunteer Force leader Billy Wright in the Maze prison. At a meeting in a week when three Roman Catholic men had been shot dead in the locality of the group, we were talking about the situation and she suddenly said with utter conviction, 'What we need is the "Ra" back on the streets, they are the only ones who will protect us.' The 'Ra' being the provisional IRA, who were, at that time, two-and-a-half years into their ceasefire. The other Roman Catholics in the group nodded in silence, whilst the Protestant members sat looking totally stunned. The most shocking aspect of this example for me was the seemingly reflex resort to the threat of violence as a means of solving the problem by a woman who considers herself, and would be regarded in the Christian community, as committed to peace.

As I pondered these and other incidents I was well aware that the Christian churches through their steady preaching of forgiveness, and their pastoral work in communities had prevented the violence becoming worse than it did. But I found myself asking: what has Christian theology to say to these situations? One of the striking characteristics among the people who attended my groups was that they did not seem to have Christian categories for reflecting about their situation that did not revolve around concepts of individual salvation. It is a line of thinking that suggests that as long as I don't do anyone any harm and I live, as far as possible, an individually blameless life, I will get to heaven. But of course, it was obvious as we progressed in the conversations that the collectivity of their individually blameless lives was not significantly influencing events in their society or their local area. Had the Christian churches developed no coherent, cooperative strategy of response to this long and bloody conflict? It seemed not.

In our work and especially in our book *Moving Beyond Sectarianism*, Joe Liechty and I sought to expose the ways in which the systemic nature of sectarianism uses the ignorant complicity and inaction of good, religious people to fuel itself. For Christians in Northern Ireland, therefore, doing nothing is not an option. The questions are: What to do? How to do it? With whom to do it? Informed by what theological understanding? It is to that theological understanding that I turn to now.

---

[6] 'And whatever you say, say nothing', Seamus Heaney, *North* (London: Faber and Faber 1975).

Embrace: Created for Reconciliation and Wholeness

In his article 'The Social Meaning of Reconciliation', Miroslav Volf, professor of theology at Yale University, argues persuasively that the 'social agenda of the church has been isolated from the message of reconciliation', with the result that Christians have difficulty in fostering reconciliation and in avoiding being drawn into conflict.[7] Volf points to the fact that the church has focused on the reconciliation of an individual with God without taking into account the wider social scene which is riven by conflict.[8] Similarly, in the face of radical injustice, the church has adopted a 'justice first' agenda, regarding reconciliation as possible only after justice or liberation has been attained. In a detailed exegesis of Paul's use of the notion of reconciliation, Volf contends that Paul's vision was one of social reconciliation and that central to it is the fact that God reconciles human beings to Godself, not vice versa. Therefore, he argues, there is a pre-eminence of grace over justice.[9] He relocates the struggle for justice as 'a dimension of the pursuit of reconciliation whose ultimate goal is a community of love'.[10] His overarching framework, then, is reconciliation.

Volf eloquently makes the case for there being inherent social dimensions to a theology of reconciliation and not simply social implications that can be drawn from it. He uses the powerful metaphor of 'embrace', opening arms, waiting, closing arms and opening them again, to elucidate the reconciling encounter between two parties in their otherness. Embrace, whilst it suffers the limitations of being drawn primarily from the world of individual relationships (unless you are systematically into group hugs!), nevertheless encapsulates an encounter which allows for fluidity of identities, a non-symmetrical relationship between participants, and through its gentle, non-invasive nature an openness about outcomes and change following an encounter.[11] Embrace, as I will argue below, is a powerful symbol of God's relationship to the world in both creation and salvation.

The vision of reconciliation that informs Volf's position is 'the creation of dynamic harmony in a world ravaged by life-impairing strife'.[12] This vision seems to me to be too limited and too focused on the establishment of harmony in the place of strife. Human relationships entail a measure of conflict and struggle, if only in the differentiation of identities. Such conflict and struggle can be both necessary and positive. In our book, Joe Liechty and I define

---

[7] Miroslav Volf, 'The Social Meaning of Reconciliation', *Interpretation*, Vol. 2 No. 54 (April 2000), 162–3.

[8] Volf, 'The Social Meaning of Reconciliation', 162–3.

[9] Volf, 'The Social Meaning of Reconciliation', 164–9.

[10] Volf, 'The Social Meaning of Reconciliation', 163.

[11] Volf, 'The Social Meaning of Reconciliation', 165–7.

[12] Volf, 'The Social Meaning of Reconciliation', 167–8.

Christian reconciliation as 'the processes and structures necessary to bring all the elements of the cosmos into positive and life-giving relationship with God and with one another'.[13] I understand reconciliation as both an ongoing process, which because it is human requires structures, and which because it is a movement of God's grace, is also an eschatological event. In this vision, the inherent social meaning of reconciliation, for which Volf argues, is expanded beyond the interpersonal, and beyond the ecological into the cosmic dimension. I am positing reconciliation as both the *telos* of creation, including, therefore, rational and non-rational aspects of being, and as the process of salvation.

Reconciliation as the *Telos* of Creation

Much theological reflection about human personhood gives primacy, explicitly or tacitly, to conscious rational thought and regards the process of hominisation as the pinnacle of creation.[14] Even Wolfhart Pannenberg who develops his anthropology in dialogue with the depth psychology of Sigmund Freud, and who regards the self as an unconscious psychological structure, tends to concentrate on the rational dimension of personhood in which the ego, as the centre of consciousness, plays a dominant role.[15] These approaches suggest an evolution of consciousness in creation from the primordial towards the development of the capacity for human rational thought. The creation which always sang the glory of God now becomes conscious of itself in the act. They, however, leave out of account the intra-psychic, unconscious, non-rational level of human being. Yet it is precisely in the psychological processes of integration of the rational and non-rational in human consciousness that human beings experience reconciliation at its most immediate, reconciliation with the ever-present, unconscious 'otherness' of self. The development of human beings towards wholeness is an ongoing process of integrating aspects of the self, in such a way that the person's being and presence in the world becomes more and more positive, and open to her or himself, to others, to the created order, and to God. At the core of human

---

[13] Liechty and Clegg, *Moving Beyond Sectarianism*, 292.

[14] See, for example, Jürgen Moltmann's Trinitarian theology, which is posited on socially co-constituted, and therefore conscious, rational personhood, in Jürgen Moltmann, 'The Social Doctrine of the Trinity', in James M. Byrne (ed.), *The Christian Understanding of God Today* (Theological Colloquium on the Occasion of the 400th Anniversary of the Foundation of Trinity College, Dublin; Dublin: Columba Press, 1993); Alistair McFadyen's notion of personhood as socially co-constituted through communication in Alistair McFadyen, *The Call to Personhood: A Christian Theory of the Individual in Social Relationships* (Cambridge: Cambridge University Press, 1990) and Gabriel Daly, *Creation and Redemption* (Dublin: Gill and McMillan, 1988).

[15] Wolfhart Pannenberg, *Anthropology in a Theological Perspective* (Edinburgh: T&T Clark, 1990).

development, then, is a fundamental drive to integration, which, according to both Sigmund Freud and Carl Jung, is carried on in dreams even when people's consciousness is suspended in sleep.[16]

We do not yet know whether this process, which is still ongoing, will result in another stage of evolution into what might be a type of 'super-consciousness' in creation. Nor do we know what the contours of such 'super-consciousness' might look like, since it will entail both rational and non-rational elements.[17] What is clear is that at the heart of God's creative activity in human beings is a structure of development that is driven by a movement of reconciliation between rational and non-rational aspects of being. This reconciliation, as both process and event, when lived fully in relationship with self, others, the earth and God, can be considered wholeness.

If we now examine God's act of creation through the metaphor of 'embrace' it is possible to say that in this continuous dance of creation God reaches out to reconcile the cosmos to Godself, waits, enfolds those who and that which responds, and releasing them reaches out once again. Within this framework, the event of the incarnation arrives as simultaneously God's reaching out to reconcile the cosmos and the cosmos, through humanities' conscious and unconscious being, and reaching back to be reconciled, to be both enfolded by and then released by God. In the faithful life and innocent death of the God-man, Jesus of Nazareth, one complete cycle of embrace comes into being. It is in this limited sense that I would describe Jesus of Nazareth as the fulfilment of creation. He is the first of many and opens the way for the grace of God, through the presence of the Holy Spirit, to inspire further response to the offer of embrace. Reconciliation, then, understood as the structures and processes necessary to bring all elements of the cosmos into positive life-giving relationship with God and one another, is indeed the *telos* of creation. It is at this point that the orders of creation and redemption overlap. In the life, death and especially in the resurrection of the God-man, the fulfilment of creation is revealed as, at the same time, the offer of salvation.

Reconciliation as the Process of Salvation

Paul asserts, 'God was in Christ reconciling the world to himself',[18] and behind Paul's simple statement lies the complex interplay of processes of

---

[16] See Carl Jung's notion of the 'transcendent function', Carl Gustav Jung, *Collected Works* (ed. W. Maguire; trans. R.F.C. Hull; London: Routledge & Kegan Paul, 1957–79), Vol. 8; and Sigmund Freud, 'The Interpretation of Dreams', in *The Standard Edition of the Complete Psychological Works of Sigmund Freud* (trans. J. Strachey; London: Hogarth Press, 1953), Vol. IV (I) (1900).

[17] Peter Russell, *The Brain Book* (London: Routledge, Kegan Paul, 1979).

[18] 2 Cor. 5:19.

creation and salvation. For me, the salvific role of Jesus Christ is best viewed in two distinct but inseparable stages: Jesus of Nazareth as provisional salvation – that is, reconciliation or embrace present, but not yet achieved – and Jesus, the risen Christ, as salvation – that is, reconciliation or embrace achieved but not yet fulfilled. In Jesus of Nazareth, the reconciling embrace of God has been offered and is in process of response. The embrace, however, is not yet achieved because the response depends upon the total 'yes' of Jesus throughout the duration of his earthly life, and this yes is by no means certain. It is reasonable to assume that if Jesus was truly human he must have had the same structure of conscious and unconscious being as every one else. He must have experienced, therefore, natural positive and negative movements at both the conscious, rational and unconscious, non-rational level and the drive towards integration and development. He must have faced also the choice of self-contradiction, of choosing against love, against God, through sin.

Jesus is, nevertheless, attested in Scripture as a person capable of living love and positivity to the extent that it literally radiated from his body and healed those around him.[19] Such an image suggests a man who was achieving a high degree of reconciliation between the conscious and unconscious levels in his being. In this state of integration, he would have been increasingly conscious of the strong positive and negative movements which were active in him, and he was clearly able to choose consistently to live in a way consonant with love and reconciliation, whatever it cost him in terms of suffering.[20]

In this way of understanding Jesus, I am arguing that he differed from other human beings in that at the unconscious level, the archetype of self, that is, the God-image of human being, corresponded completely to God because Jesus was divine.[21] In the depth of himself and unconsciously he must, therefore, have experienced himself as one with God in a way that other people do not; they experience themselves as other than God. This position appears to entail the logical contradiction that Jesus was whole by virtue of his identity with God, but not whole as a human being. The contradiction is more apparent than real because the wholeness of Jesus through the archetype of self was precisely only archetypal, that is, an inherent possibility, and had yet to come to actual realisation in and through the human life of Jesus of Nazareth.[22]

---

[19] Cf. Jairus' daughter and the woman with the haemorrhage in Mark 5:21–43 and Matt. 9:18–26.

[20] For example his consistently loving choices in the temptations Matt. 4:1–11, and in the agony in Gethsemane Mark 14:32–42.

[21] For the concept of archetypes, see Carl Gustav Jung, *Collected Works*, Vol. 5, 264.

[22] Jung believed archetypes to be inherited possibilities: 'In the pre-natal phase archetypal images appear no longer connected with the individual's memories but belonging to the stock of inherited possibilities of representation that are born anew in every individual'; Jung, *Collected Works*, Vol. 5, 264.

The pivotal event of salvation is the final triumph of Jesus' total 'yes' in his death on the cross and in his resurrection. This fulcrum point of salvation has two aspects. From the perspective of his death, the faithful human life of reconciliation expressed in loving self, others and God becomes reconciliation achieved. In other words, salvation as a punctiliar event happens in Jesus Christ. It is a complete response to the embrace of God, a movement into the enfolding arms of God. It is not, however, fulfilled because the participation of the rest of the cosmos in this salvation has yet to occur.

From the perspective of his resurrection, the faithful, reconciling life of Jesus of Nazareth is validated. Through this validation, the definitive wholeness of human being, possible only in reconciled relationship with God, becomes present in the cosmos. In the final sequence of the embrace, the reciprocal movement of opening arms between Jesus and the Father releases the power of the Holy Spirit into the cosmos. The grace that initially was offered by God, who might be perceived as distant and other, comes to the cosmos in Christ Jesus as the power of the reconciling wholeness of human being, which while still other, is no longer distant but near. With theologians such as Karl Rahner, I would affirm that whilst in principle God might have created the cosmos without the gift of grace, it was given, in fact, always, from the beginning, in view of Christ.[23]

Through the gift of the Holy Spirit, God reaches out anew to embrace the cosmos and to offer the possibility of fulfilling salvation. Such a process of coming to fulfilment depends upon the free historical choices of human beings for or against reconciliation and wholeness. The event of reconciliation in Jesus Christ, however, has introduced a new level of being, a new level of consciousness, into creation. This consciousness since it is a new perception of reconciliation and wholeness must be present both consciously and unconsciously in humankind. It is present consciously in the oral and scriptural witness to Jesus. It is present unconsciously though an alteration in the archetype of Self. In other words, the reconciliation and wholeness of human being made present in the resurrected Christ alters the archetype of self to reflect the possibility of reconciliation and wholeness as a reality that has come about for at least one human being.[24] It still remains a fact that human beings can choose self-contradiction, and my argument is in no way intended to limit human freedom. I am, however, implying that through the salvific action of Jesus Christ, humankind has been offered the possibility of radical transformation and given the enabling power to choose this transformation.

---

[23] Karl Rahner, *Theological Investigations* (trans. E. Quinn; London: Darton, Longman and Todd, 1983), Vol. 18, 189–210.

[24] This proposition depends upon Carl Jung's concept of the 'Collective Unconscious'. Jung's elucidation of this complex concept is scattered through his writings. For an overview, Carl Gustav Jung, *Collected Works*, Vols 5 and 8.

Reconciliation as the Mission of the Church

This view of reconciliation as both the culmination of creation and the process and event of salvation resonates with the understanding in the World Council of Churches study of the nature of the church, that the church is God's instrument to 'bring humanity and all of creation into communion'[25] – and it goes beyond it. If reconciliation has inherent personal *and* social dimensions, then churches are called to live, worship, socialise and evangelise in ways that promote positive human relationships, individually and corporately, and to promote ecologically sound living, not just outside the boundaries of their congregation but also within them. If reconciliation is the mission of the church, then Christians are called to work to ensure that all church structures and actions, corporately as well as individually, internally as well as externally, reflect the loving, boundary-crossing, truth-seeking, right-relating, work of Jesus Christ. If this social vision of reconciliation had informed the communities in which Bill and Catherine, about whom I spoke at the start of this lecture, live, their situations would have been unlikely to occur.

Reconciliation as salvation has some important implications for Christian life and mission, individually and corporately. Individually and within a church or community, it first implies that part of the discipline for Christians, of all ages, and especially for those in teaching and leadership roles, should be to work actively at developing their personal consciousness and human integration. In other words, they are to be actively engaged in learning to embrace the otherness within. This in turn requires that Christian communities create the conditions, in terms of structures, worship and teaching, which are conducive to fostering such personal growth. The often dry, verbal, rational form of so much Christian worship simply will not do. Its lack of symbolism, colour and movement fails to address and engage the whole human person, conscious and unconscious.

Second, it means that actively fostering a social culture of peace and reconciliation within Christian communities is a priority for mission. In other words, learning to live in reconciliation within a church community and between Christian communities is a means of being congruent with the gospel preached and a living witness to the reconciling embrace of God in Christ. Third, it requires that theology and Christian education take seriously the insights of psychology with regard to the structure of consciousness of human being, and adapt content and methodologies to reflect these insights.

---

[25] 'The Nature and Purpose of the Church: A Stage on the Way to a Common Statement', Faith and Order Paper No 181 (Geneva: World Council of Churches, 1998), section 26.

The vision of reconciliation that I am sketching here demands the recognition that the gift of grace engages Christians in a collaborative project with one another and with Christ not only to overcome conflict and division but also to establish relationships of embrace towards otherness in themselves, other people, the natural world and God. An individually blameless life is less than half the story, and the fact that we, as churches, in Northern Ireland have often taught little more than that is a cause of deep regret and repentance. It is particularly so because it has given space for exclusion, the opposite of embrace, in the form of separation, destructive denial and contradiction, to flourish.

Exclusion: Separation, Destructive Denial and Contradiction

Building on an understanding of creation as both 'separating and binding', Miroslav Volf describes exclusion as transgressing against both elements in the form of disconnection which destroys binding, and assimilation, which nullifies separation. Assimilation is the absorption of the other who is regarded as inferior.[26] Disconnection, on the other hand, pushes the other away either as an enemy or as a non-entity.[27] Since 1910, through the ecumenical movement, positive relationships between Christian churches have developed and the types and prevalence of exclusion have diminished – but not disappeared.

Separation is still very much evident and takes a number of forms, with varying degrees of actual separation. Within Roman Catholicism, since the Second Vatican Council, there is an apparent openness to Protestant churches, though the closed communion table enforces a separation at the heart of its sacramental celebration of unity that is stark, and attitudes evident, for example, in the circulation of the document *Dominus Iesus* seem to belie a real intent to embrace.[28] Within Protestantism, an anti-Catholic form of separation entails adherents refusing joint worship and sometimes even contact with Roman Catholics on the grounds that they are not Christian. But Protestant churches also have internal anti-liberal, anti-evangelical and anti-charismatic forms of exclusion. As a Roman Catholic living in North Belfast I still find it mesmerising that in Christian Unity week a pulpit exchange between Protestant churches is sometimes the height of the relationships we can risk or achieve. But this is the reality of a situation of antagonised

---

[26] Volf, *Exclusion and Embrace*, 67.

[27] Volf, *Exclusion and Embrace*, 67.

[28] Cf. the controversy surrounding the text which accompanied this document and stated that Protestant churches were not to be regarded as 'sister' churches; *Declaration Dominus Iesus: On the Unicity and Salvific Universality of Jesus Christ and the Church* (Rome: Congregation for the Doctrine of the Faith, September 2000).

religious and political difference that has endured for decades and cost thousands of lives. What is most striking is that these forms of exclusion are not reserved to small fringe groups or churches but are alive and well in the very heart of the larger denominations which are, formally at least, committed to ecumenical relations.

Each one of these forms of separation, Roman Catholic and Protestant, whilst being destructive in themselves, can lead to pressure on ecumenically minded ministers and members to refrain from developing positive relationships with the other for fear of splitting their congregation, parish or church. This, in my view, is a particularly pernicious face of exclusion, which, because it is not overt, is sometimes underestimated.

A second form of exclusion is destructive denial. I use the adjective 'destructive' to qualify denial because I have learned that there can be a blessed type of amnesia, which is a form of denial, but is sometimes, at least initially, the only way for severely traumatised people to move beyond their trauma into positive relationships. This amnesia is not the type of denial I have in mind here; rather it is the destructive denial of both difference and commonality between traditions and denominations.

The tendency to minimise difference is, in my experience in Northern Ireland, a particular temptation for Roman Catholics, though it is not exclusively Roman Catholic. There is a universalising and inclusive dynamic that characterises a typical Roman Catholic approach and which in inter-church settings can lead to a premature and therefore destructive assertion of commonality. One of the counter-balances for this is an appropriate concern for the Faith and Order issues that divide the churches, without allowing them to become stumbling blocks to developing authentic relationships in a locality.

On the other hand, the tendency to maximise difference is a particular, but not exclusive, temptation for different types of Protestants. There is a profoundly individualistic and differentiating dynamic, which characterises typical Protestant approaches and which in inter-church settings can lead to a persistent focus on, and therefore destructive assertion of, difference. One constructive way of balancing this tendency is to encourage people to express their different denominational identities in strong, positive terms, to give them space to be themselves, and an affirmation that their identity is respected, before attempting to make any connections of commonality. People need to be standing in a secure place in terms of their own identity before they can risk making space for meaningful connection with the other.

Conclusion

There is, however, one question that has lurked just below the surface all the way through this chapter: if reconciliation is the *telos* of creation, the process of salvation and the mission of the church, why is it not more fully advanced between the Christian churches? This question is particularly pointed in a situation like Northern Ireland, where religious-political division has led to such carnage and distress. It is not sufficient to point to the lack of doctrinal consensus. The fifty years of conversations which led to the Lima document in 1982,[29] and the subsequent significant bilateral conversations, such as the Anglican-Roman Catholic International Commission (ARCIC), Roman Catholic-Lutheran, and Church of Ireland-Methodist, are concrete evidence that many, though not all, of those obstacles are, largely, behind us.

We in the Christian churches must face the question of the place of memory, history, power and wealth in our failure to live in congruence with the gospel of reconciliation that we preach. We have the mission, we have many of the resources, but we seem to lack the will to embrace one another in any sustained way. And so we linger between embrace and exclusion. What is needed, in my view, is an option for reconciliation in much the same way as the option for the poor was adopted by some churches a number of years ago. The events of 11 September, the emergence of global religious ethnic violence, indicate that we have reached a crossing place, in Irish, 'Trasna', and we have a choice. So let me end with a reflection on this crossing place, by Sr Raphael Consedine, a Presentation Sister.

Trasna

The pilgrims paused on the ancient stones
In the mountain gap.
Behind them stretched the roadway they had travelled,
Ahead, mist hid the track.
Unspoken the question hovered:
Why go on? Is life not short enough?
Why seek to pierce its mystery?
Why venture further on strange paths, risking all?
Surely that is a gamble for fools ... or lovers.
Why not return quietly by the known road?
Why be a pilgrim still?
A voice they knew called to them, saying:
This is Trasna, the crossing place.
Choose! Go back if you must,
You will find your way easily by yesterday's road,
You can pitch your tent by yesterday's fires,
There may be life in the embers yet.
If that is not your deep desire,
Stand still. Lay down your load.
Take your life firmly in your two hands,
(Gently ... you are trusted with something precious),

---

[29] See 'Report of Faith and Order Commission WCC, Lima, Peru 1982', in Harding Meyer and Lukas Vischer (eds), *Growth in Agreement: Reports and Agreed Statements of Ecumenical Conversations on a World Level* (New York: Paulist Press, 1984).

While you search your heart's yearnings:
What am I seeking? What is my quest?
When your star rises deep within,
Trust yourself to its leading.
You will have light for your first steps.
This is Trasna, the crossing place.
Choose!
This is Trasna, the crossing place.
Come!

CHAPTER 9

Respecting Boundaries and Bonds: Journeys of Identity and Beyond[1]

Geraldine Smyth OP

Strangers and Guests: The Call to Cross the Jordan

> There are those who 'cross the Jordan' and seek out truth through a different experience from the one they are born to, and theirs is the greatest struggle. To move from one cultural ethos into another, as I did, and emerge embracing them both demands more … than any armed struggle. For here is the real conflict by which we move into … maturity … Those who struggle through turbulent Jordan waters have gone beyond the glib definitions of politics and religion. The rest remain standing on either bank firing guns at one another. I had had enough of gunfire, the rhetoric of hate and redundant ideologies.[2]

These words of Brian Keenan, Belfast man and former Beirut hostage, from the opening pages of his memoir, reflect a wise insight on the ambivalence of identity. Here he is recalling his farewell walk though Belfast before taking off for a teaching post in the Middle East. His eyes fix on the dividing walls and their atavistic murals that staked out territory and tribe, and functioned through their violent mythological imagery to reassure or intimidate. It was as if people were drinking of a sectarian poison, out of a sense of frustration, of fear, of a raging thirst for identity and purpose. Shrinking even then from labels like Protestant, Loyalist or British, Keenan both values his place and knows it is time for him to make the mythic leap across the Jordan. He senses that the boundaries that strengthen a sense of identity must be opened up and transcended. If he is to come home to himself, there must be the possibility of encounter with the stranger from the other shore. Keenan was not then to know that he would soon be drawn into another rage for identity as intractable as any witnessed on the streets of Belfast. A teacher of English literature, Keenan was not beyond conjuring up the shade of James Joyce as prototype of his refusal to be bound by his background and its shibboleths, as he prepared for his own 'mythic leap across the Jordan'. The author looks back as one who has travelled an infinite distance from the point of first starting out. We note, however, that his purpose was not to reject his own cultural

---

[1] This chapter is a reworking of the paper originally offered as the formal response to Marc Gopin's Keynote Address at the Irish School of Ecumenics' 'Boundaries and Bonds' Conference, Belfast, 1997.

[2] Brian Keenan, *An Evil Cradling* (London: Hutchinson, 1992), 16.

ethos in favour of another, but to emerge, 'embracing them both'. The imagery and the holding of contrasts in tension associate themselves with Jesus' baptism in the River Jordan initiating him into a ministry that crossed ancient divisions of imperial politics and local religion.

The different human ways of hiding behind, negotiating or reaching across boundaries are a key symbol in Keenan's story. But his story is also about the way boundaries can be structured to intensify both the bonds of oppression and the bonds of love. And Keenan maps his story between the extremes of hatred and love: on the one hand, 'How men misdirected their anger and aggression onto one another, and mutual support turned into mutual dislike and seething silence';[3] and on the other, a disclosure of the power of love between his fellow-hostage John McCarthy and himself. This bond plumbs the depth of shared despair, intimacy and defiance. In the 'bonding of our innermost selves', Keenan touches into the mystery of redemption as an 'act of transformation and transcendence [which] could be seen as a metaphor for the times we live in'.[4]

Keenan's story brings us into that magnetic field of 'identity politics' and 'identity religion', now all too familiar whether in Beirut or Belfast, and through analytic insight, such as that of Charles Taylor, Michael Ignatieff or Julia Kristeva. Thus, the general and particular conflicts among persons, groups and cultures, in that magnetic field where ethnicity, politics, culture and religion oppose one another, are viewed increasingly as configured around the boundaries and bonds of identity and relationship with those whom we have come to regard as the stranger.

In the particular context of Northern Ireland, the negotiation of personal and social identity has been deterred by the presence in a contested space of a majority group and a sizeable minority group. Compounding this, the reality is rendered more complex by being enmeshed in differing, and even oppositional, self-understandings of Christian identity, linking back historically and in folk memory to post-Reformation and Plantation conflicts, with their religio-cultural reservoirs of bitterness, distrust and bloodshed, and the attendant legacy of respective particularist self-identity on the 'Protestant-Unionist' side, as God's divinely appointed people sent into the land to be the City on the Hill, besieged on all sides but never defeated. On the Catholic-Nationalist side, the palm of martyrdom, whether as a result of famine, brutally suppressed rebellion or hunger strike, was prized as a badge of religious superiority and bearing the promise of victory to come. To each cultural group, ironically, God was on the side of their irreproachable cause. It is not difficult to see how such conflictive political history and antagonistic self-understanding would look for biblical assurance. One can relate this

---

[3] Keenan, *An Evil Cradling*, xii.
[4] Keenan, *An Evil Cradling*, xiv.

struggle to that in the Hebrew Bible between the election of Israel as God's chosen people (linked with the Mosaic covenant), and the universal covenant with Abraham and Sarah and through them with all the nations, though with scant attention to the latter strand in the tradition, and to the prophetic impulses running cross-grain within it. The challenge of Jesus' teaching and example in welcoming outsiders and reaching out to enemies, it would seem, is curiously easy to set aside. The understanding of the cross as costly forgiveness and salvation for all is easily disremembered. The meaning of the resurrection of Jesus as new hope sprung in the midst of the apostles' betrayal and loss, and then as the 'irruption of the utterly gratuitous other' is too incredible to grasp[5] – once it is a matter of those beyond the boundaries of one's own cultural tribe or religious flock. Sectarianism, as we have already noted, has its narrow geography, as well as its preferred versions of history. The effect of hedging one's political boundaries with the sharp rhetoric of sectarian exclusivism has achieved its dire effect of mutual separation, exclusiveness and enmity, even whilst mantling these with a transcendent aura of self-legitimacy and the justification of violence.[6]

Frank Wright classified Northern Ireland as 'an ethnic frontier society', in which relationships are structurally antagonistic.[7] Thus, the border, which delineates the Northern Ireland state as part of the United Kingdom, evoked opposing attitudes to its legitimacy from the Unionist-Protestant and Nationalist-Catholic population, the former looking for support to Britain and the latter to the Republic of Ireland. Thus, even since the declaration of ceasefires in 1994, the traditional antagonistic stances of trust and distrust have maintained themselves, whether *vis-à-vis* the unstable political arrangements, the judicial system, structures of economic access or civic equality. Each group continues to draw comfort from the relatively powerful position of its respective church or political leadership. Social relationships have continued to be governed by the threat of repeating outbreaks of violence, and, at times, by a religious sanction for violence.[8] Even in the post-ceasefire era, there is no reason to doubt the persisting relevance of Wright's analysis of the social system as one secured by a 'tranquillity of mutual deterrence', and where, on a frequent basis, old rivalries spill out in spates of violence and counter-violence executed by rival paramilitary groups. During recent decades, we have continued to see a systemically contested interpretation of past history and contemporary events framed in this paradigm of mutual deterrence – from the Civil Rights Campaign of the late

---

[5] Cf. James Alison, *Knowing Jesus* (London: SPCK, 1993), 9–18.

[6] Cf. Geraldine Smyth, 'Sectarianism – Theology Gone Wrong?', in Alan Falconer and Trevor Williams (eds), *Sectarianism* (Dublin: Dominican Publications, 1995), 52–76.

[7] Frank Wright, *Northern Ireland: A Comparative Analysis* (Dublin: Gill and Macmillan, 1992), 20ff.

[8] Frank Wright, *Northern Ireland*, 112–16.

1960s to the Anglo-Irish Agreement of the mid-1980s, to the Good Friday agreement of the mid-1990s, to the breakdown of political structures of power-sharing in the first decade of the new century.

The seeds of an alternative possibility have been sown but have not easily taken root. For the 'tranquillity of mutual deterrence' to give way to other patterns of interrelationship would demand the exposure of its dependence on a rivalry that is indeed mimetic. This is no mean task, because each group has accommodated its identity to this pattern and tends to see violence as a necessary evil. Walter Wink's observations on the 'myth of violence as redemptive' are *à propos* here, [9] Wink, like Wright, drawing upon the insights of René Girard on the interplay of religion and power (through a cycle of mimetic rivalry, demonising, scapegoating, exclusion and sacral violence as a way of restoring of the uneasy tranquillity of the *status quo ante* – though only on a temporary basis).[10] According to such analysis, within such a paradigm, religion becomes the transcendent legitimisation and fuelling power of the cycle of deterrence and violence. Influenced also by their Christian faith, both writers point to the need to demythologise and unmask this claim to violence as redemptive, as fundamentally and repeatedly destructive. One can also infer from their writing that no solution to violence can be found within the old paradigm – for it is driven and fed by violence. Other authors, writing from different conceptual bases, posit not dissimilar conclusions. Julia Kristeva, for example, from a Jewish and psychoanalytic perspective, treats of oppositional relationships between foreigners and natives: 'The rooted one who is deaf to the conflict and the wanderer walled in by his conflict thus stand firmly facing each other. It is a seemingly peaceful co-existence that hides the abyss: and abysmal world, the end of the world.'[11]

A shared weakness of Girardean and psychoanalytic probing alike is that they operate mainly from a negative moral stance, saying next to nothing about positive responsibility *vis-à-vis* the creative demands of truth, the role of rituals of repentance, or formation for peace and reconciliation. We shall look at this later particularly in relation to the churches. Suffice to note here that while the churches do indeed need to reflect on their collusion in violence and living too comfortably in its penumbra, the gospel also calls them to recognise the needs of strangers and to work with others to generate relationships of trust and charity, and in collaborating with others to sustain cultural and social bonds, attempt to create an alternative paradigm premised on peace and shared life. For this to succeed, the churches must be

---

[9] Walter Wink, *Engaging the Powers: Discernment and Resistance in a World of Domination* (Minneapolis, MN: Fortress Press, 1992), 133ff.

[10] Cf. René Girard, *Violence and the Sacred* (trans. Patrick Gregory; Baltimore, MD: Johns Hopkins University Press, 1977).

[11] Julia Kristeva, *Strangers to Ourselves* (trans. Leon S. Roudiez; New York: Columbia University Press, 1991), 17.

among the agents of change who are themselves renewed by their inner symbolic ritual and practice that lead towards forgiveness and reconciliation. As well as exposing and seeking to disarm the myth of redemptive violence, all who are concerned for peace must tap into the symbolic wellsprings of peace, understood, for example, in such regenerative symbol structures as *Shalom*, Jubilee, the Reign of God, or the Eschatological Banquet. Overcoming hostility is not simply a matter of breaking down the enmity, but of offering hospitality and enabling one another to flourish and have life to the full.

Beyond 'Single Identity'

By the same token, I would argue, one must entertain a certain suspicion of the current enshrining in the Northern peace process of the notion of 'single identity'. One often now hears the claim – posited not simply as justifiable but as desirable – that members of a particular ethnic group, before moving to engage in dialogue and encounter with the group across the boundary, must first intensify a sense of their own identity. Difficulties arise when attachment to 'single identity' becomes an end, and behind talk of necessary 'self-confidence in one's own culture' lurks an undisguised ideology, which precludes any truck or traffic with those beyond the boundary.

W.R. Rodgers suggests that we discover ourselves only by going out of ourselves, and, just like the three Magi, we may have to travel a far distance and discover the paradox that encounter with what is most different and strange will bring home to us a fuller sense of self-knowledge:

> Strange that, in lands, and countries quite unknown,
> We find, not others' strangeness, but our own;
> That is one use of journeys; if one delves,
> Differently, one's sure to find oneselves.[12]

The journey into self-understanding requires that we 'delve differently'. To see ourselves in depth, we need somehow to stand outside ourselves. Rodgers, like fellow-Ulsterman Keenan, marvels that identity is intrinsically plural, that it is disclosed in journeying far from home, and that in order to become itself, it must encounter what is deemed wildly different. So too, the poet's diction intimates the need to be active and concretely located if we are to attain increased self-understanding. To be confronted with another's

---

[12] W.R. Rodgers, 'The Journey of the Magi', in Michael Longley (ed.), *W.R. Rodgers: Poems* (Oldcastle, Ireland: Gallery Press, 1993), 59–63 (60, 61). See also Paul Ricoeur, *Oneself as Another* (trans. Kathleen Blamey; Chicago, IL: Chicago University Press, 1992), 181–2.

strangeness evokes an impulse to protect ourselves by strengthening the boundaries – the Freudian *dictum* of fight or flight. Northern Ireland has its own versions of these in the twin impulses for sectarian attack or sectarian withdrawal.

In the context of the current quest for peace and reconciliation between conflicting cultural groups, the current vogue for 'single identity work', as it is called, is a contradiction in terms and also lends false legitimacy to a staged segregation, in some bid to bolster the self-confidence and self-consciousness of traditionally segregated cultures. I would argue that this current penchant for 'single identity work' is ill conceived. This is not to disclaim the relative value in certain situations for particular cultural groups to withdraw in order to reflect on themselves and on their own internal narrative and desired direction. What must be challenged is a continuous practice wherein the group's withdrawal reinforces a deliberately self-referential scheme that is thus put beyond question. In such cases, the group is more likely to harden the boundaries of its political or religious identity rather than take a discriminating pride in its own cultural distinction and potential contribution to society at large. Unless it keeps the other in view, the process falls into solipsism. Furthermore, modern psychology, both developmental and social, demonstrates that a self, nation or culture defines itself in relationship, both negatively and positively, to some significant others.[13] For the very rift that separates is a bond in which each is alter ego to the other. It is also evident that persons in society share in a range of overlapping identities and communities of belonging. We inhabit each other's memory and histories. We are implicated across a rift that is a bond structured and weathered by conflicts, intimacies and interests.[14] The vision of another kind of bond needs to be nurtured and encouraged. The grittiness of differences can serve to unite us across the boundary, even at such times when a church or civic group finds it salutary to stand back from the other in a step of critical distance, to reflect on what it can bring to the relationship or to some collaborative undertaking. As inter-church and inter-cultural groups discover through encounter that their identity is irreducibly relational, members often attest to the paradoxical experience of increased self-awareness and confidence in their own self-understanding.[15]

---

[13] Cf. Kristeva, *Strangers to Ourselves*, 170, 181–3, and *passim*. See also John Macmurray, *Persons in Relation* (London: Faber and Faber, 1961), 86–105, on the necessary rhythm in all relationship of 'withdrawal and return', where the withdrawal is always for the sake of the return: 'My withdrawal from the Other is itself a phase of my relation to the Other. The isolation of the self does not annul the relation; it refuses it … to annul the relation is to annul oneself' (92).

[14] Kristeva, *Strangers to Ourselves*, 183–4, on Freud's concept of the 'alien double', with the 'compulsion to repeat'.

[15] One can also adduce a narrative hermeneutic here. Students at the Irish School of Ecumenics, who study alongside others from church traditions, year by year, testify to

The Double Drive for Freedom and Security

With the bi-polar need for freedom and security, a common human temptation is to reject the inherent tension.[16] Repeatedly in history, the dynamics of political and religious worlds can be construed as in the grip of these oppositional drives which find their origin in irreducible instincts and needs – for freedom and for security. At a deeper level they correlate with aspirations to integrity and solidarity. When such instincts are frustrated, they may convert to rage, and a grasping after 'more of the same', whereas what each really needs is 'more of the other'. Thus, instincts for security/order/certainty (often salient in the landscape of a politics of identity) tend to throw a fog of suspicion over what is strange, interpreting it as threatening, and intensifying the clinging to settled assumptions of the other as hostile.

Conversely, the drive for unrestrained social freedom, spatial power and independent thought involves a distortion of human need, prompting denial of limits and rejection of any external principle of accountability. At this extremity drive turns to rage. Both represent a refusal of the mutuality that is the condition for self-realisation, each mirroring its opposite, issuing in self-destructive behaviour and a refusal to recognise the *otherness* of the other, the refusal of the other's boundaries and of tentative possibilities of bonds across boundaries. Acutely aware of this fateful interplay, Marc Gopin has argued that recognition of self-limits and the limits in one's surrounding world is the condition of self-fulfilment and indeed of the survival of the planet: 'Where there is no boundary there is no recognition of anything but the self. Where there is nothing but the self there is only demonic destruction and putrid self-worship. The human failure to live within limits may well turn out to be not only the aboriginal failure (Gen. 3) but also the ultimate disaster.'[17]

Julia Kristeva suggests that the foreigner lives within us as 'the hidden face of our identity' and that the challenge is not so much to live with others as to live *as* others.[18] Also probing the Jewish understanding of the foreigner as '*ger*',[19] she warns against objective and subjective pressures of assimilation, preferring the more precise '*ger-tochav*' (resident alien) as intimating the need

---

achieving a new depth of understanding of their own church doctrines and practice as a result of broader base of study, exposure and reflection than had been possible while reflecting within their own denominational family.

[16] Marc Gopin, *Between Eden and Armageddon: The Future of World Religions, Violence and Peacemaking* (Oxford: Oxford University Press, 2000), 5–6.

[17] Gopin, 'The Heart of the Stranger', lecture delivered at 'Boundaries and Bonds' Conference, Irish School of Ecumenics, Belfast, 1997.

[18] Kristeva, *Strangers to Ourselves*, 1.

[19] See also Gopin, *From Eden to Armageddon*, 6–7; and Gopin's chapter 'Embracing the Stranger', above.

to safeguard the tension and underlining the importance of refraining from co-opting the foreigner – respecting and welcoming without the demand for conformity.[20] Kristeva's words hark back to those cited above of Presbyterian poet, W.R. Rodgers, with their reverberation in the Ulster psyche, as in other situations of sectarian conflict. She claims that 'The foreigner comes in when the consciousness of my difference arises, and he disappears when we all acknowledge ourselves as foreigner, unamenable to bonds and communities.'[21]

Making much play of the fact that, through the narrative of Ruth the Moabitess, foreignness is inserted into the very heart of Jewish identity, Kristeva notes the perennially disturbing truth that through her, 'foreignness and incest were ... at the foundations of David's sovereignty'.[22] She underlines the ironic reality that what one most treasures as distinctive in one's identity is prototypically constituted in the face of otherness and involves a *transgression* from royal sovereignty and indeed self-sovereignty:

> Ruth, the foreigner, is there to remind those unable to read that the divine revelation often requires a lapse, the acceptance of radical otherness, the recognition of a foreignness that one might have tended at the very first to consider the most degraded ... Perhaps damaged, worried at any rate, that sovereignty opens up – through the foreignness that founds it – to the dynamics of a constant, inquisitive, and hospitable questioning, eager for the other and for the self as other.[23]

In settings of contesting identities, and settled views of purity of origin, of who is in, who out, such tantalising ironies need to be pondered.

The Politics of Identity in Contexts of Ethnic Conflict

In reflecting upon the dynamic of boundaries and bonds in the concrete context of Northern Ireland – marked by the relative stability of ceasefires, yet without having attained to a political settlement – one can fruitfully adduce the interdisciplinary discourse which has in recent decades conceptualised the notion of ethnic boundaries and cultural bonds in some precise and inflected fashion.

It was Frederick Barth, the Norwegian anthropologist, who coined the term 'ethnic boundary' in 1969 – the date usually ascribed to the start of the recent phase of the 'Irish Troubles'.[24] One central thematic in Barth's challenge to

---

[20] Kristeva, *Strangers to Ourselves*, 67–76. Ruth, the Moabite is, of course, the classical and exemplary *ger-tochav*.

[21] Kristeva, *Strangers to Ourselves*, 1.

[22] Kristeva, *Strangers to Ourselves*, 75.

[23] Kristeva, *Strangers to Ourselves*, 75.

[24] Frederick Barth, 'Introduction', in *idem* (ed.), *Ethnic Groups and Boundaries: The Social Organisation of Culture Difference* (London: Allen and Unwin, 1969).

earlier notions of fixed identity and his assertion that ethnic identities are forged through transactional encounters both positive and negative is the distinction between the 'ethnic boundaries' and 'ethnic contents'. For Barth, ethnic boundaries have more to do with subjective identity *perception* (us *vs* them) than with objective cultural *substance* (contents/practices *within* the boundary), and as such, ethnic boundaries are less amenable to modification in the formation and maintenance of group identity. There is an obvious hazard here, however unintended by Barth (who sought to release the notion of cultural identity from the more common belief of cast-iron typological fixities and ancestral ascriptions), of tipping the scales in favour of invisible psychological dynamics and of constructivist influences on boundary fluidity, which can serve to minimise the actual significance of ethnic culture in the forming and sustaining of identity. One also must guard against the kind of romantic heroicising of culture, which history has often shown serves to institutionalise cultural exclusion as a hindrance to social and political transformation.[25]

In the past quarter of a century, the notion of the boundary has been further theorised across a range of disciplines – in anthropology, psychology, social theory, human geography, religious studies and political science, for example, issuing in a fertile interdisciplinary field of discourse.[26] In linking ethnic identity, ethnic culture and violent nationalisms, some generalised comments can be noted: the increasingly recognized importance of *intra-* (alongside *inter-*) relationships in ethnic and political identity patterns; a growth in anti-essentialist views of identity with a corresponding emphasis on spatial, relational, constructivist and strategic factors in identity formation and boundary intensification; a postmodern revalorisation of difference, pluralism and multiculturalism and a complex ambivalence towards cultural homogenisation and political assimilation and secularisation.[27] It can also be asserted that because ethnicity is defined by boundaries, even when and

---

[25] One thinks of Nationalist Socialism in 1930s Germany with its sports and fitness culture harnessed to the ideology of Aryan purity of race; or *Voortrekker* cultural re-enactments of the Great Trek in South Africa; closer to home, certain sectarian aspects of the Parades culture or graveside commemoration rhetoric also come to mind. In subsequent writings, Frederick Barth warned against any tendency to falsely dichotomise 'ethnic boundary' and 'ethnic contents' and argued rather for a focus on the functioning of the boundary in mutual influence with the cultural contents enclosed within it. Cf. Frederick Barth, 'Enduring and Emerging Issues in the Analysis of Ethnicity', in Hans Vermeulen and Cora Govers (eds), *The Anthropology of Ethnicity: Beyond Ethnic Groups and Boundaries* (Amsterdam: Het Spinhuis, 1994), 17ff.

[26] For a brief overview, see Daniele Conversi, 'Nationalism, Boundaries, and Violence', *Millennium: Journal of International Studies* 28, no. 3 (1999), 555–9.

[27] Cf. Vamik Volkan, *Bloodlines: From Ethnic Pride to Ethnic Terrorism* (Boulder, CO: Westview Press, 1997), with illustrative reference to the fraught but evolving relationship of Russia and Estonia (215–18).

although the internal cultural 'contents' of a group may indeed adapt and shift, it is the maintaining of the boundary controls and mechanisms which are increasingly relied upon to delineate the group's self-identity. According to John Bell Armstrong (writing on nationalism), 'groups tend to define themselves ... by exclusion, that is, by the comparison to strangers'.[28]

Boundaries in Belfast

It is the boundary, rather than what lies behind it, that is seen as the indicator of ethnic endurance, one constantly reinscribed with symbolic or mythic significance. So, in Northern Ireland, the delimiting defiant functions of flag-flying, kerbstone painting and murals on interface boundaries tell less about the reality of territorial control or cultural experience *within* the boundary, than about insatiable need to keep the boundary 'hot', to keep reinvesting it with intensity of feeling, asserting distinctiveness or territorial hegemony, provoking fear of others, warning outsiders against trespass. Territorial demarcation and self-delineation are two sides of the same coin. Notably, however, there is little visible *content* of cultural life, little vital sign of ethnic distinctiveness beyond the crude slogans and image.

Seen thus, the claims and counter-claims to boundary-space in terms of the right to 'distinctive culture' have a certain hollow ring. The right to parade down a particular route, the counter-right not to have to be subjected to this, assertions of entitlement to bi-lingual street names and public signs (Irish or Ulster-Scots) in predominantly mono-lingual settings – these betray an actual confusion of ethnicity and culture, and manifest a fixation with strengthening the ethnic boundary rather than developing cultural 'thickness'. Clearly, some theoretical and practical distinctions need to be teased out. Here I adduce Conversi's comprehensive analysis, making my own points of interpretation and extrapolation into the Northern Ireland scene.

Conversi, building on Barth's distinction between 'ethnic boundary' (as subjectively fixed, exclusionary and closed identity marker, based primarily on *perception*), and 'cultural contents' (understood in more substantive terms associated with such objective variables as language, heritage, putative ancestry), marshals a range of cross-disciplinary analysis to corroborate and extend this basic insight.[29] Culture or 'ethnic contents' is in this understanding more open and accessible to outsiders, having an inviting communicative quality: thus a language can be learned; musical or literary traditions fruitfully cross-fertilise, with an effect of cooling the boundaries

---

[28] John Alexander Armstrong, *Nations Before Nationalism* (Chapel Hill: University of North Carolina Press, 1982), 5.

[29] Daniele Conversi, 'Nationalism, Boundaries and Violence', 561–3.

and creating bridges across. Once more the boundary is also a bond: the rift that binds, the perpetual sign of the destabilising perception of danger from without, becomes the possibility of a bridge that would connect the separate realms. The implication is that without such a bridge, territory becomes a trap, and power is rendered impotent to promote a culture of the commonweal or of freedom for exchange. Rather, the stakes are heightened further and the total focus must be fixed upon the boundary rather than on any objective assessment on what the boundary is designed to shut out or safeguard within.

Here, what has been said above about the ensnarement of 'single identity' consciousness bears some modification, though I would still argue it to be a misnomer. Where communities have been structured around the boundary demarcation of insider and outsider, where the other is perceived as ever-encroaching threat, the boundary itself becomes the repository of identity, and culture is driven by fears for security. In such fraught settings, survival and defiance inevitably become the normative *modus vivendi*. Thus, in the years following the 1994 ceasefires, those living on interfaces claim to have enjoyed little improvement in the sense of security or inward socio-economic investment. They have continued to be plagued by violence and have been more liable to suffer the grip of strategically-driven paramilitary rioting inside and 'low-grade' harassment from outside – tactically welcomed by the vigilante powers within as reconfirming the necessity of the boundary, the frequent flexing of paramilitary muscle, and securing the reliance of residents on paramilitary 'protection'. Following the Holy Cross School protest,[30] a Protestant clergyman, while unequivocally condemning the intimidatory tactics of the protesters, told me of the wholesale public disregard of the plight of a small enclave of elderly residents on the 'Protestant' side of the interface, who were subjected to nightly intimidation and prevented from shopping by day. No one of influence was lifting a finger – whether to rein in the bully-boys or negotiate with opposite numbers across the divide. One resident was left with all her broken windows left unattended for a week, despite the clergyman's efforts to act as go-between with the City Council and with local Unionist politicians. Over time, social confidence had dwindled; there was an absence of on-the-ground leadership, while political and civic

---

[30] The pupils of Holy Cross Catholic Primary School, in a troubled interface area in North Belfast, were prevented over a number of months in 2001–2002 from gaining access to their school whose main entrance was located in a predominantly Unionist enclave. Incredible to any general onlooker, scenes of intimidation of terrorised five- to eleven-year-olds and their parents were flashed across the world's media, most notably when Archibishop Desmond Tutu, on a visit to Belfast, lent his solidarity by walking alongside the children. Inevitably, the highly charged situation was politicised, representing many dimensions of a volatile boundary conflict. See the subsequent wider-ranging study by Paul Connolly, Alan Smith and Berni Kelly, *Too Young to Notice? The Cultural and Political Awareness of 3–6 Year Olds in Northern Ireland* (Belfast: Community Relations Council, 2002) (jointly commissioned by Channel 4 and the Community Relations Council, Belfast).

authorities at one remove seemed content to let the pot simmer, according to their own popular advantage. Small wonder that with such thin lived experience or benefit of 'bonding capital' in the internal culture behind the boundary, there is correspondingly little will to invest in cooperation across the interface ('bridging capital'), or of venturing out into cross-community dialogue, mediation or potential partnership to achieve a desired end.[31] In such contexts the boundary is the 'bond-age' whereby no 'peace dividend' has been enjoyed and the favoured currency of speech is about heightening the 'peace-line' boundary. And so politicians or local community leaders trade in talk of their people's perceived or real losses, and in the perceived or real gains of the other community, calculated always in inverse ratio, one community to another, with little internal analysis of the disposition of power within and between communities or between a community and the state system.

There is a good deal of theorising on the evidence of the comparatively stronger existence and access within Nationalist communities of a distinctive social and cultural capital, ranging from sport and music to language and literature, in which people take pride and experience social joy and solidarity. Nationalist communities set a trail in forms of social organisation – credit unions, neighbourhood associations and citizens' advice structures, for example, as well as in widespread skill in securing resources for projects of capacity building and of social inclusion and economic access. In the past decades many Unionist neighbourhoods have found some parallel success and adeptness in organising creative enterprises of social up-building through a wide range of educational, cultural and micro-economic endeavours. Some of these were of a joint nature; others of a cross-community nature, and still others internally geared to human uplifting in socially disadvantaged areas. But for those on the interfaces, lived experience is not a whole lot different from before, with regular experience of violence at flashpoint times of year as well as random attacks, intimidation and forced flight from homes. There have been considerable achievements in the expansion of housing stock,

---

[31] See, for example, Robert Putnam (ed.), *Democracies in Flux: The Evolution of Social Capital in Contemporary Society* (Oxford: Oxford University Press, 2002), 11–12. It is important, however, in adverting to this 'bonding'/'bridging' model, not to neglect the critical significance of the underlying disposition of power relations. A critical corrective is advanced in Pierre Bourdieu's fourfold distinction between different types of capital within the 'field' of power politics: economic; cultural (involving different types of knowledge); social (involving valued social relations between people), and symbolic (arising from one's honour and prestige). An analysis of the field must also take objective account of the hierarchical locations of power relations; and of the nature of the '*habitus*' of the agents occupying these structured positions. See Pierre Bourdieu and Loïc J.D. Wacquant, 'The Purpose of Reflexive Sociology', in P. Bourdieu and L.J.D. Wacquant (eds), *An Invitation to Reflexive Sociology* (Chicago, IL: University of Chicago Press, 1992), 61–215 (101, 167). For a discussion of Bourdieu's insights, see George Ritzer, *Agency-Structure Integration* (Singapore: McGraw-Hill Book Company, 1983), 532–42.

although official surveys show that almost a decade after the ceasefires, more people choose to live in housing arrangements that are more sectarian in social structure than at any other time.[32]

One church minister – who has painstakingly dedicated the past decade to pastoral and structural ways of confidence-building within and across communities, developing projects of social analysis, mediation and social regeneration – recently bemoaned, after another spiralling outbreak of boundary rioting, that everything she and her collaterals were building up could be dismantled in a night. 'It is so frustrating,' she said, 'that so much in North Belfast is driven by what is happening on the interfaces.' One recognises the astute insight here that both ethnic boundary and ethnic culture require a bi-focal attention subtly held together in ways that recognise their respective complexity and their interrelated dynamic impact.

Two Necessary and Interrelated Approaches to Peace

It is interesting to observe that in particular locations of transition there is an intuitive realisation that where perceptions of violence are softening and the controlling power of the boundaries is being cooled, changes in mural iconography tend to reflect amelioration of the fragile cultural life within. Recently, for all the enduring paramilitary emblems on boundary murals, there are also hints of different cultural contents being exhibited. Where social renewal schemes have borne fruit, there have been accompanying signs of cultural regeneration, for example in local festivals, art exhibitions, writing workshops, intra-nationalist and intra-Unionist debating events. Creative signs of imaginative vitality have appeared on boundary murals. In Nationalist West Belfast, some depict children dancing and playing in a carefree way, with trees and flowers replacing masked faces and armalites. In Loyalist East Belfast, some gable walls display names and symbols of famous local writers such as C.S. Lewis alongside football legend George Best. One can be cynical about cosmetic gestures, but as such they do intimate how communities are engaging in a new level of self-reflection and generating a sense of self-confidence and a pride in a *distinctive* cultural heritage that is none the less sturdy enough to be communicated. Images of self-protection have given way to ones that suggest something more substantive within,

---

[32] See Malachi O'Doherty, 'Religious Legacies', in *Nothing But Trouble? Religion and the Irish Problem – Papers Presented to the Irish Association* (Belfast: Community Relations Council, 2004), 8–17: 'The flags on your street tell the world that people from only one half of the community need bid for your house. They reduce the competition and therefore the price. Look at the little villages between Larne and Carrickfergus, in some of the most beautiful parts of Northern Ireland. No tourist will be drawn to them … They are suffocating under their flags and bunting' (p. 11).

culturally vital and resistant to assimilation, something which can be shared across the boundary – a cultural bond.

There have been other public enterprises of artistic imagination such as 'Different Drums' bringing the Orange Lambeg drumming culture into interplay with traditional Irish musicality in a dazzling display of ethnomusical conversation. Plays like Marie Jones's *Pentecost* or Frank McGuinness's *Observe the Sons of Ulster Marching to the Somme* reveal a hitherto unsuspected capacity for cultural self-questioning, and empathetic exploration of the political and religious landscape of the other tradition in ways that lift moral sensibility to a new place. The quiet enduring work of the Cultures of Ireland Association, or, at a more popular level, the narrative exhibitions of 'The Cost of the Troubles' or of '*An Crann* – The Tree' spring to mind as opening new forms of cultural remembering and memorialisation, therapeutic breakthrough or dialogical analysis. These diverse creative expressions of both an internal and boundary-crossing kind have nourished imaginations and imbued the interpretation of history with more subtle and vital possibilities. Some such ventures have been staged locally – but have progressively been staged in spaces deemed neutral, and with increasing confidence, within the heartland of the other culture or with guests invited inside from the opposing culture. While reiterating the need to eschew easy simplifications, in recognition that the creative spring can so easily be muddied by ideological interests and fresh insights hitched to fundamentalist wagons more practised in closing the *laager* than in the open exchange of the public square, such risk and imagination are to be encouraged and reflected upon. Strangers come with new stories which confuse the coordinates of familiar reality. The exigencies of encounter, dialogue and the revisiting of history are rarely without contention. Conversation with strangers risks blurring the edges of oppressor and victim, and of control and responsibility. It is a necessary risk.

It is helpful to recall what was said earlier about negatively constructed moral responses to violence in contrast with more positive or formative expressions of peacemaking on the one hand, responses whose main purpose is to set limits to violence, reduce hostility and safeguard boundaries, and conversely, approaches whose starting point is the vision of peace and narratives of reconciliation which celebrate life for all. The former operates by preventing violence, reducing damage and closing rifts. It involves the addressing of conflicting rights, seeks to establish equity on clear grounds, and redress by negotiation and arbitration. Its logic is exclusive and its aim security in a defensive sense. It relies on methods of legal justice and political enactments whereby claims can be asserted and appeals weighed by testable principle and criteria. In situations where minorities have been excluded, this conflict model, for all its limitations, does forge a necessary path in the securing of human rights, equality of access and cultural parity. To date, both Nationalists and Unionists rely heavily on this politically-based, conflict-driven approach.

But, as experience also shows, it issues forth in situations of impasse, whether over 'rights to march' or 'rights to govern'. Tribunals for establishing the truth of what happened (Bloody Sunday) or Ombudsman's Reports or Commissions of Inquiry (alleged police corruption), while satisfying or partly satisfying one side, have left the other more aggrieved than before.

This conflict model of society has been developed along defensive lines of protection *against* infringements of a human rights or cultural entitlement, functioning to protect the citizen against violence, putting political constraints on oppression and discrimination. But, in this embattled world, as Michael Ignatieff reminds us: 'Rights language offers a rich vernacular for the claims an individual [or individuals within a sub-group] may make on or against the collectivity, but it is relatively impoverished as a means of expressing individuals' needs for the collectivity ... and there is more to respect in a person than his [*sic*] rights.' [33]

Thus, in this time of transition, ways must be adopted which take into account human *needs* as well as human rights, ways of opening up and cooperating within the contested space, not by relying on arbitration or competition, but by tapping into the capacity for solidarity and conviviality. In addition to a political ethic, we need an ethic of life. The language of this moral discourse is life-centred, expressive and symbolic, and it is concerned to sustain the moral and spiritual substance of communities through practices of hospitality towards stranger and outcast. For Christians this is embodied in the gospel culture of peace. It is summed up in the Beatitudes (Matt. 5) and is rooted in sensitivity to the other's aspirations, in relationships of trust and the struggle to live in charity and forgiveness.

In a now-classic essay, Charles Taylor demonstrates the inadequacy of procedural liberalism in the matter of accommodating cultural difference. Referring to cultural identity clashes in Canada, he notes that there is a form of 'the politics of equal respect, as enshrined in a liberalism of rights, that is inhospitable to difference ... [and] suspicious of collective goals'. He goes on to argue the need to accommodate difference in areas of non-fundamental rights over against the blind uniformity of a 'culture of judicial review'. Thus, he points up the need for a more flexible model of liberalism 'grounded very much on judgments about what makes a *good life* – judgments in which the integrity of cultures has an important place'.[34] Rowan Williams argues for a counter-balancing of this necessary but over-dominant moral discourse of

---

[33] Michael Ignatieff, *The Needs of Strangers* (London: Hogarth Press, 1984), 13.

[34] Charles Taylor, 'The Politics of Recognition', in Amy Gutmann (ed.), *Multiculturalism* (Princeton, NJ: Princeton University Press, 1994), 25–73 and 60–61. Taylor clearly has in mind the limits of Rawlsian 'difference-blindness' in situations where multi-culturalism must be accommodated within a politics of equal dignity. His conclusion that the 'rigidities of procedural liberalism may rapidly become impracticable in tomorrow's world' (p. 61) have a prophetic but also an empirical ring.

claim and counter-claim by the risk of 'civic vitality' (preferring the term to 'social cohesion' with its assimilationist overtones) and grounded in people's shared history and actual needs. He might have had the current Irish political impasse in mind, asserting that such risk 'does not wait for the restoration of a situation in which all entitlements are satisfied before engaging in social converse, challenge and even co-operation'.[35] While insisting on the prior necessity of recognition, Williams, *pace* Taylor, asserts that full recognition

> ... entails a move beyond the idea that my good, my interest, has a substantial integrity *by itself*: no project is *just* mine, wholly unique to me. I have learned from others how to think and speak my desires; I need to be heard – but that means that I must speak into, not across, the flow of another's thought and speech ... [so] I may gradually understand the sense in which the robust, primitive, individual self, seeking its fortune in a hostile world, and fighting off its competitors is a naïve fiction.[36]

To engage in this ethic of life with its hospitality to difference is then a necessary correlative to a political ethic of rights, and it requires that we deepen our capacity for imagining and risking relationship across the boundary. This preferential option for the stranger within an ethics of life comes towards us as a radical disruption of our dependency on mutual deterrence as a means of maintaining the social contract. Such a preferential option for the stranger is a transcending human need, which will be fostered in trust and risk across the rift that can also become an undreamt-of bond that is strong enough to bear difference.[37]

Boundaries and Bonds: The Gospel Way of Right Relationship

Doubtless, churches in Ireland have played a role in boundary-pacifying and boundary-crossing, not least in the worst times of violence. There have, too,

---

[35] Rowan Williams, *Lost Icons: Reflections on Cultural Bereavement* (London: T&T Clark; New York: Continuum, 2003 [2000]), 141.

[36] Williams, *Lost Icons*, 113.

[37] This alternative ethic of life is rooted in particular spaces, and has in NI been generated by community groups, women's associations, neighbourhood and cross-community bodies and ecumenical groups. These operate by processes that affirm life within and between communities, enabling people to express and celebrate their potential as bearers of life and hope. It is all the more regrettable that with the suspension of the formal Legislative Assembly in 2003, the Civic Forum (so much resisted by most of the political parties) has also been prorogued, thereby obstructing the vital under-stream of dialogue and development that constitute other ways of doing politics in the 'lifeworld' of civil society. Rowan Williams reminds us that it is by such community engagement that 'the self' or one's culture, or history, by being put into question, is capable of being rethought, remarking also on the significant coincidence of the 'decay of critical perspectives on the self' and the 'decay of 'charitable' space in social transaction.' One cannot but agree with his conclusion that 'one is not going to be restored without the other' (Williams, *Lost Icons*, 114).

been some outstanding gestures of Christian leadership that have kept open the way of reconciliation. But the churches have not been to the fore in sustaining relationships of shared life. Their relationships have been more characterised by the manner of boundary-keeping in regard to their own identity, minimalist in creating opportunities for contact and celebrations of common lament or intercession. The normative pattern is comparative and competitive. Exchange has been too often constrained by political considerations, both secular and ecclesial, bent on securing denominational identity. This is not to deny the political ethic its rightful role, with its protective procedures for regulating church life, doctrine and worship. But one also expects churches to witness together in acts of repentance and new vision, and to contribute to movements of ecumenical hospitality, in the belief that 'where sin abounds, grace does more abound'. It is therefore the more to be welcomed that Archbishop Brady, the Catholic Primate of Armagh, speaking on 1 September 2004, the tenth anniversary of the first ceasefire, adopted a more explicitly magnanimous rhetoric affirming the risks taken by Protestant clergy in engaging with Republicans to achieve the early ceasefires and calling for their renewed help through the current stalemate. In like manner, Archbishop Eames, the Anglican Primate, called on people to move beyond the suspicion that had overtaken the initial euphoria of the ceasefires, encouraging the 'reinstatement or creation of a new sense of trust – that they can believe what they are being told'.[38] These statements call for a renewed commitment to the Gospel way of reaching across boundaries and sharing life. It is with a short reflection on a typical Gospel narrative that I conclude.

The Gospel of Mark, as intimated above, geographically dramatises Jesus' frequent crossing of boundaries between Jews and Samaritans, Jews and Gentiles, as well as of gender and social status. Particularly significant is the frequent lake crossing, manifesting Jesus' constant movement between his own place and the alien territory on the far side.[39] One agrees that Jesus' mission was deeply shaped by the 'double bind' within his own tradition of

---

[38] Maeve Connolly, 'Protestant Clergy Can Aid Peace: Archbishop', *The Irish News* (31 August 2004), 1; and Gerry Moriarty, 'Churches Urge Politicians to Take Risks to Build Peace', *The Irish Times* (1 September 2004), 7.

[39] This pattern is not peculiar to Mark and it is, of course, related to emerging developments and controversies in the post-Resurrection community. In both Matthew and Mark there is a replication of the feeding of the multitude on both sides of the lake, representing on the one hand 'home territory' (Matt.14:13ff; Mark 6:30ff, with a reference to the left-over food gathered into 'twelve baskets' – with reminiscences of the Twelve Tribes of Israel), and on the other, 'the other side of the lake' (Matt. 14:13ff and Mark 8:1ff, where the remaining food is gathered up into 'seven baskets', possibly symbolising the Gentiles, if one also recalls the choice of *seven* deacons in Acts 6:1–6, from among the Hellenists). It is clear that the main purpose of the redactor at this point is to show that Jesus was in touch with both sides of the lake, anticipating the dissolving distinction in the early church between Jew and Gentile (cf. Gal. 3:27ff; Col. 3:11; 1 Cor. 12:13).

particularity and universality, and like other prophets before him, it cost him his life. Mark – the starkest of the gospels – evokes a sense of dread in the face of the foreign territory on the far side of the lake. Yet Jesus, as if impelled to extend his mission there, is seen crossing the waters in a manner which symbolically evokes the primeval chaos of the opening words of Genesis. The man with the unclean spirit confronts him. He had been wandering among the tombs – realm of the dead and of the social outcast. The encounter is portrayed in terms of struggle and crisis. Jesus upbraids the unclean spirit which possesses the man. They question each other, and Jesus asks to know his name. At this point, 'the one' takes on the form of 'the many': 'My name is Legion.' Sending the spirits into a herd of swine which proceed to destroy themselves, Jesus proceeds to heal the man, and then sends him back to his own home – to tell others of his experience of the Lord's mercy (Mark 5:2–19). Jesus himself moved on to the deeper strangeness of the Decapolis region (Mark 5:20–43). Only then does he return to his own side of the lake.

Not long after, we hear that his own people in Nazareth 'took offence' at the wisdom of his preaching, resenting that this could come from the local carpenter's son, as if to set bounds to his identity and to keep Nazareth a trouble-free zone. Jesus, we are told, 'could do no deed of power there ... and he was amazed at their unbelief' (Mark 6:3–6). One recognises here that the defensive erecting of a boundary *within* one's own group can be a threatening experience. Here it confronts Jesus with a limit to be transcended. Some time after this, and subsequent to his feeding the five thousand on his own side of the lake, Jesus once more crossed to the opposite shore, where the Gerazenes rushed to meet him bearing their sick. It was they, rather than his own, who recognised that Jesus was a bringer of healing and grace.

Furthermore, these journeys to the other side had the effect of provoking resistance and fear in his followers. This is dramatised in the narrative of the storm on the lake as they made their first journey to the other side. Jesus slept through it and they cried out in terror of sinking. The cosmic upheaval of wind and wave is the outward symbol of the terror that must be embraced and stilled if his disciples are to stand on the other shore, if they are to be bearers of healing and liberation beyond their own. The raging lunacy of the Gerazene demoniac shouting abuse at them did not exactly have the ring of a welcoming committee. One could describe the situation as suffering from an ecumenical deficit. The Gerazenes and the disciples – like ourselves – could be described as 'ecumenically challenged'. Jesus' healing of the ecumenical deficit took him and his disciples into the deeper reaches of themselves where they had to face their own fear, sink into their own vulnerability and find some empathy with the other's need in all its strangeness.

Recent scholarship on the origins of Christianity has shown that these stories cannot be understood outside the early Church's contested relationship with Judaism, particularly in the light of the destruction of the second Temple in 70 CE. While it is beyond our scope to examine the dynamics at work between the two groups, some safe assertions can be made: for example, that Jesus and the Jesus movement that became the church were profoundly Jewish in their primary identity; that Christian identity and Jewish identity as these came to emerge in the inter-testamental period were forged in contexts of opposition, polemics and the gradual mutual hardening of boundaries; the emerging Christian community maintained many points of continuity in belief, ritual and worship, while investing these with new meaning (ritual meals and baptism, for example), reflecting the logic of the Resurrection that transgressed the boundary between life and death, sin and grace, exclusion and communion.[40]

I acknowledge here a critical insight from a conversation with Jerome Murphy O'Connor, who is in fact of the opinion that this Marcan text relating to the Gerazene demoniac portrays Jesus as crossing a boundary in his own self-understanding, re giving priority in ministry to his own (suggested by the initial stage of his conversation with the Syrio-Phoenician woman (Mark 7:27). For Murphy O'Connor, the cure of the raging demoniac and of the daughter of the Syrio-Phoenician woman (Mark 7:29), these are not 'post-Resurrection loopholes', but examples of Jesus breaking his own rules on boundary-crossing. Even without such a strong claim, however, there are good warrants indeed from the social-critical tradition of biblical scholarship and from feminist biblical scholarship for a reconstructive reading of the Gospel texts from the perspective of boundary-crossing. These texts speak for themselves of the need to respect boundaries and the blessed ties that bind within the community of the tradition. But they contain within them also the seed of a countering, inclusive vision. Their inner self-correcting tension is recalled in the words cited in Leviticus 19 or Isaiah 49, or indeed anticipate those of Brian Keenan about the imperative to cross the Jordan, or Kristeva's on the restless ambiguities and inescapable disturbance in the encounter with Strangers. They speak into our own reflection on boundaries and bonds of culture in our necessary journeying beyond sectarianism.

---

[40] This new logic relates to the opening-up of the boundaries of the young Christian group to those not at first envisaged as its members. Thus, while one cannot minimise the work of post-Resurrection redaction, and while one should not expect the historicity and authoritativeness of every word and deed of Jesus to explain the emergence of Christianity, one should nevertheless resist the positivist temptation to drive a firm wedge between the 'Jesus of history' and the 'Christ of faith'. Followers of Jesus must constantly seek to correlate the example and teaching of the Jesus of the gospels with the emergent understanding of the significance of Jesus Christ in the life of the early church. Like the contemporary churches in Northern Ireland, this church was doctrinally conservative and highly conscious of maintaining boundaries; hence the well-attested interpretation of events related in Acts 10 as a turning point for the early church in terms of the admission of Gentiles, despite Peter's undoubted reluctance in the first and second instance.

Index

A TREASURY OF
BRITISH
FOLKLORE
Maypoles, Mandrakes & Mistletoe

DEE DEE CHAINEY

A TREASURY OF
BRITISH
FOLKLORE
Maypoles, Mandrakes & Mistletoe

National Trust

Dedication

For my granddad, who always sat me on the Wishing Chair, and listened for whispers in the Fairy Glen; and for Cyrus, who has walked every step of the folklore journey with me.

First published in the United Kingdom in 2018 by

National Trust Books

43 Great Ormond Street

London WC1N 3HZ

An imprint of Pavilion Books Company Ltd

Text © Dee Dee Chainey, 2018

Volume © National Trust Books, 2018

Illustrations by Joe McLaren

ISBN: 9781911358398

A CIP catalogue record for this book is available from the British Library.

10 9 8

Reproduction by Mission, Hong Kong

Printed and bound by Toppan Leefung Ltd, China

This book can be ordered direct from the publisher at the website www.pavilionbooks.com, or try your local bookshop.

Also available at National Trust shops or www.shop.nationaltrust.org.uk

CONTENTS

INTRODUCTION

Britain's culture and traditions are steeped in legends filled with giants, heroes and heroines, centuries old and from various origins. These are Britain's stories, and they belong to everyone who has ever lived here, or chosen to make Britain their home, and to every visitor who has marvelled at the legends of Britain and taken some of their magic back into the wider world. As we get older, we still sense the wonder of those tales we know from childhood. They whisper to us with every fleeting glimpse of what might just be a fairy in the woodlands, or a giant peering through a crevice in the rocks. They're our stories – they grow with us and live on inside us. We tell them to our children and to their children, who will in turn breathe new life into these tales and traditions, carrying them forward in their own way.

There can be no definitive guide to the 'truth' of British folklore. The only real truth is that folklore is the lore of the 'folk', passed on as a whisper, a tale or a tradition that goes on to become a thing that is shared. Folklore is made up of stories, songs, dances, customs and crafts that are passed from one person to another, and often from generation to generation. Folklore is the soul of a community: it lives, and changes, as it moves from the lips and mind of one person to the next. Folklore, including mythology and legends, comes from an oral culture that is in constant change, and there is no 'true' version that is better or more 'real' than the others. What we have of much early folklore is pieced together from old manuscripts, and not all of these survive. Those tales that were heard, recorded and written down – often from memory and by hand – were the versions of a particular storyteller, and a particular scribe. In the same way, we add our personal interpretation to folklore quite innocently: we retell the bits we love most, we emphasise the parts that strike a chord with us and we leave out things that seem irrelevant to us (even though others might find them fascinating).

In addition to personal interpretations, regional cultures in different parts of a country have an influence on its stories. Versions of a tale evolve as it moves across the land to different groups of people. Regions have their own local lore and traditions, distinct from their neighbours. The uses of folklore are many, and it is often used with intent. Its stories can underpin a sense of identity and belonging and reinforce the ideas people hold about themselves. It can be used as a cultural 'weapon', wielded against rival groups to prove how they are wrong, inferior or illegitimate. Folklore is alive and impossible to pin down, and can be dangerous. It presents people with a mirror to their own face, and can reveal the darker, more primal side of life. It is, after all, a thing written in the wind and the rushing waters.

Studying the shared myths and legends of the past show us that while empires may rise and fall, a sense of place and landscape can endure over thousands of years. These stories put our own lives in perspective. They reveal the vastness of time, and the reassurance that everyone, and perhaps every living being, is born, lives, may have fears and dreams, and eventually returns to the soil. In this way folklore is comforting, reminding us always to look at the wonder in the world. Folk tales and legends let us step outside of 'normal' life for a little while, to think about something wonderful and magical, something other than our everyday worries. These tales offer the hope of heroes and gods, and the often the promise that – in tales at least – good will triumph over evil.

There are great swathes of folklore from the countries of Britain and Ireland going back thousands of years; too much to include in a small book such as this. Instead, the book features examples that illustrate the vastness of British folklore as a whole, with the aim of giving the flavour of the subject across a number of Britain's regions. There is little room to dig deep into the intricacies of various debates that have raged for centuries on many of the topics, but I hope readers will enjoy the book for what it is – a celebration of the folklore of a nation, in all its wondrous complexity and diversity, and an invitation to understand more about humans and the cultures they create.

PART ONE:
OF THE LAND, PLANTS, AND ANIMALS

1

OUR SUN AND SEASONS – THE FOLKLORIC YEAR

T hrough all times and in all places people have conjured festivals to honour the changing of the seasons, the rising and setting of the sun, or the spinning of the stars. Each region has its own ways of marking the turning of the world, even if the importance of the darkening year and browning of the fields is a nostalgic memory of yesteryear for many. It's difficult to experience the changing landscape from our homes in built-up city areas. Even so, the turning of the world still lingers at the edges of our modern culture, in the crevices of our imaginations and in the corners of our traditions. This is what connects us with our animistic – and animalistic – past.

As people have done for centuries, we still look up to the sky, marvelling at the burning grandeur of the Sun, and the gentle beauty of the Moon, and folklore reflects our continuing wonder. In Scotland it's seen as very good luck to always move 'sunwise'

– in the same direction as the sun moves across the sky – while moving 'widdershins', or against the Sun, is associated with bad luck and evil. It is, apparently, very bad luck to point at the sun at any time, and it's often thought of as bad luck to see the moon through tree branches. For the antiquarians and folklorists of the past, the ancients were said to have many practices and observances surrounding the heavens. More recently, archaeologists have mapped out extraordinary solar and lunar alignments at ancient stones, from Land's End to John O'Groats. We can imagine people of times long gone, watching the shadows trace across the land and solemnly taking measurements of the Sun's rays, in order to build great megaliths and stone circles that marked special occasions in the year – one such is Castlerigg in Cumbria, one of the earliest stone circles in Britain, dating from around 3000BC. Until the late eighteenth century in Britain, when artificial light through gas began to be developed, the period of darkness 'between the sun and the sky' – that is, between daybreak and sunrise – was seen as a magical time, particularly potent for incantations and the best time for performing exorcisms. Just like us, in the Middle Ages people looked up to the night skies and saw the Man in the Moon. For them he was a 'rustic', or country dweller, bound in rags and carrying a faggot (or bundle) of sticks. Weighed down by his burden, both physically and symbolically, he was seen as a moral lesson on how stealing never profits.

As each new day dawns, marking the Sun's travel, the named individual days of the week have come to have special significance in different places. Getting rid of the floor sweepings in Ireland on a Monday is said also to get rid of your luck for the week to come, while a sneeze on a Wednesday in Hertfordshire means a letter is coming. To begin anything on a Friday, from a journey to a business deal, is regarded as bad luck in Devon. In Norfolk, rain on Sunday morning apparently means rain all week.

Seasonal festivals that developed over time in rural Britain continue to break the year into segments, following the changing weather and reflecting the activities that happen, or used to happen, at different times of the year. Some festivals, like harvest, honour the autumn as the fleeting or 'flitting' season while others, like Halloween (also known as All Hallows' Eve), mark a more symbolic time, welcoming the darkening of approaching winter, in which remnants of pre-Christian beliefs still linger.

Allhallowtide lasts from 31 October to 2 November. The festival dates from pre-Christianity in Britain, and includes Halloween (or All Saints' Eve), All Saints' Day, and All Souls' Day. This feast is a time dedicated to honouring the dead, thought to have its origins in the Celtic festival of Samhain, and traditionally marked the end of summer in Scotland, the Isle of Man and Ireland, and welcomed the dark half of the year. Huge bonfires were built, where animals would be burned, and a great feast would take place. Well into the nineteenth century, people believed that this was the time when the spirits of the dead roamed the earth.

To many, 1 November was thought of as New Year's Day, and a particularly auspicious time for predicting the future. The Welsh Halloween is *Nos Calan Gaeaf*, one of the nights when in Welsh folklore the *Cŵn Annwn* – the spectral hounds of the Welsh underworld, *Annwn* – ride high in the sky on a wild hunt. Anyone who sees or hears these hellish beasts is said to be doomed to die. The procession is led either by Arawn (king of the underworld) or by Gwyn ap Nudd (king of the *Tylwyth Teg* or Welsh 'fair folk'). It's said that Gwyn ap Nudd holds his court at Glastonbury Tor in Somerset, an entrance to the Otherworld. In Cornwall, Halloween is known as *Nos Kalan Gwav*, meaning the 'eve of the first day of winter', and is celebrated with a great harvest feast. The Tudors marked the festival as an opportunity to pray for the souls of the departed – especially those in purgatory – and would ring bells to comfort the souls trapped there, light bonfires and ward off evil spirits with protective charms. Traditional Allhallowtide activities regularly take place at Little Moreton Hall in Cheshire and regional

variations are often revived and celebrated elsewhere in Britain. Mumming has taken place across Britain since the fourteenth century, in celebration of various seasonal festivals. Traditionally, actors dress up as characters to perform folk plays around All Souls' Day, Christmas, Plough Monday, and Easter, and they are now often seen along with Morris and sword dancing groups at village events. Similar characters appear in folk plays in many regions, and often include Saint George, the hero, and his opponent, who is a Turkish knight in southern England and known as Slasher in other areas. A quack doctor who has the power to restore life to the dead generally makes an appearance, while Father Christmas, Beelzebub, the Fool, and a horse are other characters that sometimes take part, depending on local tradition. Each region has its own version to add their particular local flavour to the custom. In Scotland, mumming is known as 'going galoshins'. Mumming that takes place around Halloween (or All Hallows' Eve) is called souling, or soul caking – remembered in the particularly haunting 'Souling Song' by the folk group The Watersons. At this time of year, the mummers would knock at doors and sing for soul cakes, made for the poor in return for their prayers for the dead and used to remember loved ones who had passed away over the previous year. Soul caking is still very popular in Cheshire, and plays are performed annually by such groups as the Jones' Ale Soul Cakers, although nowadays to raise money for local charities.

In Lincolnshire, it's very unlucky to eat the whole Christmas cake on Christmas Eve.

Christmas traditions abound in Britain, and many customs are still common practice today – such as kissing under the mistletoe, hiding lucky charms in the Christmas pudding, and having a Christmas tree. There are some other more strange examples of Christmas folklore in different regions and countries. In Lincolnshire – a warning for those eager to start the celebrations early – it's very unlucky to eat the whole Christmas cake on Christmas Eve. More ominously, a Scottish bannock or fruit cake that breaks in the middle predicts the death or illness of the intended recipient within the year. In Westleton, Suffolk, the lights were turned off in many households on Christmas Eve because the furniture was thought to jump about. In London it's said that a white Christmas leads to a brown Easter. Elsewhere, a saying that a green Christmas means a full graveyard doesn't bode well for many. Similarly, having wet things hanging in a house on Christmas Day is said to invite bad luck, and even a death. Another luck-related custom is that you should always bite into a mince pie because cutting it will cut your luck. Today, many people still believe that Christmas decorations should be taken down before Twelfth Night – either 5 January or 6 January – or bad luck will follow, although originally it was acceptable to leave them up until Candlemas, on 2 February.

Wren Day is celebrated on St Stephen's Day, falling on 26 December (now known as Boxing Day in Britain) in places

like Pembrokeshire and Suffolk, and also across Ireland. Mummers known as strawboys or wrenboys would dress in masks, straw suits and colourful clothing, then go about hunting a wren, which would be tied, alive, to a pole or pitchfork. The revelry would include music and parades through the villages and towns. Money would be collected to host a 'wren ball' in January.

In Wales, St Stephen's Day is known as *Gŵyl San Steffan*, and was observed by bleeding livestock – for health and stamina – right up until the beginning of the nineteenth century. A practice called 'holming' – hitting female servants on the arms with holly branches until they bled – was also traditional, supposedly to ensure good luck for the coming year. *Nos Galan*, the Welsh New Year, would follow soon after. A horse's skull – the *Mari Lwyd* – with hinged, snapping jaws and covered in a sackcloth or a white sheet with colourful ribbons and bells, would be carried from house to house, accompanied by other traditional characters, such as Punch and Judy. The mummers would knock on the door, singing traditional songs to gain entry, and the householders would reply in song, eventually allowing them to come in to share food and drink, after the horse had cavorted around the house, and often giving money for their collection. This tradition dates back to at least the 1800s, and can take place any time between Christmas Day and Twelfth Night, and revivals of this pageant are today seen around Christmastime in cities such as Chepstow, Aberystwyth, and Chester. Hodening, or hoodening, is a similar tradition that took place in Kent around Christmastime from the eighteenth century. A wooden hobby horse was mounted on a pole and carried around the local villages, accompanied by musicians, a groom to lead the horse and a man dressed as a woman, called a 'Mollie', collecting money as they went. The horse still makes an appearance in local

> *The mummers would go from house to house singing traditional songs to gain entry.*

mumming plays, even though the traditional form of hoodening no longer takes place.

'First footing' is a traditional custom on New Year's Eve in Scotland and the North of England. According to tradition, the first person to enter a house once the clock has struck midnight should be a man, for a woman would cause disaster. Some say a fair-haired man is the luckiest, for instance in Scotland, while others believe it should be a dark-haired fellow, as in Lancashire, where a dark-haired man brings the most luck with him. Some say a flat-footed person bodes ill. In Yorkshire the first foot must always bring a glass of spirits, while in Northumberland it must be a bachelor who brings in the luck for the year, and he should always carry coal. Today, the first foot carries a combination of items when entering the house: a coin, bread, salt, coal, evergreen, and whisky, to represent wealth, nourishment, protection or flavour, warmth, a long and healthy life and a dose of good cheer! It's also important that the person should already be outside the house at the stroke of midnight. In Lincolnshire, the first foot should say the following rhyme:

Take out, and then take in,
Bad luck will begin;
Take in, then take out,
Good luck conies about.

It's said to be very bad luck to carry fire out of the house on New Year's Day, or indeed any implement made from iron. In some places it was seen as very bad luck to lend anything on that day, even a light for the fire.

In the nineteenth century in the West Riding of Yorkshire, groups of child mummers would go 'wassailing' across the festive season, which meant visiting houses and singing traditional hymns in return for a little money or refreshments, similar to carol singing today. They would dress up for the occasion and carry the 'wassailing cup', along with little boxes containing figurines of the Virgin and Child called 'milly-boxes', a corruption of 'My Lady'. These would be lined with sugar, spices, and oranges. Wassailing took place in many other parts of Britain as well, although in most areas 'wassailing' meant something else entirely, and was an orchard custom that took place after Christmas. In Exeter, Devon, many farmers and their families would gather around their orchard trees, pour cider over their roots and dangle cake from the branches, while songs were sung and traditional rhymes chanted to bless them for the coming year, ensuring an abundant harvest of apples for cider making. A Surrey rhyme about this goes like this:

> Here stands a good apple-tree,
> Stand fast at root,
> Bear well at top;
> Every little twig
> Bear an apple big:
> Every little bough
> Bear an apple now;
> Hats full, caps full!
> Threescore sacks full!
> Hullo boys, hullo!

Wassailing events still happen today throughout the country, for instance at Isaac Newton's orchard in Woolsthorpe Manor, Lincolnshire, around 'Old Twelfth Night' in January – another traditional time for wassailing. Other events take place at Cotehele Orchards in Cornwall, and at Birmingham Crescent Theatre.

Yuletide has long been a time of all-night celebrations in Shetland, with the beat of drums, blowing of horns and banging of kettles; over time these celebrations have become more elaborate. In 1840 tar barrelling was introduced, where youths would set the barrels alight on rafts, which would then be dragged through the streets. A torch procession replaced this mischief in the 1870s when the name Up Helly Aa was introduced. A galley was first burned during the event in 1889, and the tradition has now turned into a huge affair at the end of January, where the townsmen dress up as Vikings and process to the coast in a parade of flaming torches. These are thrown into a replica Viking longship that is burned at the end of the festivities.

Candlemas falls on 2 February, the day before Imbolc and St Brigid's Day. On this day candles are carried for the Virgin Mary and blessed, and it is said to represent the beginning of spring. Soon after that, Shrove Tuesday is celebrated across much of Britain on the day before Ash Wednesday, when the Christian period of Lent begins. For many, the religious overtones of this day have become lost over time, and Shrove Tuesday is popularly known now as Pancake Day, when pancakes are eaten – the more the better, in fact, since this was traditionally a day for gorging, to use up food before the Lenten fast. Pancake races were, and still are, held throughout Britain to celebrate the day, and from the seventeenth century 'mob football' also accompanied the feast. The latter fell out of favour when football on public highways was outlawed in the nineteenth century.

Many villages across Britain still celebrate the ancient spring festival of May Day with Morris dancing, fairs, and a maypole festooned with coloured ribbons that are entwined as children holding them dance around it. Even today, Jack-in-the-Green still makes an appearance, while a May Queen is crowned in some places, for instance at Ickwell Green in Bedfordshire. The 'Obby 'Oss (hobby horse) still plays a central role on May Day at Padstow in Cornwall. The original tradition involved a man dressing in a horse's skin: a trickster figure, he would cause mischief as crowds followed him through the streets – like throwing dirty water into the mouths of the onlookers, much to their amusement – according to C.S. Gilbert who watched the pageant in around 1820. In 1919, a second horse was introduced, known as the Blue Ribbon 'Obby 'Oss, Temperance 'Oss, Peace 'Oss, or merely the

Blue 'Oss. The supporters of this 'oss tried to combat the riotous behaviour that often ensued at the festival, yet to no avail. Even today, local people still don the colours of the 'oss they support for the day. In Wales, the May festival is called *Calan Mai*, and spirits are thought to roam on the evening before, another traditional time when visions of the future are sought. May Day festivities have long been linked to Beltane celebrations (the name for the Gaelic May Day). In the past, it was traditional to light huge bonfires, and leap through the flames for luck and also to drive cattle through them – supposedly as a protection against disease and to make them fruitful. This practice fell out of favour by the nineteenth century in Devon and Cornwall, but was recorded as late as 1810 in Perthshire, where local stories also relate how boys from the surrounding villages would meet on the moors and bake a huge oatcake. This would be broken into bits, and one piece covered in charcoal to make it black. Each boy would be blindfolded, and then choose

Anyone who gathers the first dew of May will be granted protection against the evil eye.

a piece from a bonnet. Whoever picked the blackened piece would be 'sacrificed to Baal' (symbolic rather than literal!) and would have to jump through the flames three times. Less dramatic,but rather more magical, it's said that anyone who gathers the first dew of May will be granted the power of witches and protection against the evil eye, and on a mountainside near Brecon, in Powys, it is only on May Day that a doorway opens to the garden of the fairies.

Celebrations have historically been held at Midsummer in Britain, often involving feasting, bonfires and parades. Midsummer Day is traditionally celebrated on 24 June in the United Kingdom, around the time of the summer solstice, which is the longest day of the year. Like other events in the

Christian calendar, St John's Day, which is also celebrated on this date, incorporated many Pagan customs, such as jumping through a bonfire for luck, in an attempt to Christianise them. In Cornwall, it is traditional to light fires along the highest peaks on Midsummer Eve, and it was said that in the nineteenth century people would climb up high to count these fires and make predictions based on their number. A few villages in the area still preserve this tradition, and while the custom was already dying out by the beginning of the nineteenth century it was revived by the Old Cornwall Society at the beginning of the twentieth. A long tradition of festivities exists in Cheshire, where the Chester Midsummer Watch Parade took place from the fifteenth until the seventeenth century. This was revived in 1995 but although in the past the pageant involved giants, a unicorn, a dragon, hobbyhorses, and 16 naked boys, it is a little different today! Today at Midsummer, modern-day Druids meet to watch the sunrise on the longest day of the year at Stonehenge in Wiltshire, one of their sacred sites, along with other Neo-pagans and others who enjoy celebrating the summer solstice.

> *Lammas – meaning 'loaf mass' – welcomed the first bread baked from the new crops.*

Following Midsummer, the harvest season traditionally began with *Lughnasadh* in Scotland, the Isle of Man and Ireland, celebrated on 1 August with feasting and dances, and linked with the god Lugh. On the same date in the medieval period, Lammas – meaning 'loaf mass' – was celebrated as the first harvest festival, welcoming the first bread baked from the new crops. This would be offered up on the altar in churches in thanks for a fruitful year. Once all of the crops had been harvested the season would end with the great feast of Harvest Home, and the annual cycle would begin again at the next Halloween.

2

LEGENDS OF
ROCK AND STONE

T he legends that pervade the mountains and valleys of
Britain have a deep-rooted mythology that seeps
through the landscape, revealing the fears and suspicions
of people now long gone. Those stories that surround ancient
mountain rocks and the great ritual monuments of prehistoric
Britain are age-old tales that echo from the distant past, as if the
land remembers the stories for us. Even now, walking ancient
pathways, our legends unravel before us. If we listen carefully,
we might fancy we can still hear the whispers of giants, witches,
fairies, and the ghosts of the warriors that still sleep under verdant
mounds. When we gaze over the meadows, we might just
glimpse the elf-arrows glittering in the sunlight, peeking through
ploughed fields from their hiding places in the ancient brown loam
of history.

Not only megalithic tombs and stone circles but also natural
markers, such as rocks and headlands, have attracted legends as far

back as the communities around Britain can remember. These are often tales of mythological races, legendary creatures, ghosts, kings, and the heroes and heroines of old. Stories of fairies are some of the most common found still lingering around megalithic tombs and Bronze Age barrows across Britain; many people over the centuries have recounted tales of hearing haunting music flowing out from the cairns and barrows. Many still refer to them as 'fairy mounds', or as doorways to fairyland. At Nafferton Slack in East Yorkshire, there's a tale of a large stone at the roadside that was said to have miraculous powers. In certain seasons it would glow, and seemed as if it might be a doorway to a grand, well-lit hall. On one occasion, a stone-breaker reported hearing wonderful music coming from within, and on another he swore to seeing a parade of gaily-dressed elfins going into the hall, some even in carriages.

Stone circles were often said to be people turned to stone after breaking laws or customs.

According to many legends, anyone disturbing ancient stones will face retribution. Storms are said to follow those who trouble Long Meg, the largest stone of a circle in Cumbria, while illness, diseased cattle, death, tornadoes and explosions are promised for similar crimes in the rest of the country. Many stone circles were said to be people who were turned to stone as a result of breaking laws or customs, such as working or dancing on Sunday, or refusing to accept Christianity, or commonplace crimes such as milking someone else's cows, deserting a wife or stealing church property. The story around the stones at Stanton Drew stone circle in Somerset is that they are wedding party revellers, petrified for daring to continue the festivities through the night into the Sabbath. Stones at some sites are said to move, dance, turn around, or to go to drink at midnight, when the cock crows, or when the church bells ring. The story is that the Diamond Stone at Avebury in Wiltshire actually crosses the road when the clock strikes 12, while the Rollright Stones on the Oxfordshire/Warwickshire border go to drink. Coetan Arthur in Glamorgan drinks or bathes in the sea on Midsummer's Eve, and does the same at All Hallows' Eve. Others are said to return automatically to their position when they are moved, or cannot be moved at all.

Many of the ancient sites of Britain were thought to have healing powers. The Toothie Stane (Carraig an Tàlaidh) in Argyllshire was said to cure toothache if someone knocked a nail or screw into the portal stone. The numbers three, seven, and nine often have magical properties at these places: children must be passed through the hole in the Crick Stone – against the sun – either three or nine times at Men-an-tol in Cornwall to cure a crick in the neck, while if a person walks three times around Stenness in Orkney they will be cured of whatever ails them. To run seven times around the Giant's Grave long barrow in Wiltshire will raise the Devil.

A common tradition is that the number of stones in certain stone circles can never be counted accurately, even though many

have tried. It's recommended that you visit the Rollright Stones, Long Meg and Her Daughters or Stanton Drew, and try to count these for yourself. Yet you may want to beware, because it is also said to be incredibly bad luck to even attempt to count the stones wherever this superstition is held, and can lead to an untimely death! At Lower Kit's Coty a story goes that an Aylesford baker tried to count the stones by placing a loaf on each, yet as he did so one loaf disappeared – and there in its place sat the Devil himself. As always, there are different versions; another tells that when he had finished, he found an extra loaf – one more than he'd actually brought – while yet another says that before he had chance to call out the number of stones he dropped down dead. King Charles II managed to count the stones of Stonehenge, Wiltshire, accurately twice in a row in 1651, and was praised for his miraculous powers that apparently surpassed those of ordinary folk, though many had tried to rival his feat.

Some sites are said to have been created when a woman dropped a 'skirtful' of stones.

Stone-carrying women are said to be responsible for the creation of many ancient tombs and mountains. Some are giantesses, and others are old women. Some sites, like Beinne na Caillich (The Hag's Hill) in Skye, are attributed to the Cailleach herself – a veiled woman, seen as a timeless symbol of winter. Tales of an old woman carrying stones also appear in Yorkshire and Northumberland, and many old sites are said to have been created when a woman dropped an 'apronful' or 'skirtful' of stones while bounding across the land. Barclodiad y Gawres in Anglesey literally translates as 'the giantesses' apronful'.

Megaliths of epic proportions are scattered across Cornwall, and throughout Scotland and Wales, so it's unsurprising that tales of giants echo through the land. Stories of two rival giants competing to hurl the stones the furthest are passed down through the centuries, while in some tales the second giant is replaced by the Devil. The well-known megalith of Lanyon Quoit, in Cornwall, is also known as the Giant's Quoit or the Giant's Table. A giant skull was found in a stone cist at Tigharry in the Hebridean island of North Uist, and is said to have been so big that it could cover a man's shoulders!

Up until the seventeenth century many Iron Age hill forts were named after giants because of their immense size. Long barrows and cairns are also often named after giants, and it's easy to imagine that such huge mounds cover the bodies of these enormous creatures as they slumber under the earth in death. The story goes that if someone runs around Adam's Grave long barrow in Wiltshire seven times, the giant will come out. Many mountains are also steeped in giant legends. One of the most famous is Cadair Idris, or Cader Idris, in Wales. Legend tells that the mountain was the home of Idris, the chief of the giants in the region – an astronomer who used to gaze up at the stars from his chair (*cadair* or seat), which people now say is the volcanic lake on the mountainside. It's said that anyone who spends the night on the summit of the mountain will either wake as a philosopher, a poet, or will succumb to madness.

Natural rock formations have also attracted many legends. The Chiding Stone at Chiddingstone village in Kent still holds legends of judgement and sacrifice by the ancient Druids and, while unlikely, it is possible that the stone was a Saxon boundary marker. It's also remembered as a place of judgement and retribution for nagging wives and witches in medieval times.

3

WORMS, WELLS
AND WATER HORSES

T he rivers of Britain meander peacefully through the
countryside and it's easy to imagine boats gliding along
them through this rolling landscape, while butterflies
flit along the grassy banks. Yet this view of nature stemmed only
from the Victorian imagination, and that of their Romantic
predecessors – times when the natural world was celebrated
through poetry and art as a counterpoint to the increasing
industrialisation faced by the British people; it is also at this
point that fear of the harsh reality of the wilds was lost. Behind
the pastoral haze of long summer days there are darker tales of
Britain's rivers and streams that arise from a more brutal, primeval
past. In these we can still sense the churning power of the water
spirits of old, with their demands for votive offerings. We secretly
fear the mysterious creatures snaking through the unknowable
depths of the wild lochs of the far north or skulking just below

the surface of the murky pools of the Welsh hills. Perhaps we don't like to admit that these springs and rivers still seethe with the mystery of our old myths, and we relegate the creatures that slink in the depths to stories that keep our children awake at night. Yet these tales surface when we dare to dip a naked toe into a deep, surging river. We laugh nervously, for a moment fearing we'll be dragged into the cold darkness by whatever lies beneath.

Many have heard of the notorious Loch Ness Monster but there are tales of other creatures that, legend has it, lurk in the rivers and pools of Britain. The Welsh Afanc is a monster that lived in Llyn-yr-Afanc in the River Conwy, and caused regular flooding until lured from the waters by the song of a beautiful young girl. Once caught, he was bound in chains and dragged to Llyn Ffynnon Las, a lake near the summit of Snowdon, where he remains trapped to this day. In Sussex, a famous knucker – a water worm, or dragon – lived in the knucker hole near Lyminster, which

The Lambton Worm could only be appeased with the milk of nine good cows.

was reputedly bottomless and had healing properties. The knucker was able to fly, carousing through the air, terrifying the local population and stealing their livestock. Legend tells that the King of Sussex offered the hand of his daughter to anyone that could slay the beast. A wandering knight succeeded, and the couple settled in the area, where they lived until the end of their days.

A longer tale is that of the Lambton Worm, a small creature resembling an eel that was fished out of the River Wear in Durham by John Lambton. Thought to be the Devil, it was thrown into a well, but poisoned the water and grew to a huge size, later escaping to devour sheep and snatch away village children. The worm could only be appeased by offering it the milk of nine good cows each day, a ritual that was observed by the local lord, who happened to be John's father. On John's return

from the Crusades, he vowed to slaughter the creature that had
terrified the village in his absence, and managed to slay the worm
after taking the advice of a Durham witch: to modify his armour
with spears and lure the beast back to the River Wear. The tale
has a sorry end; the witch decreed that he must kill the first living
creature he saw after his victory or be cursed for nine generations.
John arranged for his father to release his faithful hound, to be his
sacrifice. But his father was so overjoyed to see John return that
he forgot the promise, and rushed out to greet his son. Loath to
take the life of his father, John ignored the warning and killed the
dog instead, in an attempt to avoid the curse. It was to no avail,
and the next nine generations of Lambtons were destined never to
die in their beds. This last tradition proved true for at least three
generations, possibly adding credence and infamy to the legend of
the terrible worm.

Water horses come from all regions of Britain, and in
many shapes and sizes. Kelpies are shape-shifting spirits found in
the rivers of Scotland that carry people off into the water to be

devoured, after becoming so sticky that the rider can't get down.
A tale about Lochan-na-cloinne in Thurso tells of a small boy
who found himself stuck to the horse's shoulder after touching
it, only escaping after cutting off the guilty finger, while the
other children were all dragged away and devoured – the only
evidence left behind was their entrails, found the next day on the
riverbank. The Ceffyl Dŵr is a Welsh water horse who entices
people to ride him but then flies up into the sky, only to dissolve
into thin air and drop the unsuspecting rider to their death. The
Manx water horse is the cabyll-ushtey, who drowns victims at sea,
while the nuggle of Shetland is more known for playing pranks
than maliciousness. The nuckelavee of Orkney was more sinister, a
cross between a human and a
horse, with breath that could
cause droughts, as well as
ruin crops and livestock alike.
Shellycoats are mischievous
creatures that haunt the rivers
and streams of Scotland and Northern England, with rattling coats
made from shells.

Shellycoats have rattling coats made from shells and haunt rivers and streams.

Much folklore gives magical properties to the waters
themselves, not just to the creatures that live in them. Many
ancient springs and wells reputedly have miraculous properties that
range from healing to predicting the future, so it's unsurprising
that remnants of ancient well worship still exist today. In the
Black Isle of Scotland, an ancient spring sited near Munlocky is
dedicated to St Curidan, or Boniface, and was once said to be the
site of a church. Here, ribbons of cloth and rags – called clooties
– stream from the trees in the wind. People dip the fabric into the
sacred waters and then tie them to branches while saying a prayer.
Each pilgrim has their own reason to make this act of devotion
to the ancient spirit of the well – to ask for healing, or to make a
wish. In the past, desperate parents left their children overnight
at the site, ardently believing that the well had the power to heal

them. The sacredness of such places is always tinged with an air of sadness, and we can wonder how many prayers and wishes were answered. Clootie wells, as these sites in Celtic areas are known, often remain the focus of pilgrimages today.

The Petrifying Well at Mother Shipton's Cave in North Yorkshire was viewed with deep suspicion by the Knaresborough townsfolk who, they said, had seen small birds and creatures turned to stone near it. Yet the antiquarian John Leyland, who visited the well in the sixteenth century while under the employ of Henry VIII, sung its praises, saying that people would flock to drink and bathe in its waters, which had miraculous healing powers. We now know that this is one of the few wells in England with such a high mineral content, yet this doesn't diminish the magic of the wondrous well that had the power to turn any object to stone. Another famous well is the Drumming Well in Oundle, Northamptonshire, was said to give out the sound of rolling drums to warn of important events, apparently predicting both the death of Charles II and the arrival of the Scots in England at the time of the Civil Wars. Monk's Well in Wavertree, Liverpool, bears an inscription from 1414, relating the local legend that all travellers must give alms at the local monastic building when drinking from the well or, should they not, a devil chained at the bottom would laugh. Interestingly, Sir Walter Scott stated that wells at the top of high hills in Scotland lead to fairyland. In sixteenth-century Dartmoor, the notorious John Fitz of Fitzford and his lady became lost, or pixy-led, in the hills by a thick mist. Yet after quenching their thirst in a spring on a hillside, the glamour cast over them by the little folk of the moor dissipated, and they were once more able to find their way and reached Tavistock before nightfall. As a mark of gratitude, the Fitz family erected a granite structure to commemorate the spring's healing properties against the pixies' mischief, and the marker still stands to this day on the same site, now known as Fice's Well, and is said to have healing properties against eye problems.

Well dressing is a popular custom in Derbyshire and Staffordshire from May to September. The wells are first blessed and then they are decorated with elaborate panels of clay and flower petals in intricate mosaics that often depict Biblical scenes. Once banned as an idolatrous practice stemming from the worship of ancient water deities, little can be said of well dressing's true origins. Some attribute the custom to the period following the Black Death, where villages such as Tissington, in Derbyshire, were untouched, and it was presumed to be because of the blessing of their fresh water supply. Some say Tissington, where crowds flock every year to see the dressed wells, has the oldest and most authentic customs now practised in England. A 'Blessing of the Wells' also takes place in Bakewell.

Strange properties of water are not restricted to wells, as attested by a wealth of supposedly bottomless pools in Shropshire. It's said that Llynclys Pool never had a bottom to it, and contains a submerged city or palace. Also in Shropshire, Jenny, or Ginny, Greenteeth was

> *Well dressing was once banned as an idolatrous practice, stemming from the worship of ancient deities.*

a water-witch: an old woman skulking under the weeds that cover stagnant pools, ready to drag in any unsuspecting child that ventured too close to the water's brink with her long arms. Thought by many to have origins as an ancient deity or water nymph, she is remembered today only as a tale to scare children enough to stop them from teetering at the water's edge, where they might fall in and drown. While the same legend remains in Lancashire today, the nineteenth-century version was a little different. Jenny was known more by the name Green Teetir, also called Bloody Bones or Old Nicli, and said by local children to hide under the willows that overhung the water, while the bubbles of gas in the pools were signs of the water sprites lurking below the surface. Peg Powler is a hag who lives in the River Tees. She has green hair and sharp teeth, and also pulls children to their doom. Grindylows are creatures from Yorkshire and Lancashire with long arms that drag children into pools to drown them. Water sprites are rife in legends from the north of England, where it's said they must claim a life regularly, to appease them. The Ribble is said to claim one life every seven years; the Trent takes three a year with the spring tide; the Devonshire Dart takes one; while the Tweed is said to be bloodthirsty, and can only be appeased by throwing salt over the nets before fishing. Yet the Chester Dee is seen as a sacred river that gives up the bodies of the drowned for burial, rather than demand lives be given to it. Strange measures were often taken to find those who were drowned. In Ilkeston, Derbyshire, the tale is that beating a drum over water will reveal where a corpse lies. It's said a woman's body was recovered using this method in 1882, when the drum fell silent as it passed her lifeless form. To find a corpse in Durham, hollow out a loaf, fill it with quicksilver, and put it out on the river. Legend says the loaf will float onwards until it finds the place the corpse lies, when it will stop.

In Derbyshire rivers, you must beat a drum over water to reveal where a corpse lies.

36

4

TREES, PLANTS
AND FLOWERS

Many forests and woodlands in Britain are ancient, and their history is replete with legends of elves and woodwose (wild men) who watch on, unseen by us everyday folk. Walking through the forest, tracing the gnarling tree roots while leaves brush your face and sunbeams dance among the leaves, it's easy to be seduced by their magic. As you breathe in the scent of the mouldered loam, you can get lost in the dense wilder woodlands, both bodily and metaphorically. Getting physically lost in the wild is less common today but it was a palpable and dangerous reality in earlier, pre-industrial times when people's livelihoods were closely tied to the landscape. Legends arose as people mythologised their fears. In the North-west Highlands of Scotland in the eighteenth century, the Gille Dubh of Loch a Druing was said to live in the birch woods of Gairloch. A shy, well-meaning guardian fairy with dark hair, clad only in moss and leaves, legends say he would guide any lost child home. A common version of the tale relates the Gille Dubh's meeting with a little girl named Jessie Macrae, said to be the only person with whom he conversed. Mackenzie, in his *A Hundred Years in the Highlands* from 1921, tells that the fairy looked after the lost child kindly for the night before returning her safely home the next morning.

Certain trees are so magnificent that they attract their own legends and histories. Rumour tells that the avenue of sweet chestnut trees at Croft Castle in Herefordshire was grown from nuts salvaged four centuries ago from a shipwrecked boat of the Spanish Armada; the 1,000-year-old Quarry Oak is also found at the castle. An 1807 poem by William Thomas Fitzgerald regales the tales of the imposing Ankerwycke Yew, near Runnymede, Surrey, said to be 2,500 years old and to have born witness to the signing of the Magna Carta, as well as being the site of clandestine meetings between Henry VIII and Anne Boleyn, before he divorced his first wife to marry Anne. On a smaller scale, a 400-year-old apple tree at Woolsthorpe Manor, Lincolnshire, the birthplace and childhood home of Isaac Newton, reputedly inspired his ideas on gravity.

The avenue of sweet chestnuts at Croft Castle is said to be grown from nuts salvaged from a shipwreck.

People have felt close to trees and built stories and beliefs around them for centuries, in Britain as elsewhere. A Northumberland tale tells that on the feast of St Oswyn – on 20 August – in 1384, a wright (the archaic local term for a carpenter) set about cutting down a tree to build a ship. With every stroke of his axe, blood poured from cuts in the tree. Thinking it must be because it was a holy day, he abandoned the task. But his companion, having no reverence for the miracle that had just happened, took his axe to the tree, which only resulted in more blood from the tree. A similar tale from Syresham, Northamptonshire, tells of a man who cut a branch from an elder tree for a boy to play with, only to find blood poured forth from tree. In this tale, a local woman appeared soon after with her arm bandaged. Believing the tree to be a bewitched form of the woman, the locals put her to trial by swimming her in the pond. There was a longstanding belief that blocking up any holes in a tree's trunk with concrete or bricks would better its health, and this 'brickwork' can still be seen on the beech stumps at Dunham Massey in Cheshire. In the forests in Scotland, near Dunkeld, one might stumble upon Ossian's Hall, a folly where a wishing tree can be found. People have recently begun to hammer coins into its stump as an offering for health and luck, and many of these coins are from overseas. Legend tells that if a coin falls from the tree, the wish will not be granted.

Special significance is given to certain types of trees. While it's commonly advised not to stand under a tree during a thunderstorm, in Gloucestershire there's a belief that it is safe to shelter under an elder tree because this was the wood used to make the cross on which Jesus was crucified, so lightning will never strike it. But it's unlucky to bring elder into the house for the same reason. In other regions, placing an acorn at the window is thought to keep lightning out, and it's said that oak trees groan and shriek when they are cut down. Trees are also supposedly good for warding off evil: yews, often planted in graveyards to ward off witches, should never be brought into the house as this will lead to a death. In Lancashire, the folk belief is that the mountain ash, called the wicken or wiggen tree, will repel a witch. Even a tiny twig in her path will halt her misdeeds, and cattle should be adorned with sprigs of this wood, and churn-staffs made of it to stop the milk or butter from being bewitched.

A folk remedy found in Gloucestershire is to carve your initials into the bark of an ash tree that still has keys (husks with seeds), and cut as many notches into the tree as you have warts

– as the bark grows the warts will fade. Holly can be used to cure colic, and in Cornwall it's said that any man with a walking stick of holly will never suffer from rheumatism. Plant remedies have been used for millennia, and played a major part in Anglo-Saxon medicine. The British Library has recently completed a project to digitise many of these early herbal texts. Some of these, written between the ninth and seventeenth centuries, give lists of plants and animals and the ailments they were used to treat. The texts include legendary plants, but also folk beliefs attached to actual plants – like mandrake, a root with a strangely human-like form that was used as an anaesthetic in ancient Rome. It is alleged to shine in the dark, shy away from anyone impure, and scream when it is pulled from the ground. One text summarises the tools for collecting mandrake: an iron implement and ivory rod for digging, and a dog to pull it up, since the root's scream will kill any living thing that hears it.

Walnuts resemble the brain, and so can be used to treat illnesses of the head.

'The Doctrine of Signatures' has its roots in classical antiquity. Developed by Paracelsus in the sixteenth century, it was based on the premise that any plant, animal, or object that resembled a part of the human body could be used to treat afflictions of that corresponding body part. It was believed that God had designed this resemblance as a sign to humankind of each plant's healing properties and their purpose in creation. In this way, walnuts can be used to treat illnesses of the head, as they resemble the brain; while the tiny holes in the leaves of St John's wort resemble the pores of the skin, so can be used to treat related afflictions. In the Doctrine the mandrake, with its resemblance to human form, was used to attract love, or to conceive a child when placed under the bed (as depicted in the film *Pan's Labyrinth*, directed by Guillermo del Toro). The Doctrine was a well-established accepted practice in Britain in the seventeenth century, used by polymaths and botanists alike, including Sir Thomas Browne and William Coles. Many of these remedies remained in medical texts until the nineteenth century, including *Culpeper's Complete Herbal*, which many people still use today as a source of herbal remedies. Today, medical science considers the theory itself to be archaic, without relevance to modern medicine.

Some plants have links to the infernal. Strange tales abound about the Devil and his blackberries. In Northumberland, it's believed that the Devil throws his club over the blackberries in late autumn, rendering them poisonous, while others say that blackberries should never be eaten after Old Michaelmas, in October, which is indeed when blackberries tend to go out of season. But folklore reasons vary: in Yorkshire it's said that the Devil spits on them on this day, while in Cornwall he urinates on them! Parsley is a slow-growing plant, supposedly so because the seed goes to the Devil nine times before breaking through above ground, and to move it is very bad luck. Other plants are peculiarly sensitive: in Gloucestershire, mushrooms will not grow after they have been seen and rosemary only grows at a house ruled by a woman. Finally, it's thought that caraway seeds ward off thieves.

> *Blackberries should never be eaten after Old Michaelmas.*

Flowers, too, have been given meanings for thousands of years, in Britain as elsewhere. In the Victorian era, 'the language of flowers' was adopted as a secret language to convey hidden messages to a lover. In the language of flowers, roses and red tulips are traditionally a declaration of love, while yellow tulips signify hopelessness. Daffodils and lilies are unlucky and linked to death, while white lilies symbolise purity, and yellow falsehood. Daisies symbolise innocence, and the first daisy of the year should be stepped on for luck, but never touched by a toddler or disaster will follow. Bluebells, symbolising constancy, are iconic British flowers that bloom from mid-April to May, their pretty blue heads waving in the breeze, carpeting the floors of the ancient woodlands like Box Hill and Hatchlands Park in Surrey, and Chirk Castle in Wrexham. Also called cuckoo's boots, lady's nightcap, and witches' thimbles, bluebells were used in witches' potions. Fairy enchantment will follow if a person wanders into a ring of bluebells, or alternatively they will be visited by an evil fairy and die. Elizabethans used bluebell bulb juice as starch for ruffs, while in the thirteenth century monks used them to treat snakebites and leprosy.

5

THE LORE OF BIRDS
AND ANIMALS

I n the rural communities of centuries ago, animals were essential to human survival and Britons lived closely with them: cows slept in the byres, sheep poked their heads through the doorways of cottages and horses were trusted steeds. Dogs were for hunting, sheep shearing was an annual event, and pigs would be slaughtered as part of an age-old tradition that often involved the whole community, separating the carcass into meat to be salted for later, and the delicacies and titbits to be shared in a celebratory feast. Animals are integral to age-old folk traditions and beliefs, variously presented as omens of bad luck, able to foretell love or the weather, or to have the power of divination. Similarly, remedies to ensure animal health and breeding success also have a long history.

Protecting livestock, in particular cattle, has always been a major concern for any rural farmer, and various folk beliefs are associated with this. As late as 1899, flint arrowheads were sometimes thought to be elf-darts, or thunderbolts that had struck earth. Believed to have healing properties, they would be boiled in water intended for cattle, to cure them of common afflictions. White cattle were seen as auspicious in early times, and were said to have originally been imported by Julius Caesar, specifically for sacrificial purposes. Even up until the turn of the nineteenth century it was said that the druids would carry home ritually gathered mistletoe that they collected with golden sickles, and were

> *Julius Caesar imported white cattle specifically to be sacrificed.*

pulled by cattle of the purest white that had never felt the yoke. White cattle were also thought to have the best meat, and were bred by tenant farmers to serve abbots and other high clergy, and royalty. The tenants of Bury St Edmunds apparently kept them for the 'oblation of the white bull', a ceremony performed by

clergymen to relieve barrenness, involving a woman leading a white bull to the shrine of St Edmund.

White animals as a whole have special significance throughout history. The white hart, or stag, is a common trope, made famous in C.S. Lewis's *The Lion, the Witch and the Wardrobe*, but with roots in many folk tales. Catching sight of a white hart is considered a portent of a momentous moment for the onlooker, and also a sign of changing times for Britain. In Welsh legend, the appearance of a white hart signals that the Otherworld is near, or that one is transgressing a boundary or taboo – for instance the Arthurian tale of Peredur entering the Castle of Wonders. Arthurian legend tells that the creature can never be caught. While large numbers of deer are not such a common sight today in Britain, *Reuters* reported the sighting of a rare white stag in the Scottish Highlands in its 12 February edition in 2008. Other white animal superstitions have also retained their popularity into more recent times. In Digby, Lincolnshire, for example, it was believed well into the twentieth century that once you have seen a white dog, you should not speak until you then see a white horse – a feat that might render a person silent for some time today and possibly why this superstition died out! White headless horses are said to gallop about Hertfordshire, particularly near Welwyn Village; while in Liphook, Hampshire, the ghostly figure of a white calf can, it's said, be seen trotting along happily and jumping hedges. It's sometimes said to shrink to the size of a cockerel before disappearing entirely.

> *In Lincolnshire if you saw a white dog, you could not speak until you saw a white horse.*

Cats have long been associated with witches, an association that continues in stories today. A traditional Northamptonshire story tells of a woodsman who, on having his dinner stolen each day by a cat, decided to lay in wait for it, exacting his revenge by

cruelly cutting off its paw. On returning home, he found that his wife was missing a hand. In Lancashire and the West Riding of Yorkshire a cat frisking about the house is a warning of stormy weather. Kittens born in May were thought to be terrible mousers, and would instead bring snakes into the house. Generally, a black cat coming towards you is thought to bring luck, but one walking away will take the luck along with it. In Yorkshire it's seen as lucky to own a black cat but unlucky to meet one. A common saying about cats and their colouring throughout England was 'Kiss the black cat, an' 'twill make ye fat; kiss the white one, 'twill make ye lean.'

Animals of the British countryside too have their folklore, evidenced as far back as the Iron Age. In *Roman History*, Cassius Dio describes how Boudicca, Queen of the Iceni, released a hare from the folds of her clothing as a form of divination; whichever direction the hare took as it ran would give the prediction. Yet a hare is said to be the unluckiest animal to meet in Yorkshire. Strangely, hedgehogs were also often looked on with suspicion across many counties throughout history; seen as cunning, they were said to suckle on cows while they slept. One of the most gruesome pieces of animal folklore has to be that green frogs were said to be used to open locks – first the frog must be killed, and then dried in the sunlight for three days. Once this has been done, it should be ground into a powder, which when applied to the lock would magically open it.

Even the tiniest creatures are surrounded by folklore and superstitions as to good or bad luck. In East Monmouth and Glamorgan it was considered very bad luck to kill a spider or black beetle, well into the twentieth century, while in the East Riding of Yorkshire, to kill a beetle would ensure rain. In Northamptonshire, and elsewhere, small spiders are called 'money-spinners' and it is considered good fortune to have one land on you, while in Suffolk, to kill the long-legged spider called 'the harvest man' will lead to a bad harvest. Traditionally, seeing a ladybird means that good luck will follow (in Cambridgeshire it was considered especially auspicious when they were found crawling on the right hand). Generally, the superstition is that the more spots, and deeper red they are in colour, the more luck they will bring, and in Wiltshire the number of spots corresponds to the number of months your good luck will last. A ladybird should never be killed, but if they are, it was once traditional in Norfolk one must bury them, and stamp on the grave three times, while intoning the same rhyme that many people still say today when a ladybird lands on them:

Ladybird, ladybird, fly away home,
Your house is on fire and your children are gone.

Across England, and beyond, it's believed that if a ladybird flies off of its own accord after landing on a person, good luck with money will come. In the eastern counties there was a superstition that the direction a ladybird takes when thrown into the air will show where a lover lives, and a rhyme to go with this was collected as late as 1938 in an article in *Folklore*, 'Ladybirds in England':

Fly away east, fly away west,
Show me where lives the one I love best.

Cornish folks say that snails and bees bring luck. Up until the 1920s, on meeting a snail in their path children in the region would say:

Snail! Snail! Come out of your hole.
Or I will beat you black as a coal.

The Aberdeen Bestiary, a list of animal descriptions dating back to the twelfth century, says that bees are irritated by noise. The notion that they are sensitive creatures has been preserved into modern times. In Northamptonshire it's believed that bees can't thrive if living within an argumentative household, and it's said that one should never swear in front of a hive. It is customary to always whisper to your bees in case they feel neglected, and decide to up and leave. Penzance people firmly believe that honey should always be taken from the hive on St Bartholomew's Day – 24 August – as he is the patron saint of bees. In Devon it's seen as ominous if a swarm decides to settle on a dead tree; a death will surely follow in the house within a year. Suffolk tradition teaches that bees are intelligent and hard-working creatures that should be treated as members of the family, and never be bought or sold like other animals, as this would be a sign of disrespect. In Suffolk and elsewhere there was a superstition that when there was a death in the family it was necessary to engage in the tradition of 'telling the bees' of the loss so that they could mourn, otherwise they would become angry and desert the hive. There is a record of this tradition being observed in July 1827, when the head of a humble cottage household died. On the day of burial a black crêpe scarf was affixed to each hive, and funeral biscuit soaked in wine left at the entrance to each. In Yorkshire, dire consequences will ensue for anyone that dares kill a bee, as in other regions – a superstition no doubt arising from how bees can sting if agitated. In Tyneside one should, it's said, never be the sole owner of a hive, and it is luckiest if jointly owned by an unmarried man and woman. In Northumberland the bees are said to gather together on Christmas Eve and hum a hymn.

Birds, as lords of the skies, are often regarded as messengers of the gods. Since ancient times their flight patterns have been used for divination, their innards for prophesy and their behaviours interpreted as dire omens or predictions of luck.

Some of the most famous bird folklore in Britain relates to the ravens at the Tower of London. It's said that if they ever leave the Tower, Britain will fall. For many this supposed superstition seems

In Northumberland, bees are said to gather together and hum a hymn on Christmas Eve.

suspiciously like a fictional titbit, designed to delight tourists! Folklore from the west of Scotland tells that hooded crows are fairies in bird form. If one settles on a house a death or other misfortune is sure to follow. *The Aberdeen Bestiary* says that many omens are attributed to crows, one of the most useful is that they will caw loudly as a presage of rain. In Northamptonshire, as well as elsewhere, it is bad luck to see a lone crow, as it is to hear the chattering of magpies. In Wales, superstition says that a wild bird in the house is always a sign of death. It's also said that to obtain money one must take a swallow's egg from a nest, boil it and then return it. If the swallow brings a root to the nest after this is done, you must take that, and carry it in your wallet or purse – riches are sure to follow. In the Hebrides, superstition has it that cocks have the ability to avert the evil eye, ward off ghosts and tell the future.

They were also regarded as creatures that could banish darkness each morning just with their call – a case of getting the situation the wrong way around. In Lancashire a cock crowing while facing the door predicts the arrival of a stranger. Yorkshire folk believe that a cock crowing can always predict a death: in Eliza Gutch's 1911 book, *County Folklore: The East Riding of Yorkshire*, a farmer from Holderness is reported to have stated when confronted by a sceptic, 'Then dis thoo meean ti say oor awd cock disn't knaw when there's boon ti be a deeath i famaly!' or 'Then do you mean to say our old cock doesn't know when there's bound to be a death in the family!' In Somerset it was said that farmyard cockerels could frighten away the Devil himself. However, the fabled cockatrice– a bird, or kind of serpent, reputedly hatched by a serpent from a cock's egg – was said to have more peculiar talents. This mythical creature, and at one point seen as the scourge of England, could – like the Medusa – kill you with a single look. Legend tells that a brave hero once covered himself in mirrors and strode about the countryside, so ridding the land from the infestation of these vile fiends, who expired when they saw their own reflections.

> *The robin was granted his red breast when he plucked the sharpest thorn from Jesus' forehead during his crucifixion.*

Birds feature in much of the Christian folklore of Britain. A robin is said to have plucked away the sharpest thorn from Jesus' forehead during his crucifixion; the story goes that this act of kindness is how this small grey bird gained the red patch on his breast, in some versions he is stained with the blood of Christ. Further testament to the robin's good nature appears in the English folk tale, 'Babes in the Wood', based on a sixteenth century ballad. In the same vein as the children's author Lemony Snicket, this folk tale tells of two children entrusted into the care of an evil uncle, who decrees that they should be taken into the forest to be killed by hired thugs so that he can steal their inheritance. In this tale, the children are left to starve in the forest. On their death, a little robin comes to surround their bodies with leaves. Robins are well-loved birds in Britain, as evidenced by many tales. It was said that bad luck would follow any child vandalising a robin's nest, and in Suffolk the story goes that anyone taking the eggs of a robin will suffer two broken legs, while an Essex rhyme, recorded by Ernest Ingersoll in his *Birds in Legend, Fable and Folklore*, warns that:

> The robin and the redbreast,
> The robin and the wren;
> If ye take out o' their nest
> Ye'll never thrive again.

> The robin and the redbreast,
> The martin and the swallow;
> If ye touch one o' their eggs
> Bad luck will follow.

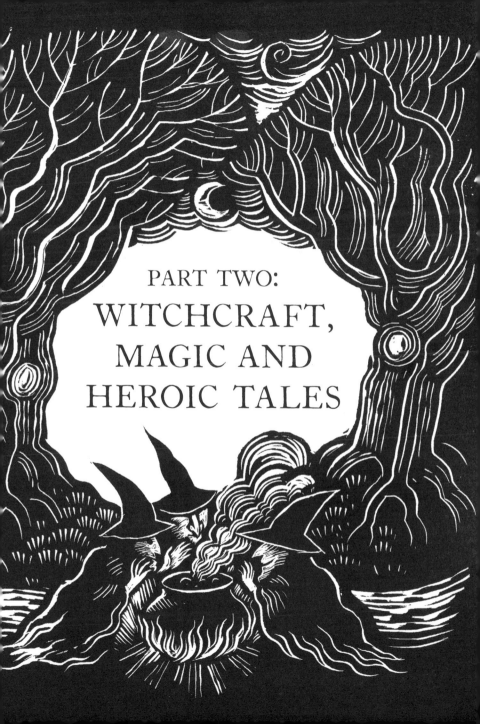

PART TWO:
WITCHCRAFT,
MAGIC AND
HEROIC TALES

6

OF GIANTS,
WARRIORS, KINGS
AND HEROES

―――――――――――――

Some of the earliest humans may have arrived in the British Isles as long ago as 800,000 years ago, at the beginning of the Palaeolithic Period – the Old Stone Age – when people first stared to make stone tools like those at Happisburgh in Norfolk, the earliest ever found in Britain. Later, Mesolithic hunter-gatherers began to make the slow transition from moving around the landscape to settled rural life. In museums we can see hand axes that these early humans left behind them, and in ancient rock art, such as at Creswell Crags in Derbyshire, the imagination of people in the mysterious past reaches out to touch our own time. Legends and myths abound as to early human habitation. Some stories imagine that ancient Britain was first inhabited by giants who roamed the land. These myths are perhaps celebrated in gigantic figures carved into the chalk hillsides, such as the Long Man of Wilmington in East Sussex, and the Cerne Abbas Giant in Dorset, although their origins are unclear: folklore says that the Cerne Giant may in fact be the outline of the corpse of a real 'giant', others adding that the outline is of a Danish giant, who was drawn around and beheaded by the locals as he slept.

One of the most famous British giants features in an old legend of the founding of London, linked with Welsh and Cornish traditions and related by Geoffrey of Monmouth in his *Historia Regum Britanniae* ('The History of The Kings of Britain') in the twelfth century. This tale tells how after the fall of Troy a band of Trojans fled to the seas, led by Brutus. After many adventures, they finally arrived on the shores of Albion (now Britain), which had been inhabited by a race of brutal, cannibalistic giants. Gogmagog was their fearsome leader, and now the only one left of their ancient race. One of the Trojans, Corineus, fought the giant in single-handed combat, which led to Gogmagog being thrown from a cliff to meet his doom. The end to the tale is murky, and it's unclear whether the giant died or was taken captive. At this point the story shifts to how the city of *Troynovant*, or New Troy – now the City of London – was founded by Brutus and his crew. Brutus supposedly chose to erect his great palace where the Guildhall now stands. The London Stone is a well-known London landmark that is usually situated nearby at Cannon Street (though currently housed at the London Museum). Its origins are disputed, but it is certainly a relic of an ancient building that may date from Roman times or even earlier. Two statues now stand in the Guildhall to commemorate this tale: some say one is the giant Gogmagog and the other his captor Corineus, while many simply call the statues Gog and Magog – two giants of legend mentioned in the Bible (the Gog Magog hills south-east of Cambridge are also named for them). The original statues, recorded as appearing at the coronation of Queen Elizabeth I in 1559, were remade in the eighteenth century, yet these replicas were destroyed during an air raid in the Second World War. Remade once more, the giants have regularly taken part in the Lord Mayor's show, held in November each year.

Jack the Giant Killer is an infamous figure in Cornish folklore, said to have killed the giant Cormoran, who built the castle on St Michael's Mount. The story goes that the giant was famous for terrorising the local people, and a reward was offered to whoever could rid them of this scourge. A young boy named Jack decided to try his luck, and one morning dug a huge hole in one side of the Mount, after which he awoke the giant by blowing his horn loudly. Blinded by the bright sun, the giant stumbled down the mountainside, and fell into the hole. Jack filled it in on top of him, becoming a local hero instantly. Even today, when taking the path up to the castle, you will see a heart-shaped stone which some say is the giant's, and that if you stand upon it, you can still hear the thud-thud of its beating, underneath your feet.

Another famous British giant is Ysbaddaden, from the tale of Culhwch and Olwen in *The Mabinogion*, a collection of the earliest prose stories in British literature that comprises *The White Book of Rhydderch* and *The Red Book of Hergest*. This tale is a classic hero quest,

> *Jack the Giant Killer is said to have killed the giant Comoran.*

where a young man, Culhwch, sets out to find his love, Olwen, the daughter of a giant, after being cursed by his stepmother so that he could love no other. The hero goes to find her, with the help of his cousin Arthur. She agrees to marry him but her father, Ysbaddaden, decrees that Culhwch must accomplish a number of impossible feats before he will give permission. In the style of other great heroic tales, such as Heracles or Odysseus, Culhwch manages some of these tasks; and then Ysbaddaden dies, leaving the couple free to marry.

Another fearless figure from British and Irish mythology is Fionn mac Cumhaill, a hunter-warrior who appeared in Scottish and Manx folklore, carried from Irish tradition by settlers from across the Irish Sea and North Channel. In many tales, Fionn is a fearless hero, while in some stories he himself is a benevolent giant. He is surrounded by tales of great heroic deeds, from killing giants to defeating fearsome serpents, and his story is steeped in magic. Animal transformations play a huge part in his story: when thrown by his grandfather from a cliff, his grandmother took the form of a bird and caught him. His mistress, mother of his son Ossian, was said in some versions to take the form of a deer at night, the result of druid magic. His sister was transformed into a dog by a jealous lover, and later gave birth to two hounds, which accompany Fionn in his adventures. He was said to be able to transform into animal form by using a magical hood, and was blessed with the powers of invisibility and to raise storms. One of the most famous tales surrounding Fionn, the Salmon of Knowledge, comes straight from Irish legend. The salmon's knowledge of all, gained by eating only hazelnuts from a sacred tree, could be passed to anyone who tasted its flesh. Fionn's teacher, the druid and poet Finnegas, had sought the salmon for many years. One day he finally caught it near the River Boyne, and told Fionn to cook it for him. Fionn burned his thumb while cooking, and inadvertently put it to his mouth, tasting the salmon and gaining some of its knowledge. On seeing this, Finnegas told the boy to eat the entire fish, to gain all of the knowledge in the world, which he did. From that day forward, Fionn would put his thumb to his mouth, and evoke the wisdom of the salmon. He is said to lie at Tomnahurich near Inverness, or on the Isle of Skye, and it is said he is in endless sleep with his band of warriors, the Fianna, only to wake when called to save the country from peril.

The legendary Welsh bard Taliesin – originally known as Gwion Bach, son of Gwreang – has a similar story to that of Fionn mac Cumhaill and the Salmon of Knowledge. Servant to the great Ceridwen, the boy was charged with stirring the Cauldron of Inspiration for a whole year. Once the potion of inspiration was complete, three drops of the mixture spilled onto his thumb, which he put in his mouth and thus gained its magical powers. He fled in fear, and transformed himself into a piece of grain in order to hide, which Ceridwen ate, later giving birth to the boy, who was from that day renamed Taliesin.

Like so many great heroic tales, the legend of King Arthur began with a story that might have had some truth but was subsequently added to and embellished. Fragments of text about a warrior who drew together the tribal chiefs and petty kings of Britain against the Saxons, after the Romans left, are scattered in old texts. Nennius, a ninth-century Welsh monk, speaks of him as a great battle commander in his *Historia Brittonum*, and Arthur is shown early on to be a warrior bent on defending Britain from a tide of marauding forces. Gildas, a sixth-century British monk, tells us that Arthur fought the Saxons in a number of battles, culminating in the success that led to his reputation at the legendary Battle of Mount Badon. Possible contenders for the site of this semi-mythical battle include Badbury Rings hill fort in Dorset and Liddington Castle in Wiltshire, as well as the

Gwion Bach gained magical powers after spilling liquid from the Cauldron of Inspiration onto his thumb.

city of Bath. With each passing age, writers took the legends of Arthur and added their own twists, weaving old tales with new, in feats of imagination. For those in the Dark Ages, he was a warrior who would return as a saviour of the people in a time of need; later, he became a medieval symbol of chivalry, yet for the Victorians, his was a story filled with Christian virtues.

Arthur's final resting place was also shrouded in mystery, some say so as not to stir the ambitions of the Saxons. One legend tells that he was buried at Glastonbury Abbey, which incidentally is near Cadbury Castle. In the twelfth century, monks at the abbey claimed to have unearthed the bones of both Arthur and his blonde-haired queen, along with a cross inscribed with his

name. More recent research has shown that a grave of the correct type was indeed located in the area the monks claimed. However, there is also strong folk tradition in Britain that imagines King Arthur as a sleeping warrior, ready to wake to save the land when needed. This legend places him in many possible locations: Avalon, Richmond Castle in North Yorkshire, Alderley Edge in Cheshire, and at the ruin of Sewingshields Castle in Northumberland. Other notable sleeping kings in Britain include Owain Lawgoch, a Welsh soldier, who is said to sleep at Llandeilo in an underground cave illuminated by lanterns, until the time when he will awake to become king of the Britons. Another is Owain Glyndŵr, a Welsh ruler who led a revolt against the English, who is said to have powers of invisibility using a magical stone, and the ability to raise storms. He is thought to lie in the Vale of Gwent. Finally, the cairn on the summit of Brown Willy is said to house the sleeping king of Cornish folklore.

> *King Arthur is imagined as a sleeping warrior, ready to wake to save the land when needed.*

Another famous figure from Arthurian legend is the wizard Merlin. Legend has it that King Vortigern chose Dinas Emrys in North Wales as the site for his castle, yet the workers would return each morning to find the newly built walls in ruins. The King's sorcerers advised that the only solution was to sprinkle the ground with the blood of a child born to a mother of this world and a father of the Otherworld. When the child, Myrddin Emrys (who became the great Merlin) was found, he declared that two dragons lay under a lake within the mountain, and were destroying the foundations of the castle each night. On digging down, a lake was indeed discovered, and two sleeping dragons were found at the bottom – one red, one white. When they awoke, a great battle ensued between them, ending when the white dragon fled and the red fell back into a slumber underneath the hill. The castle was successfully built, and the red dragon – now immortalised on the Welsh flag – is said to sleep there still.

Many battle leaders have been deemed heroes for their warlike prowess. Examples from ages past include Boudicca, Queen of the Iceni tribe who defended her people patriotically against the Romans, and of course Robert the Bruce and William Wallace, both surrounded by legends of their glory in the fight for Scottish independence against England. Other folk heroes were always outside the law, and some were loved despite their dark deeds and misadventures. For centuries, none has been so famous a symbol of hope as the infamous outlaw Robin Hood. Cast out to live in the forests and forced to survive through hunting and robbery alone, the tale of this medieval yeoman is now steeped in legend. Perhaps the first mention of the tales of 'Robyn Hode' is in a fourteenth-century narrative poem by William Langland, 'The Vision of Piers Ploughman', while ballads about him were first printed nearly a hundred years later. Early on, many believed that Robin Hood was a real man, who became a hero to the common people in a time of great need, and was made famous during a time of political oppression. Later it was thought that he was an imaginary hero, conjured as a figure that poor people could identify with, being very different from the heroes and kings of the more affluent in society. Whatever the case, Robin Hood was a political hero who despised the exploitation of the poor by the rich, fought back against laws that restricted hunting on the king's lands (at a time when people faced starvation and hardship) and refused to harm any woman. He and his band of Merry Men were said to roam throughout Sherwood Forest in Nottinghamshire, and Barnsdale Forest in Yorkshire. In stories he is characterised by his great bowmanship and his hatred of both the law and the clergy. He reputedly shot and cut off the head of his arch-enemy, the Sheriff of Nottingham. Whatever the truth, it's undeniable that Robin Hood has been, and still is, a people's hero who will live on in English legend for years to come. A new Robin Hood

play, based on a traditional legend, *Robin Hood and the Friar of Fountains Abbey*, was written as recently as 2012, and performed at the Furness Traditional Festival, and then at Fountains Abbey in Ripon, North Yorkshire, said to be the place of Robin's legendary riverside meeting with Friar Tuck.

Robin Hood is famous for never hurting the poor; the same cannot be said of the notorious highwayman Dick Turpin, who certainly existed, and in his own way became a folk hero. His story originates in Hempstead, Essex, but ends in Yorkshire, and it's thought that the feats of many highwaymen across the country were wrongly attributed to him, which only added to his fame. Despite his reputation as a great villain of British history, he won people's favour through tales of his gallantry, charming those he robbed. This respect was far from deserved since in reality he had no qualms about robbing and beating anyone that stood in his way, including the elderly and infirm. One of the most gruesome tales of his deeds was the attack on a 70-year-old pensioner, Joseph Lawrence of Edgware, who was dragged around by his nose, beaten heavily with pistols and then tortured by being sat on a fire unclothed.

Lady Godiva is depicted as a compassionate figure, who rode naked through the streets of Coventry.

Lady Godiva, too, could be called a heroine of the people. There is no doubt that Godiva was a real woman: she was a countess who lived in the eleventh century and governed Coventry with her husband, Earl Leofric of Mercia, one of the four magnates chosen by King Cnut to rule over England after it was conquered by the Danes. Legend paints her as a compassionate and brave figure, who rode naked through the streets of Coventry, only covered by her long hair, to gain remission for the high taxes levied on the tenants by her husband. She ordered that every citizen should stay indoors, with the windows covered, out of respect. A later addition to the legend is that only one man – Peeping Tom – ignored her request and tried to watch, yet was struck blind before he could catch a glimpse of her. It's said that the Earl did indeed keep his word – considering it a miracle that she could accomplish such a feat without anyone seeing – and removed all taxes except for that on horses. The annual Godiva Procession, recently revived, re-enacts the story.

St Winifred or Winefride – *Grenffrewi* in Welsh – is sometimes known as the Welsh Lazarus. The story goes that in the seventh century a Welsh nobleman charged Beuno, his brother-in-law, with the task of erecting a church and providing religious instruction for his daughter Winefride. However, a local chieftain named Caradog wanted Winefride for his wife, and made advances – which she ardently refused. Caradog's rising passions soon got the better of him, and he tried to force himself on the girl – at which point she fled to the safety of the church. He then became mad with lust and rage, and cut off her head. The story then takes an unusual turn, as a spring gushed from the ground in the place where her head fell, after which it rolled among the feet of the congregation, calling out to God for vengeance. Beuno, now holding the head in his hands, invoked a holy curse against the murderer, who was wiping his sword on the grass next to Winefride's lifeless form. Caradog died at once, disappearing entirely. Beuno placed Winefride's head on her body, and called the congregation to pray with him to restore the girl to life. At this Winefride sat up, revived, yet a thin white line would from thenceforth encircle her throat in the place where her head had been severed. Rumour tells that the blood from that fateful day still stains the stones of the holy well, which gives its name to Holywell in Flintshire, and people still visit the spring for healing.

7

ANCIENT GODS, DEVILS AND WILD MEN

M any still sense the ancient gods and goddesses of Britain in forests, sacred stones or when leafing through historic tomes to read age-old words about them. Even so, the gods of the ancient Britons are difficult to piece together because all that is left are fragments, in stories and under the soil. When the Romans invaded Britain they allowed people to continue with their worship of native gods and drew parallels between these gods and their own, often fusing the names together. Cocidius became Mars Cocidius, the god of war near Northumberland and the Scottish Borders. Maponus became Apollo Maponus, said to have become the character Mabon ap Modron in medieval Welsh literature. The Romano-British goddess Coventina was worshipped at a spring at Hadrian's Wall, while Boudicca herself called on the goddess Andraste, a goddess of war, before going into battle with the Romans. It's thought that many of the Celtic gods that were worshipped in continental Europe were also worshipped in Britain. These include Cernunnos, often called 'the Horned One' and seen as a wild god of the animals; Lugus (Lugh in Irish; Lleu in Welsh), identified with the Roman god Mercury and associated with the harvest festival of Lughnasadh; and Belenus 'the Shining One', who is linked to the annual celebration of Beltane. It's thought that Britain had a long oral tradition before the Romans came to our shores, with myths of ancient gods and goddesses passed down from generation to generation, yet these were only written down centuries later, once these deities had been dwarfed by the Christian God, and were often only remembered as heroes and fairies. Some say that with the arrival of Christianity the symbolic power that belonged to these old gods dissolved. We can only speculate on this, and look to archaeology and folklore for clues.

Modern Pagan traditions revere an ancient mother goddess in many forms.

Some historians point to the many Palaeolithic Period (Old Stone Age) figurines of ample-breasted women as evidence of an early belief in a mother goddess figure. Modern Pagan traditions in Britain today also revere an ancient mother goddess, in many forms, and many celebrate the triple goddess – who manifests as maiden, mother and crone – symbolising the stages of the female life cycle. Some archaeologists have argued for the worship of a triple goddess across ancient Europe. While the idea of a primordial great mother goddess in Britain is still widely debated, mythology tells of the Welsh goddess Dôn, often likened to the Irish Danu, and of the goddess Modron, who some believe to be derived from the primordial mother goddess Matrona, later filtering down into Welsh myth. Some scholars argue that a milk and dairying goddess existed for the Romano-Britons, since many legends and myths speak of spirits of the herd, dairy and home, who will treat humans how they in turn are treated. Others believe that water goddesses were already worshipped by the time the Romans came to Britain, associated with fertility and often petitioned for healing at sacred pools, springs and wells. Dedications to Minerva have been found throughout Britain, linked with the goddess Sulis, whose worship centred on the thermal springs at Bath, Somerset.

There is a long tradition of mythical figures in both legends and folk customs throughout Britain that conjure images of ancient nature gods and woodland sprites peering from behind leaves and tree trunks as we wander through our forests. These threads have been woven together in a coherent picture of a series of vegetation gods, many of whom are worshipped throughout Britain today by modern Pagans, who revere nature through both a goddess and counterpart god, while others worship a whole pantheon of such deities. The Green Man has become a prominent figure in modern Paganism in Britain, often representing the male aspects of the religion. He is a figure commonly seen throughout European history, who is usually represented as a face, either surrounded by leaves and branches or with these sprouting from his mouth – sometimes even from his nostrils and eyes. Kathleen Basford, author of *The Green Man*, believed that he symbolised 'the spiritual dimension of nature' as a vegetative deity, a symbol of death and rebirth, and of the seasonal cycle. Many Pagans see the Green Man as a symbol of Robert Graves' Holly King and Oak King, who do battle twice a year at the autumn and spring equinoxes when seasons change, the winner presiding over that half of the wheel of the year. The Clun Green Man Festival is held each year during the May bank holiday in Clun, Shropshire, where the Green Man battles the Spirit of Winter.

His image appears in many churches, perhaps as a spiritual link between Christianity and older practices. It's often said that the term 'Green Man' was coined by Lady Raglan in her article of 1939 in *Folklore* journal, exploring 'The "Green Man" in Church Architecture'. Previously these kinds of carvings were called

foliate heads, but Lady Raglan suggested that the carvings must have been based on the figure of Jack-in-the-Green or the Garland King from local pageants. However, the sculptures predate these British festival figures, first appearing in Britain in the late twelfth century. One example from Ightham Mote, a moated manor house in Kent, dates to the early 1300s, while further examples of Green Man carvings can be seen in 23 counties of England, including at the cathedrals in Norwich, Lincoln, Wells and Ely, as well as in Midlothian in Scotland. Brandon Centerwall, a researcher on the topic, sheds some light on the figure in his 1997 article in *Folklore*, 'The Name of the Green Man'. He argues that the Green Man appeared as a character in English pageants as early as the sixteenth and seventeenth centuries, for instance in the Lord Mayor's Pageant, but usually only as a 'whiffler' – people who would clear the way through the crowds with flaming torches or fireworks. They would appear as comic relief, acting as if they were drunk, possibly also why many pubs are named after them. The characters also appeared on St George's Day, on 23 April 1610, at a Chester pageant to celebrate the birth of the new heir, Prince Henry. They were disguised in ivy leaves, with black hair and beards, and garlands on their heads. It's said that they carried clubs, and were accompanied by a dragon that was eventually killed, but only as a last-minute idea to please the crowd. Brandon Centerwall suggests that the carvings probably gave rise to the pageant characters, rather than vice versa. Although we cannot know the original symbolism, some still see the heads as a survival of a pre-Christian hope that the harvest will be fruitful each year.

Often associated with the Green Man today, the traditional figure of Jack-in-the-Green was a popular figure at May Day celebrations from early on in England. It's said that he originated with people making huge garlands for the parades in the sixteenth century, which became so elaborate that they eventually enveloped an entire person. Others believe that he was a moneymaking invention of chimney sweeps in the late eighteenth century. He can still be seen in parades today in revivals of the tradition in places like Whitstable, in Kent, and Hastings, where he is dressed in a conical frame covered in leaves and vegetation, almost resembling a walking Christmas tree. Other parades can be seen in Greenwich and Bermondsey in London, as well as in Oxford, Bristol, and Knutsford in Cheshire. The Garland King is a similar figure, who appears covered in flowers on Castleton Garland Day on 29 May, to coincide with Oak Apple Day in the Peak District, Derbyshire. An interesting tradition of celebrating Burryman Day still exists in South Queensferry, Edinburgh, each August,

Some believe Jack-in-the-Green was a moneymaking invention of chimney sweeps.

where a man is covered entirely in burrs from head to foot, and paraded around the town. People offer him whisky and money in order to ensure good luck for the coming year – possibly derived from an ancient tradition, either to ward off evil spirits or using him as a sort of scapegoat.

The Wild Man, or Woodwose, was another prominent figure in British folklore from the medieval period onwards. These woodland creatures reminiscent of fauns are found throughout European folklore and mentioned in *Sir Gawain and the Green Knight*, an Arthurian romance from the fourteenth century. Wild Men would often play a similar role as the Green Man in such pageants, mainly to clear the crowds, but also appearing now and then in short sketches and plays. A Wild Man would be covered in hair instead of leaves, originally appearing in the medieval period as a symbol to depict what man is without god: a beastly creature that might take the shape of a man, but behaves and thinks more like an animal. Scholars believe that although the Green Man and the Wild Man might look similar, and date from the same period, they developed independently.

The Abbots Bromley Horn Dance, an ancient tradition, is still held each year in Staffordshire on Wakes Monday, the first Sunday after 4 September. Six Deer-men perform a folk dance with real antlers, accompanied by a Hobby Horse, a Fool, Maid Marian and a Bowman. After dancing in two lines to music, the group proceed through the village followed by onlookers, stopping at various points along the way to dance and take refreshment. Some people say that this might be a form of dance using sympathetic hunter's magic – many hunter-gatherer groups mimic the animals they are about to hunt, either by donning their skins or imitating their movements, while some mimic killing an animal to ensure success, or ask for the assistance of their spirits in the hunt. Others suggest it could be linked to ancient shamanic practices or the Horned God. Some consider it most likely a remnant of a medieval pageant – it dates back to at least 1226, when it was performed at the Barthelmy Fair.

The Devil figure is very prominent in British folklore, and folk tales about him abound, while many bridges, hills, and dykes are named after him – Devil's Dyke in West Sussex being just one example. Legend tells that the Devil was intent on flooding the churches in the Weald by digging a trench

Many bridges, hills and dykes in Britain are named after the Devil.

in one night. As he worked he threw heaps of earth aside, which now form Cissbury Ring, Chanctonbury Ring, Mount Caburn and Firle Beacon on the South Downs, as well as the Isle of Wight. While digging he was disturbed when a woman lit a candle. This in turn caused a cockerel to crow, making the Devil think that morning had already broken. He fled at once, leaving his deadly task unfinished, and thus the people of the Sussex Weald were saved from a terrible fate.

One of the strangest stories about the Devil comes from a 1678 pamphlet: *The Mowing-Devil: or, Strange News out of Hartford-*

shire. One summer's day in August, so the story goes, a farmer
went to a poor labourer who usually helped with his harvest and
offered him the job of mowing down three half-acres of oats in his
field – but for a very low price indeed. The labourer refused, and
they began to barter, but could not settle on a price. The exchange
ended with the farmer shouting that he'd rather the Devil himself
mow the oats than now let the labourer have anything to do with
them. On awaking next morning, the farmer was told that his
fields appeared to have 'been all aflame' through the night, at
which he ran to investigate. His crops had not been burned down;
instead, he found that they had indeed been cut, but in strange
circles – and so precisely that no man could have undertaken the
task in such a short time. The terrified farmer was left with one
conclusion: that the Devil himself had indeed come to mow.

8

THE LITTLE PEOPLE
OF THE LAND

D o you believe in fairies? At the end of the nineteenth
century, it was said that the Manx people believed that
the first inhabitants of the Isle of Man were a race of
fairies that lived in the forests and mountains, so avoiding the vice
in the towns. Similarly in Irish mythology, the *Tuatha Dé Danann*
was the race of deities that, after the introduction of Christianity,
were relegated to becoming the *sídhe*, or fairy folk. Legend has
it that they now live underground and in mounds, having being
tricked into accepting half of Ireland after their defeat in an
ancient battle, only to discover that this was the half that lies
under the soil.

British folklore gives many names for fairies: the fair folk,
the good people, the wee folk – in Scotland (and Ireland) they
are the *aos sìth*, and in Wales the *Tylwyth Teg*. Usually described
in stories as tiny, well-proportioned creatures, fairies were

often depicted with long blonde hair that gathered around their shoulders. Their clothing is usually imagined in colours that blend with the landscape, in greens or browns. Strangely, not many fairies in folklore have wings. Instead, they fly on the backs of birds or on ragwort stems.

Stories of fairy behaviour are quirky and often involve dancing and cavorting by the light of the moon. In Northumberland their night raids were notorious, and they would charge around the countryside on little cream horses that left no footprints, each with a tiny saddle – the tinkling of their bells could be heard for miles around. It's said that are most easily glimpsed in the gloaming – the time when dusk falls, and the light is fading – or at day break, playing in the fields, or dancing in circles in the moonlight to their haunting fairy music. The summit of Cader Idris in Wales is said to be the site of many fairy gatherings, and its stones carried there by them. Throughout Britain, dark

Many fairies fly on the back of birds or on ragwort stems.

rings in the grass, often in reality caused by fungus, are called 'fairy rings', and imagined to be caused by fairies dancing.

The fairies of British folklore are notorious for bestowing their blessings upon humans, with the *Bratach Sìth*, or Fairy Flag, of the MacLeods of Dunvegan Castle in Skye being one famous example. It's said that if the MacLeod's are ever in dire need, all they must do is unfurl the flag, and the power of invincibility will be theirs – yet this gift was given with a warning: the flag can only be used three times. The clan has, it's said, already used the flag twice, leaving them only one more use before the fairy magic is lost forever. Legends of the flag's origin variously describe it as given to a MacLeod chieftain by a water sprite when he was crusading in the Holy Land, having been won from a she-devil, or being the legendary Land-Ravager flag of King Harald

Hardrada that ensured victory in battle to whoever possessed it. A well-known tale describes a fourteenth-century fairy-wife giving it to her MacLeod husband on her return to fairyland.

Not all fairy objects are given freely. An article in *The Gentleman's Magazine* of 1791 related contradictory tales about the origins of a crystal fairy-cup, kept at Eden Hall in Cumberland, where the Musgrave family considered it a good luck charm. In one version of the story, a group of curious people had intruded on a gathering of fairies making merry around St Cuthbert's Well. The fairies fled, leaving the cup behind them. Another version says that the cup was stolen from the fairies by a butler, who came upon them one moonlit night when drawing water from the well. As the butler made away with the cup the fairies are said to have sung this ditty:

> If that glass either break or fall,
> Farewell to the luck of Eden Hall.

The cup – which went on show at the Victoria and Albert Museum in 1926 – appears in reality to have been a fourteenth-century drinking glass, imported from Syria.

The fairy folk are regarded as notoriously mischievous, as seen in many folk myths. Like other beliefs, fairies are often associated with springs or wells, which become the site of folk tales. A well or spring near Baysdale in Yorkshire is just one place where 'fairy butter' can appear; another is Egton Grange, near Whitby. It is actually a folk name for a particular fungus that 'miraculously' appears overnight, and looks a bit like butter that has been thrown and stuck to whatever was lying in its path – by the mischievous fairies in the night, perhaps. When fairy butter was found in a house it was said to denote extremely good luck. Indeed, any house visited by the fairies was seen as blessed, and some households would put out bowls of cream each evening both to attract fairies and thank them for bestowing luck. Superstition

had it that a fall was due to the fairies laying something in your
path for a misdeed, and anything lost and then found has without
doubt taken by the fairies. If you annoy the fairies, it's said you
can avert their wrath by spitting on the ground three times first,
although sometimes they can be more evil in their ways. At
Holme on the Wolds, a village in the East Riding of Yorkshire,
a church was to be built at the bottom of the hill. The fairies
advised for it to be built at the top instead, but their advice was
ignored. When the church was nearly finished, it was found to
be in ruins. Once more, it was built up, and once more found
destroyed overnight. The villagers finally relented, building
at the top of the hill, just as the fairies had 'suggested'.

According to nineteenth-century superstition, Saturday was
the fairy Sabbath and Friday was when fairies amused themselves
by grooming the beards
of goats. The more evil
influence of fairies was often
said to be strongest during
the first three days of May,
although it was possible to
avert it from your home by

> *On Fridays, fairies
> amuse themselves by
> grooming goats.*

scattering primroses across the threshold – no fairy has the power
to pass this flower. Some of the more menacing stories about
fairies involve human children being replaced by changelings,
which we'll come to later. Tales of adult kidnappings are also rife;
one legend has it that Thomas the Rhymer was taken off by the
Queen of Elfland. Once he had spent seven years in her realm,
the Queen granted him the gift of prophecy; he then became the
greatest prophet in all the land, even surpassing the skills of Merlin
himself. The tale appears in the *Child Ballads* – 305 traditional
ballads collected from England and Scotland, with their American
variants, by Francis James Child.

Redcaps are creatures of the Scottish borders who dye their
caps with human blood. They have the appearance of grizzled

old men with sinister red eyes, long teeth, and talons, wearing
iron boots and carrying pikestaffs. They are somewhat similar
to the German *kobold* or the Irish leprechaun, but are more
malevolent and will kill anyone who wanders into their lair, often
an abandoned castle or tower. Fortunately, they can be banished
easily by reciting scriptures or brandishing a cross, at which point
they disappear in flames – leaving only an old tooth behind.
Cornish spriggans are also grizzled old men, in this case with large
heads. They, too, reside in ruins – sometimes cairns or barrows
– and are often intent on causing mayhem. Seen as notorious

thieves, they're conveniently blamed for cattle rustling, child abduction and thefts in the home, and credited with the ability to raise storms and winds to destroy crops. Thought to be related to Scandinavian trolls, these mythical characters are said to be the ghosts of giants that still haunt the far reaches of Britain around Land's End, and are the guardians of treasure.

Native to Cornwall and Devon, pixies are of an entirely different disposition altogether, being helpful rather than malevolent. In modern times pixies are often depicted as cute little creatures, with pointed green hats, and equally pointed ears, who like to gather to dance in the countryside through the night. Older tales of pixies are very different, however. In these, pixies are indistinguishable from bundles of dirty old rags. A tale of 1853, from Dartmoor, tells of a mother who arrived home after journeying in the dark with her three small children one night, only to find that one child was missing. After a frantic search the wayward

Redcaps dye their caps with human blood.

child was found under a tree, having been pixy-led by two bundles of rags, which disappeared on seeing the lanterns of the search party. The tree was supposedly a notorious haunt of the pixies. Despite being mischievous, pixies are said to help around the house. For example, as frequent nocturnal visitors to a cottage in Belstone, they were apparently heard hard at work at the loom night after night. It's said that a gift of clothing will banish any pixie. A Cornish washerwoman named Betsy was said to find this out to her cost. She noticed a ragged, pitiful creature had been washing and folding her clothes for her, and left it a yellow petticoat and red cap – the delighted pixie disappeared through the window, and was never seen again. Joan-the-wad and Jack-the-lantern are often linked with wildfire or will-o'-the-wisp – strange lights that were often referred to as pixie-lights. These lights, which appear over the moors, are now known to be marsh gas, but were traditionally thought to either lead travellers away from their path on dark nights or else sometimes to act as their guide to safety. In the east of Cornwall, the lights can be invoked with a simple charm:

> Jack the Lantern, Joan the Wad,
> That tickled the maid and made her mad,
> Light me home, the weather's bad.

Goblins are generally regarded to be among the most malevolent type of 'little people', playing tricks and causing mischief around the home. Famous for upsetting furniture around the house and bothering animals, it's said they can be dumbfounded by throwing flaxseed in the air – every goblin succumbs to the need to pick up every last seed, so keeping them busy until sunrise. Folk tales often have it that the attentions of goblins can be avoided by wearing your clothing back-to-front, or inside out.

Brownies are creatures considered to be half man, half spirit. They are found in folklore throughout Scotland, but particularly in the Shetlands, the Highlands, the Western Isles and the Borderlands. They will do chores around the house and village in return for food. Bowls of cream can be left for them, while a common treat for them in Berwickshire is meal cakes smothered in honey. Tradition has it that they must never receive wages, because the chores they take on are penance for sins committed. Like the Cornish pixies, brownies will leave if garments are offered to them; they appear to become highly offended at any gift of clothing. One from Glendevon apparently muttered the following words before taking his leave: 'Gie Brownie coat, gie Brownie sark, Ye'se geb nae mair o' Brownie's wark,' or, translated, 'Give Brownie coat, give Brownie sock, You'll get no more of Brownie's work.' Some say that brownies are also called 'dobies'; others argue that dobies are entirely different mythical creatures: either spirits of the dead that haunt the place where their lives came to an end, or demons similar to the ghostly barguest, which often guards hidden treasure. Hob-thrush, or hobmen, similar to elves or brownies, are also purported to help with the housework, and apparently often turn up nude! One particular hob-thrush, called Robin Roundcap, was said to haunt Spaldington Hall, in the East Riding of Yorkshire – demolished in the nineteenth century. He was reputed to help the maids and thrashers with their work, but would often play tricks on the inhabitants by extinguishing the fire, or tipping over the milk pails. Eventually, it's said, three clergymen prayed him into a holy well, later named after him, so that the could trouble the family no more.

Some say that the infamous trickster Robin Goodfellow, also called Puck or Hobgoblin, is a type of brownie or domestic spirit who either causes pranks or helps around the house. Other sources have him as a type of fairy or even as linked to devils and evil spirits. Usually appearing faun-like, with horns, furry legs,

cloven hooves and a huge phallus, he is often said to be a woodland sprite and nature spirit who haunts the English countryside. He appears in Shakespeare's *A Midsummer Night's Dream*, as well as in a seventeenth-century jest book that contains a series of humorous anecdotes about his escapades. Tales about this imaginary character abound – on how he assists maids with their housework, leads people astray in the countryside, tries to help reform the slovenly or, on the other hand, to reward the hard-working folk of rural England.

> *In Scotland, fairies can be warded off by hanging a pair of trousers off the end of the bed.*

Whether you welcome the fairy folk or not, it's always useful to know of ways to banish them, just in case. In Scotland, an old nineteenth-century method to ward off the fairies was simply to hang a pair of trousers off the end of the bed, while fishermen and their families would place a basket filled with bread and cheese, or a fir-candle, on the bed to keep the fairies at bay.

9

WITCHES, THE CUNNING FOLK AND ALCHEMY

The world in which the witch hunts of the sixteenth to eighteenth centuries arose was a dark one, full of ignorance, fear and suspicion. The fear of witchcraft and its maliciousness became very real and could turn families and neighbours against one another. Pope Innocent VIII decreed witchcraft to be heresy in the fifteenth century, and the words of Exodus 22:18, 'Thou shalt not suffer a witch to live', echoed in the minds of many. King Henry VIII made witchcraft a felony in 1542, and the horror of the witch trials prevailed until the first half of the eighteenth century. After this, the earlier acts were repealed as belief in witchcraft began to fade.

With the rise of Puritanism in the late sixteenth century the ritualistic ways by which Catholicism had kept the threat of witchcraft and black magic at bay – the swinging incense that could cleanse the soul, the eyes of the Virgin Mary and the crucified Christ staring down from above the altar – were taken away and condemned by the new church. Reformation swept across Europe, and a firm belief in Christ was all that was needed to keep the Devil from your door. The illiterate, more suspicious, common people of Britain and beyond were not so easily convinced, and still sought traditional ways to keep him at bay, since even the most pious soul could fall prey to the Devil and his temptations – and so become embroiled in witchcraft in return for earthly delights. People went to great lengths to protect themselves and their homes from witchcraft. Witch bottles, filled with pins, human hair and urine, were concealed around the house to ward off witches. Protective witch marks were often inscribed on the beams of houses to keep evil spirits at bay. There are examples at Knole, in Kent, thought to date back to the early 1600s, the time of the Gunpowder Plot. Etched on hidden beams around the fireplace and under floorboards of the Upper King's Rooms, they are thought to have protected King James I from evil spirits, and even from death, on his visit to the estate. Witch marks can also be seen inside the door at The Fleece Inn, a fifteenth-century longhouse in the Vale of Evesham in Worcestershire, and folklore tells of witch-circles being chalked before the hearths of this same building to keep witches from entering the house through the chimneys.

Protective witch marks were often inscribed on the beams of houses to keep evil spirits at bay.

Witchcraft could be conveniently blamed for ill fortune such as sickness, bad luck, or even a cow refusing to give milk, and an individual or group might be accused of harming their enemies through malefic magic. There were various ways of supposedly identifying if someone was a witch. Suspects were sometimes 'swum' (cast into water – if they sank they were believed to be innocent and hauled out; if they floated they were guilty), weighed against the church Bible, or forced to recite the Lord's Prayer or the Apostles' Creed. Irregular and entirely innocent marks on the body could be interpreted as signs of the Devil's Mark, indicating someone had given over their soul to the Devil in exchange for the often empty promise of earthly delights and magical powers. For impoverished rural dwellers scratching out a meagre existence, even having shelter or a full belly might be regarded as a rich reward. Other marks or 'teats' on a person who was thought to be a witch were believed to be where she had suckled her familiar spirits. Superstition had it that these marks should not bleed, and that the witch should not feel pain when a long, sharp copper pin was inserted by her accusers into the suspect mole, flea bite or mark. In Scotland and areas of the North of England this task was often undertaken by a 'pricker'; these men (and in at least one known case, a disguised woman) were paid handsomely for their work. After the humiliation of being stripped and searched by the pricker's grasping hands, the accused would be made to confess.

In England in the 1600s torture was illegal. Instead, 'confessions' from witches were drawn out by starvation, or by questioning them after sleep deprivation. This practice was particularly prominent in Suffolk and Essex in the mid-seventeenth century under Matthew Hopkins (who claimed the notorious title of 'Witchfinder General', despite the fact that this was never sanctioned by Parliament) and his associate John Stearne. In Scotland, and in the Channel Islands, odious methods of torture were used to break the prisoners, cruelly inflicting pain until the accused could take no more and gave up stories of the Devil, and the wicked deeds he had bade them do. Among the many torture devices, the witch-bridle was a common instrument, as were the iron shoes, which would be clamped on to the suspected witches' feet, and then heated. Whipping with cords until the flesh was ripped from the bones was a common occurrence. It's shocking to think of the sheer brutality that was inflicted on so many in the face of what seems, today, preposterous accusations. While nowadays we might find these crimes bizarre, the threat to one's immortal soul was taken more seriously than life itself – and we should not forget that people are still put to death for the crime of witchcraft in many places around the world today.

A supposed witch from Orkney, Alison Balfour, was subjected to repeated torture with the 'caspie-claws' for over two days – these were iron frames that held the legs and were then heated over a brazier. In order to make her confess, she was also made to watch as her family were also tortured. Her 81-year-old husband was put in heavy irons, and heavy weight loaded on, to crush his frail body. Her son faced the agony of the 'boots', a shin press where a wedge was inserted and hammered in, and his legs were crushed with 57 lashes of the mallet. Even her seven-year-old daughter did not escape, and was tormented with the 'pilnie-winks', or thumbscrews. At this last she capitulated, confessing she had used witchcraft against the Earl of Orkney, and plotted his murder. During the subsequent trial she proclaimed her innocence, naming the foul torture as the sole reason for her admission, but to no avail. She was strangled and burned for witchcraft a few weeks before Christmas, in 1594. Just two years later, the same evidence was presented at a different trial in Edinburgh, where the Master of Orkney was accused of consorting with witches in the same plot. In this case the evidence was thrown out of court because it had been obtained under torture, and the man was acquitted of the crime.

Suspected witches would be tortured with iron shoes, which were clamped to their feet and heated.

Confessions under torture ranged from the sedate to the extreme and fanciful. Suicide was not an option for the accused; any person taking their own life when being investigated for the crime in Scotland would be dragged behind a horse and then buried under the gallows. The only escape from the excruciating pain was to confess, and be condemned to death. In England, fewer than 500 people faced execution for the crime of witchcraft, yet, shockingly, 2,500 people in Scotland were executed for this crime. The fate of those who confessed under horrendous torture in Scotland and the Channel Islands (and in Europe) was often to be burned alive at the stake.

A notorious witch trial in Britain was the case of the Lancashire Witches, in Lancaster in 1612. The 12 people accused were charged with murdering ten people using witchcraft. The most dangerous and malicious of the accused was said to be Demdike, an 80-year-old widow from the Forest of Pendle, who was accused of being an agent of the Devil. She confessed to meeting a devil – in the guise of a boy – in the depths of Pendle Wood one day, who had offered anything she asked for in return for her immortal soul. In her 'confession' she described how this familiar, called Tibb, appeared to her time and time again until, in the sixth year, the visitations became more dramatic, with him appearing as a dog, jumping up onto her knee to drink blood from under her arm, only disappearing when she called upon Jesus to save the child sleeping on her lap. Tibb's activities supposedly also included helping her to exact revenge on a miller's son who had wronged her. Demdike also confessed to knowing how to injure or take a life by making clay images ('poppets') that were pricked with pins or thorns, or thrown into flames.' Yet Demdike denied responsibility for undertaking acts such as these, instead accusing members of the rival Chattox family of similar behaviour, described to her by Tibb.

In reality, beneath all this fabrication, the Lancashire Witches were caught up in a feud between two warring families – the Demdike and Chattox families – both thought to have been in the business of serving the community in the guise of witches by offering services such as healing. The rift between the rival households was heightened by fabricated accounts of the evils committed by each opposing clan. All that this achieved was to ensure that members of both families faced trial for witchcraft. Out of the nine women and two men from Pendle who went to trial, ten were found guilty and sentenced to death by hanging. Gawthorpe Hall, reputedly one of the most haunted buildings in Lancashire, has nefarious links to this infamous trial, being then owned by Hugh and Anne Shuttleworth, and their son Colonel Richard Shuttleworth – who were also landlords to both the witch Chattox and her daughter, Anne. The latter was accused of the murder of Richard's servant, Robert Nutter, and it's said that the ghost of Richard Shuttleworth walks the corridors still. With the beginning of the Enlightenment, the belief in witchcraft began to wane in polite society, but in poor, rural communities, despite Christianity, the witch hunts continued, and belief in the ills of witchcraft lingered for many years, with people still freely assaulted and killed by their communities, all under the biblical guise of condemning the evils of the Devil.

In the past, witchcraft was regarded as evil, a thing of the Devil, but sorcery and folk magic were seen as divided into two realms – either white or black magic – roughly equating to good and bad. British folklore is full of tales of 'cunning folk', folk healers who served the community by dabbling in 'white' magic. While references to such figures are found as far back as the Dark Ages, the name itself only came into use in the early modern period. Before this, magical folk of this sort were known simply as *wiccan*, or witches, and later enchanters, sorcerers, and *nigromauncers* (necromancers). All took on the same tasks: performing magic for the illiterate folk of the towns and villages who needed rid of some malady, or a charm to avert evil forces or a spell to attract love. The charms often called upon plants, herbs, and the planets – naming the signs of the zodiac or constellations – and also on the saints and angels for their help and protection. White magic was called upon for such tasks as finding hidden treasure, identifying thieves, and warding off evil spirits, elves, and witches. Despite their tendency to mix Christianity with arcane white magic, the Church condemned all kinds of magic alike.

An early example of a cunning man's talents is that of Robert Berewold who, in 1382, used 'turning the loaf' to find a drinking bowl stolen from a home in St Mildred, Poultry, in London. Turning the loaf was a method of divination that involved sinking a wooden peg into the top of a loaf of bread, then placing four knives at the sides. A list of names was then recited, either aloud or mentally, and the loaf supposedly turned when the name of the thief was uttered. Unfortunately for Robert, the would-be thief, one Johanna Wolsy, was less than impressed with his efforts, and accused him of lying. He was put in the public stocks, with the same loaf of bread used in his divining hung about his neck as a sore reminder, and also ordered to attend church

White magic was called upon for tasks such as finding hidden treasure.

the next week to confess his crime in front of the congregation.

In the nineteenth century, crystal gazing to tell the future, using herbs gathered under the influence of certain planets, for recovering lost and stolen objects, and advising in matters of the heart, were routinely practised among the fortune-tellers and 'wise men' of the common folk, throughout Britain. John Harland and Thomas Wilkinson, in their *Lancashire Folklore*, describe Owd Rollinson, a gaffer (overseer) from Roe Green in Worsley. In the evenings he would cast horoscopes, predict the future by gazing into magic glasses and employ charms against illness. One speciality was a charm against haemorrhaging, and the tale is that a young boy, sent to fetch just such a charm from Owd Rollinson when his uncle was thought to be bleeding to death, returned with a square of parchment with strange characters written on it. Instructions were that his uncle should sew the charm into a small bag, and wear it so that it touched the skin just above his heart. The man followed the instructions, and we're told that he recovered fully. The cunning-folk were often seen by later scholars as frauds and charlatans, whose practice was mired in superstition rather than in any form of science.

Alchemy in the Middle Ages in Britain was seen as the stuff of scientific enquiry – fashionable amongst the upper classes – and by the Late Middle Ages the lure of finding the elixir of life, or transforming base metals into gold, had become a seductive prospect. The thirteenth-century alchemist Raymond Lully claimed that he was invited to England at the request of Edward I who, in the secret chamber of St Katherine, in the Tower of London, witnessed him turning common crystals to diamonds, or what he called 'adamant'. In 1438, the credulous Henry VI reputedly commissioned three philosophers to make gold for him, unsuccessfully. In the fifteenth century, a law made 'multiplying metal into gold' a felony – presumably to protect the currency at the time, if the alchemy had succeeded. Both alchemy and astrology were at that time illustrious pursuits for many learned men, including the infamous Dr John Dee, warden of Christ's College in Manchester in the late sixteenth century, and his assistant, the 'seer' Sir Edward Kelley.

It was easy for even the most learned and respected men to fall in – and out – of favour with royalty, and the law, when dabbling in what were considered the 'Black Arts'. Dr Dee was given a pension by King Edward VI (which he relinquished for the rectory of Upton-on-Severn) but soon after, in 1555, was accused of practising sorcery against Queen Mary's life, and imprisoned. No charges were made, due to a lack of evidence, and he was freed. Once Elizabeth I came to the throne, Dee once more rose to favour as the Queen's trusted advisor; one occasion summoned urgently, after the discovery in Lincoln's Inn Fields of a wax effigy of the Queen with a nail driven through the chest, and on another sent on a long journey across Europe to consult philosophers about her health.

10

GHOSTS AND HISTORICAL HAUNTINGS

F olklore is full of suggestions to either banish or communicate with the supernatural. One suggestion to banish ghosts was to read the Bible backwards. In Shropshire, and elsewhere, it's said a ghost can do no harm unless you speak to it. If legends are to be believed, the lanes and historic homes of Britain are crammed with the spirits of the dead – old soldiers re-enacting marches, lords wandering through the crowded corridors of once private stately homes and kings calling from banqueting halls in the depths of the night. There are numerous accounts of spirits still walking the dark, night-time streets and hallways of Britain, and the country is filled with the ghosts of everyone from kings to countesses, highway men to infamous thieves and scoundrels.

Some of the most famous ghosts stories feature Anne Boleyn, the second wife of Henry VIII, a reputed adulteress, who was led

to her execution on the block in 1536 for high treason. To this day, some say Anne Boleyn was innocent of these crimes while others think of her as nefarious and scheming. Perhaps it is not surprising that her unquiet spirit and tortured soul is said still to roam the Tower of London and to haunt Tower Green, where she was finally beheaded. Some report blood-curdling sightings at Windsor Castle, where Anne is apparently to be seen screaming, rushing down a corridor still clutching her severed head, while at Hampton Court she often appears, it is said, dressed in a dark dress, again without her head. Yet more chilling still is a tale from 1864, at Hampton Court, when a soldier claimed to have accosted a woman in white near the Lieutenant's lodgings. When challenged she said nothing, to which the soldier thrust his bayonet into the woman, but to his dismay he felt no flesh, nor bone, and the weapon met only the night air. In this tale, an officer at the Tower corroborated his story, having witnessed the whole thing from a window. A fantastical manifestation of Anne is said to occur each year on 19 May – the day of her death – at Blickling Hall, the sumptuous Jacobean house in Norfolk that was her birthplace. Anne arrives with her head in her lap, sitting in a ghostly carriage, pulled by a headless horseman, and up to four headless horses, before wandering the house and gardens through the night, only to disappear at sunrise.

Anne Boleyn's unquiet spirit is said to roam the Tower of London.

Every stately home has, it seems, its own ghost. Oxburgh Hall, also in Norfolk, has a ghostly story of love and betrayal. The tale goes that a lady in Tudor dress is often seen roaming around the house by visitors. She is said to be the Countess Miranda, who jumped to her death from the North Bedroom, drowning in the moat below, after her marriage to the Lord's son was forbidden. In Newton House in Carmarthenshire, visitors claim to have felt invisible hands grasping them around the throats – in the eighteenth century, Lady Elinor Cavendish was strangled there by a suitor. Even more gruesome, a well-known tale from Loughton in Essex says that the highwayman Dick Turpin threatened an elderly woman with being roasted over a fire if she didn't reveal where she'd hidden her coins. His fate for this vile crime, the tale continues, is to gallop down Trap's Hill three times a year, whereupon the vengeful woman's spirit jumps on to his back and the two ride off together. Perhaps understandably, observing their ghostly ride is supposed to bring bad luck. Meanwhile, in Yorkshire, the less well-known ghosts try make their presence felt. At White Cross, between Leven and Riston, it is said that the ghost of a headless woman was the terror of passing coachmen, jumping up behind the driver to slap his ears!

A different ghostly presence said to be roaming Britain's dark places is the hell-hound, which appears with various names and forms in different regions. In Suffolk the hell-hound it is considered harmless, but only if left well alone. The tale goes that a hell-hound, with the head of a dog and body of a monk, guards a gold hoard at Clopton Hall in Stowmarket.

> *A hell-hound is described as a black dog whose footfall often makes no sound.*

More usually, the hell-hound is described as a black dog with shaggy fur and fiery saucers for eyes (sometimes having a single eye), whose footfalls often make no sound. In most areas it is regarded as an omen of death or a terrible curse. This is the case for the barguest, in Yorkshire, a similar spectre that takes the shape of a bear or black dog and is said to haunt lonely streets at night, as well as gates and stiles. Like the Irish banshee, its howls are heard in the depths of the night by the person who is doomed to die.

Other famous examples from the Yorkshire region include the Padfoot of Pontefract and the Barguest of York – the latter

said to prey on lone travellers in the narrow snickelways. In 1644
a barguest was said to have appeared to a group of soldiers, and
one (purportedly) sober guard at midnight reported grisly ghosts
skipping from their graves, and a 'barr-guest' in the form of a
bear, dog and hog. In Lancashire, the barguest is known as Trash,
Skriker or Striker, and once again its screams are meant to presage
a person's death. Although sometimes appearing instead as a white
cow or horse, the spectre is usually a huge, shaggy-haired dog – this
time with enormous feet that make squelching sounds as he walks.

If followed, he will turn his fiery eyes on the pursuer and walk backwards, only breaking his fearsome gaze once their attention waivers – at which point he will disappear either by jumping into a pool or sinking into the ground at their feet.

In Norfolk he is known Black Shuck or Old Shuck, and is famous for his eerie howling – again a clue that someone will die soon after. Local legend has it that the fearsome dog was first seen in the night by a twelfth-century servant boy at Bungay Castle, who subsequently died of shock. After several more visitations, in 1577 his appearance coincided with a storm so violent that the church itself quaked, terrifying the locals so much that they thought Doomsday itself had arrived. As related by the Reverend Abraham Fleming, in his pamphlet, *A Straunge and Terrible Wunder*, the story is that the church suddenly grew very dark, and a fiendish dog appeared with flashes of fire, cavorting around like the Devil himself. The dog ran

> *Skriker, if followed, will turn his fiery eyes on the pursuer and walk backwards.*

between two parishioners, who were knelt in prayer at the time, and wrung their necks, killing them and also harming others. A little while later, Black Shuck appeared at a nearby church at Blythburgh, swinging down from a main beam of the old roof to wreak his mischief. Here, a further two men and a boy were killed, and a fourth suffered a burnt hand, before the dog bolted from the church. To this day, marks on the church door are said to have been left by the hound's fearsome claws as he charged away on that fateful night.

Not long ago the bones of a 7ft (just over 2m) long giant hound were found at Leiston Abbey in Suffolk – just a few miles from Bungay Castle. They date back to the sixteenth century. Perhaps it's the evidence that those Black Shuck believers have been waiting for.

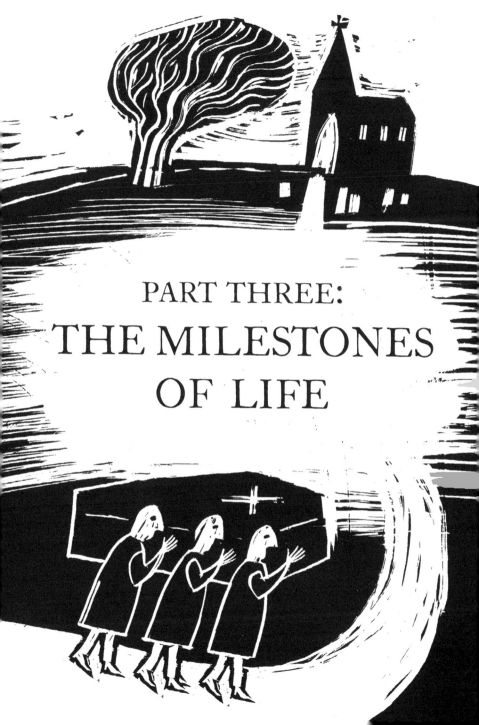

PART THREE:
THE MILESTONES OF LIFE

11

BIRTH, CHANGELINGS AND CHIME HOURS

I n the past, pregnancy and birthing were often deadly for both mother and child, and also unavoidable. Both were steeped in superstitions that were supposed to ensure the safety of their souls against spirits and other creatures that might prey upon them, as well as to avert bad luck, illness and death.

Prior to modern medicine, conceiving was in itself a complicated business that depended very much on luck and was enveloped in superstition. For those who ached for a child, rocking an empty cradle was thought to rock a new baby into it; for those who wanted to ward off such happenings, rice was believed to prevent a woman falling pregnant. This belief was so widespread that at one point there was a public outcry over giving rice to the poor, it being said that the rich did this on purpose to curb the population of unfortunates. Women on bedrest were often called 'the lady in the straw', as beds were frequently stuffed with straw. A piece of cold iron was sometimes placed in the bed of an expectant mother in Scotland to protect them from being spirited away by the fairies. Along the east coast of England it was believed that babies could only be born when the tide was in.

Customs for what to do after the birth abound, and are closely tied in with the luck the child will have through its life. The mattress was always turned after the child had arrived, right up until the mid-eighteenth century in Lancashire, yet this should not be done until a month after the birth, and a nineteenth-century Liverpool nurse insisted it would be bad luck to do so at any time before this, and would never allow it on her watch! Across the whole of Britain there is a superstition that it's lucky to take a child upstairs straight after the birth, but unlucky for it to be taken downstairs, for then it will never rise to riches and distinction in the afterlife.

For those in bungalows, it's apparently suitable to hold the baby and climb a few steps of a ladder, or even stand on a chair, for the same effect. Other birth superstitions

> *It's lucky to carry a child upstairs after birth, but bad luck to carry it downstairs.*

are that both mother and child should come downstairs for the first time on a Sunday, to ensure success. It was once said that babies should never be weighed after birth, for a weighed baby would never thrive and might even die. In Durham superstition it's bad luck for a baby to look into a mirror before it's a year old. Yorkshire tradition states that a baby should be held by a maiden before anyone else, for luck. It's often considered unlucky to cut the nails of a baby in the first 12 months after its birth, even now, and in Suffolk it's believed that this will make them a thief. It's recommended in many places across Britain that the nails should be bitten instead. In Scotland only the mother may cut a baby's nails, and it's thought good practice to burn the cuttings afterwards to stop witches from stealing them – superstition has it that the same should be done when the baby's hair is cut. Some Suffolk babies were washed with gin by nurses to ensure a fine complexion, while the mother's face was also washed in gin, as it was believed being with child would bring on an undesired tan. Here, the babies were also rubbed over with lard and then wrapped in a scorched linen rag. Finally, anyone who kisses a baby is thought to leave behind a little of their own temperament – so permission should always be asked, in case yours is deemed to be unsuitable!

The time of birth is important in folklore and children born at twilight, or midnight, are frequently said to be able to see spirits and predict the future. Those born in the 'chime hours' (these differ depending on which region you consult, but especially midnight) are thought to be particularly gifted at seeing the dead, can never be bewitched and are often called 'chime children'. One story from Sussex in the nineteenth century tells of a chime child being beckoned from her dinner by a figure outside.

In Suffolk, babies were washed with gin for a fine complexion.

The girl went out to meet the figure, yet it glided away as she drew near. Even as late as the beginning of the nineteenth century, many children were not expected to live beyond the age of five, so it's unsurprising that it was seen as incredibly lucky to be the seventh child of a seventh child. Such children are said to be imbued with special preternatural powers of the second sight in Scotland, and in Somerset bestowed with healing powers of touch, usually attributed only to kings.

In nineteenth-century Scotland a feast called a merry meht would take place to celebrate a birth. People would take away pieces of the cryin kebback, or 'indispensible cheese', to give out to their friends after visiting the new mother and child. Cheese was a prominent part of the birth customs in Lancashire

too, where the new father would provide a large cheese, along with a cake, called the 'groaning cheese' and 'groaning cake' respectively. Slices would be given out to guests, and young women would often secrete these away under their pillows, in the hope of bringing dreams of their future husbands. In the Borders, the groaning cheese can also be called the 'shooten cheese'. Here, fathers cut a 'whang-o'luck' from the edge of the cheese, which is then divided up for the unmarried female guests. Woe betide any man that nipped his finger while doing so, however, for that meant that the child would die before reaching adulthood. In Oxfordshire, a ring was cut into the middle of the cheese, and the child would be passed through it for luck on their christening day.

Although considered bad luck for the parents to buy anything for the child or accept any gifts before its birth, gifts for the newly born child were, and are still, customary – so much so that this tradition is called 'presenting' in Lancashire. It's still unlucky not to present a gift to a child in Scotland when first visiting to see it, and hanselling is still an active tradition: a silver coin is placed directly in the child's hand, or laid on the child's pillow, as a gift for luck. Not all gifts for babies are so innocent: It's said that Cameron of Lochiel received a small, silver shoe from the infernal spirits, intended to be put on the left foot of every newborn male in the family, to bestow courage and strength against his enemies. The family carried out this custom until 1746, when the house went up in flames, destroying the lucky shoe, and the tradition was no more. In Suffolk, it was once customary for each visitor to give the nurse a present as well.

From the advent of Christianity in Britain both mother and child were seen to be in peril until the baptism of the infant, and the churching of the mother was also still commonly practised until well into the twentieth century. This was a ceremony where a mother was blessed after recovering from giving birth, symbolically 'purified' of the uncleanliness of childbirth, and a thanks was given for her survival – a very real concern, before modern medicine. Christian traditions still practise traces of similar rites today, often in the form of a blessing of the mother during the child's baptism, although any ideas the mother being 'unclean' are now long gone, of course. At one time in Scotland common superstition was that churching was needed, or the fairies would steal nursing mothers away to the mountains, in order for them to suckle the fairy young. Families and local communities often mark a birth in Britain by having a drink to celebrate, either at the pub, or at the child's home after a baptism, called 'wetting the baby's head'. This tradition is relatively modern, and first appeared at the end of the nineteenth century.

Baptising a child as soon as possible was, in the past, regarded as vital because of the belief that the child would be in danger of being influenced by spirits, captured by fairies, and easily cursed by the evil eye until this was done. More importantly, to a God-fearing community, a Christian baptism would safeguard its soul if it should die soon after birth – much more common in the past than now. Perhaps as a warning, it was said that the wailing spirits of unbaptised children could be heard in the trees and dells across Scotland. It was seen as unlucky to name a child before baptism. Various other Scottish traditions include washing the newborn in salted water, which it would have to sip three times to protect it from the evil eye – coral beads were often hung around the child's neck, for the same reason.

In Devon, the pixies were thought to be the souls of children who had died before they were baptised. In Suffolk it was a very good sign for a child to cry at the baptism

Fairies would steal nursing mothers away so they could suckle their fairy young.

when water was poured on its head; if it did not, it was believed to be too good for this world and thought that it would soon die. In Yorkshire it was believed that any child baptised in a new church was destined to die. In Liverpool, the *Morning Herald* of 18 June 1860 reported a young woman who was apprehended attempting to murder her child by covering it with soil, having broken into a gentleman's grounds for the purpose. Her defence was that she had the child baptised first, and it was common knowledge that an unbaptised child could not die. In the Borderlands it was considered very unlucky to walk over the graves of unbaptised children, and anyone who dared to do so would suffer dire consequences, such as the burning skin affliction of 'grave-merels' or 'grave-scab', breathing difficulties or trembling limbs. The remedy for those so afflicted was rather complicated: it involved donning a sack made from linen produced in a field spread with manure from a farmyard that hadn't been disturbed for 40 years.

The linen itself also had to rather high spec: spun by Habetrot herself (a fairy spirit of spinning wheels) and with those involved in its manufacture, right up to the tailor who sewed the sack, all honest people. A bit of an ask.

Children throughout Britain were considered at risk of being stolen by the fairies, particularly if especially pretty. Sitting an open Bible next to a child left unattended was thought to ward off the fairies, and stop the babe from being stolen and swapped – or 'changed' – for a changeling. St John's Eve was thought to be a particular time for stealing children. The changelings that had supposedly replaced the child were said to cry a lot, dislike being touched and were often unresponsive when spoken to. Others were said to sometimes fly into a great rage, and some would have issues with eating and lose weight. Often these symptoms would appear in a child overnight, giving rise to the superstition of a sudden fairy swap for a changeling. It's now believed these folk superstitions might have arisen to explain the sudden change in behaviour of children with autism, or other conditions. In Lincolnshire, it's said that – perhaps today more in jest than genuine superstition – that if a good-tempered child becomes irritable suddenly, without reason, they must have been 'changed'. Folk tales describe some changelings as being much older than the child they replaced. One story speaks of a changeling from Emlyn, on the border of Carmarthenshire and Cardiganshire in Wales, who was as old as the real child's grandfather. In this tale, the infant was swapped one sunny day when his mother left him to go out to the fields. She returned at his cries, only to find a strange, old-looking creature in his place. The stories goes on to describe how a wizard was summoned, who placed the child before the hearth. He then ordered that a shovel be heated in the flames until it was red-hot

> *An open Bible left by an unattended child would ward off fairies.*

and then held in front of the changeling's face – at which the changeling fled. In many stories, changelings are discovered simply by showing them something odd. A tale from Corwrion, North Wales, dating back to the fourteenth century and collected by John Reece in his *Celtic Folklore, Welsh and Manx*, in 1901, tells of a mother complaining about her young twins that would bicker and cry all through the night. A witch asked the mother if she was sure that they had not been changed, and recommended a method to find out. She advised the mother to take an eggshell and brew beer inside, to see what the children would say. The children raised their heads to watch, and one remarked, 'I remember seeing an oak having an acorn', while the other said, 'And I remember seeing a hen having an egg'. One finished, 'but I do not remember before seeing anybody brew beer in the shell of a hen's egg.' On reporting this to the witch, the mother was told to take both children to the bridge and drop them off it at once, which of course she obediently did. She found her real children waiting at home on her return.

A witch advised a mother to brew beer inside an eggshell to tell whether her children were changelings.

Many of the proposed solutions to having your child stolen were harsh or brutal, and resulted in the deaths of children who were left out in the woods overnight, deliberately – a child that perished was a fairy while one that survived was a real, human child, supposedly. The Reverend James Rust, in his *Druidism Exhumed* from 1871, remarked on knowing of at least one baby recovered from the fairies in the north of Scotland, using the following rather suspect method. The child should be taken to the remains of a barrow, stone circle or cairn where fairies are known to frequent – as indicated by strange moaning, rushing sounds in the place. The parents should leave the child in this enchanted place (along with fairy offerings of bread, cheese, milk, eggs, and meat – poultry specifically, for an unspecified reason) and then creep away, to watch from a distance until after midnight has struck. If the offerings are gone when they return, they can be sure that the fairies have accepted their gift, and their own child is safely back in their hands.

Weaning a child was also steeped in tradition, some with its roots in folk remedies and stories. Good Friday was said to be the best day for weaning. In Scotland, specifically around the banks of the Ale and Teviot, mothers would wear blue woollen threads or cords around their neck until their children were weaned as a charm to ward off ephemeral fevers. The threads would be passed down through the female line. In Sussex, similarly, peony root necklaces were put on children to help with teething, as peony was thought to chase away evil spirits and work as protection from negative forces. In Durham, any teeth that were lost should be burned, and the gap filled with salt. There is a record of one young woman in nineteenth-century Sussex

In Scotland, mothers would wear blue cords around their necks to prevent fevers in their newborns.

believing that a child's tooth should never be thrown away in case it was chewed by an animal because, in that case, the child's new tooth would resemble the tooth of that animal. Apparently, the mother of an unfortunate man of her acquaintance – Master Simmons – threw the poor man's tooth into the pig trough, and he was left with a pig's tooth in his upper jaw for the rest of his sorry life.

12

LOVE AND MARRIAGE

Today, in British society, a wedding is regarded as a commitment of shared love between two people. In centuries past, in more wealthy aristocratic households, marriages were often arranged and a couple might not even know each other before they wed. In poorer communities, women were chattels, married for childbirth and to keep the home, while same-sex marriage did not exist in any form until recently in Britain. Marriage was often the only future a girl could imagine, as her status in life depended on that of her future husband. Although actually getting married was surprisingly easy – in the Middle Ages and later, simply consenting to marriage was sufficient, and this didn't have to be in church or with a priest – the reality was that women were essentially property that was handed from the possession of her father into the hands of another man. Indeed, wives could be sold at market – with their agreement, until well into the nineteenth century. A nagging wife, or 'shrew' as she might be called, could be ducked in the local pond or led around the town at the request of her husband, with a brank, or scold's bridle, fitted over her head. A prong of metal would hold down her tongue, and some of these had spikes – such as one from Stockport, dating from the seventeenth century – that would cruelly cut into her mouth when she moved. The Congleton brank could be chained to the fireplace by the gaoler in a woman's own home, to keep her there until her husband considered that she'd had enough punishment. The last known record of this barbaric and degrading practice was a late as 1834, in Kendal, Cumbria.

To predict a future partner's initial, you could peel an apple in one strip and throw it over your shoulder.

Despite the brutal realities of marriage for many in the Middle Ages and later, young girls often became enthralled with the idea of predicting what their future husbands might be like, and their were various 'methods' to find this out. To predict a future partner's first initial in Yorkshire you could peel an apple in one strip, and then throw it over your left shoulder. Whatever letter this formed was the initial of your future love. To find out his occupation, one could use the art of molybdomancy: dropping molten lead or tin into water, and the shape it forms would provide a clue. A hammer shape might indicate a blacksmith, while a sickle would indicate a farmer – given that it's so open to interpretation, you might well want to try it today to spot a computer or a stethoscope, perhaps! To see if a husband would be fair- or dark-haired, you could spin a white-handled knife; when it stops, a blade pointed towards you indicates dark-haired, away from you, fair. Another prediction sought was the years a young woman would have to wait before her marriage. In the Midlands, a rather hen-dependent method of divining this was to give the first pancake of Shrove Tuesday to a cockerel; the girl must wait the same number of years before marriage as the number of hens that arrived to share it.

It is possible to see an apparition of your future husband, particularly on Halloween, when, superstition says, their image can be seen in a mirror by candlelight. In Buckinghamshire, a nineteenth-century nurse swore to her charge that she knew of three successful instances of using the following method to obtain a visit from your future husband. Light a candle and insert two pins through the wick as it is burning, while reciting this rhyme:

> It's not this candle alone I stick,
> But [insert sweetheart's name]'s heart I mean to prick;
> Whether he be asleep or awake,
> I'd have him come to me and speak.

The nurse continued that two of the visits did not work out well. One girl had indeed married the man she had seen – but unhappily. Another broke up with her beloved immediately – he made the visit unwillingly, claiming he knew that the girl had 'been about some devilment or other' and that 'No tongue could tell what she had made him suffer', and would never speak to her again. Perhaps a safe method of conjuring an apparition of your future husband is this folk rite, found in many parts of Britain. At Halloween, place your shoes in the form the letter T – representing Thor's hammer, or *Mjöllnir* – and then repeat the following rhyme:

> I cross my shoes in the shape of a 'T'
> Hoping my true love to see
> Not in his best or worst array
> But in the clothes of every day.

Many young girls hoped to have dreams predicting a vision of their future husband on the eve of St Agnes (on 20 January), a saint martyred in fourth-century Rome for refusing to marry against her will, who later became the patron saint of virgins. On this evening, when going to bed, a girl could take a sprig of rosemary and a sprig of thyme, sprinkle them with water three times, and place one in each of her shoes, which she then placed on either side of the bed. To ensure a dream of her future husband she would then recite:

> St Agnes, that's to lovers kind,
> Come ease the trouble of my mind.

Magic was commonly used to capture the affections of an unwilling lover, or demand the return of someone who had drifted away in a relationship. One malevolent spell was to take a lamb's shoulder blade, stick a knife into it, and recite the following rhyme:

> 'Tis not the bone I wish to stick
> But my true love's heart I mean to prick
> Wishing him neither rest nor sleep
> Until he come to me to speak.

There are various spells and rituals supposed to keep your sweetheart's love. A rather gruesome love spell, recorded in the nineteenth century, says to place the tongue of a turtle dove in your mouth and then talk to, and kiss, your lover – they will supposedly become so besotted with you that they will never even glance at anyone else! If this is a little too much for you, try taking a few feathers from a rooster's tail and pressing them into your sweetheart's hand three times – it's said this will have a similar outcome.

Valentine's Day, celebrated on 14 February throughout the Western world since the eighteenth century, is by far the best-known festival that celebrates love and courting. It may have its roots in the Norman festival of Galatin's Day, or possibly earlier

in the darker Roman festival of Lupercalia. Cards and gifts proclaiming love for the receiver are anonymously sent. Divination is common on this night too, and one tradition is to write the names of potential suitors on small pieces of paper, wrap them in clay, and drop them in water. The piece of paper that rises to the surface first contains the name of your future partner. Another festival, 'Tutti Day' in Hungerford, Berkshire, is celebrated there on the Tuesday after Easter, to commemorate the day when John of Gaunt granted fishing and grazing rights in the fourteenth century. Also called 'Hock Tuesday' or 'Hocktide', the town crier summons residents to the court, and later that day the two elected 'Tuttimen', carrying poles topped with flowers and an orange, are followed by the town children as they visit each house to collect their 'dues' – either a penny, or a kiss. Traditionally, girls would bar their doors, yet the men often carried ladders, and so stole kisses through their conveniently open windows. Rather than being a sinister affair, the visits were seen as jest, and women and men would take turns to collect the dues.

Presenting your love with a knife will cut the bond between you.

By the way, a suitor should never present their love with a knife, on any occasion, as in Lancashire this is thought to cut the bond between them, and the relationship will be fraught with trouble from that day on. It's also very bad luck to go courting on Fridays in this region; in the nineteenth century, bands of musicians might follow anyone found attempting to do so, banging pan-lids until had reached their homes. Certain folklore pertains to whether a couple are a good match. A sure sign of love, or sudden marriage, is when a ring falls off the finger of a man who is not yet spoken for, and rolls to the feet of an unmarried woman. While anyone who hears a robin redbreast singing under their window on a Wednesday, while courting, is said soon to share a happy marriage. Happiness is also predicted for anyone who sees a hare run across their path on a Saturday morning.

Today, as in the past, certain things stand out as having incredibly important traditional significance at a marriage ceremony, the main three of these being the wedding dress, the rings and the cake. The colour of the dress was very important, and green was viewed as particularly unlucky, being considered a fairy colour that would invite trouble, right up until the nineteenth century. Incidentally, it was only in more recent years, after the marriage of Queen Victoria in 1840, that white became popular, in imitation of her wedding dress. Variations on the following rhyme are still widely circulating today, to warn any unsuspecting bride against the pitfalls of choosing an inauspicious colour:

> Married in red, you'll wish yourself dead.
> Married in yellow, ashamed of your fellow.
> Married in green, ashamed to be seen.
> Married in pink, your spirit will sink.
> Married in grey, you will go far away.
> Married in black, you will wish yourself back.

It's still a common superstition that the bride should never wear her full wedding outfit before the wedding. It's also considered very bad luck for the groom to see the dress before the wedding. Some say that the veil, which traditionally protects from the evil eye, should never be seen in the mirror by the bride and shouldn't be tried on before the day of the wedding. Strangely, it's good luck to find a spider crawling on your wedding dress. Many brides today still follow the requirement to wear:

> Something old, something new,
> Something borrowed, and something blue.

The charming symbolism behind the popular rhyme is that the old and new represent a link to past and future, respectively, a borrowed item connects the bride to the present, and blue symbolises the traditional purity of the bride. The rings exchanged at a wedding symbolise endless, unbroken love, and the loss of the ring, unsurprisingly, signifies loss of love. Traditionally, some see the finger a ring is worn on as significant: the index finger shows that someone is looking for love, while a ring on the little finger of the left hand shows that someone is uninterested in getting married. The third finger of the left hand is traditionally the one reserved for the wedding ring, as it was (wrongly) believed that the main artery runs from this finger directly to the heart. It's considered bad luck for anyone to lend their wedding ring, or generally take it off for any reason, while it's very bad luck indeed to wear the ring at all before the marriage. Wedding rings should always be new – never second-hand – or any issues associated

with their past use will carry over to the new marriage. It's said that if the groom drops the ring during the wedding the marriage is doomed. While a wedding band is often unadorned gold, the choice of gemstones for a ring can have great significance. Traditionally, little meaning was given to the engagement ring but, today, the list of gemstone symbolism might be better applied to it. Opals and emeralds are seen as bad luck for many, unless they happen to be your birthstone, while pearls symbolise that tears will follow. Sapphires offer good luck and happiness, while diamonds are said to be the luckiest choice of all, and lead to strong and enduring love. Some gemstone symbolism goes back for centuries, while some is more recent.

Traditionally in Britain, the timing of a wedding was significant. May was traditionally seen as an inauspicious month to marry, as it's seen as belonging to the old, and in Ancient Rome it was a month for remembering the dead. Until not that long ago, it was regarded as inappropriate to marry during Lent, while, in contrast, June is still seen as the best month for marriage, as it was in the past. Friday is an inauspicious day to begin anything – including marriage – and Thursday is a very unlucky day to wed in all but Northamptonshire, where Monday is also favoured. This traditional rhyme gives some common associations for each day of the week:

Monday for health,
Tuesday for wealth,
Wednesday the best of all,
Thursday for losses,
Friday for crosses,
And Saturday for no luck at all.

Today, confetti – or sometimes rice – is often thrown at the newly wedded couple after the ceremony. Originally in Britain this would have been corn, as a symbol of fertility. Chimneysweeps were often paid to attend weddings, well into the twentieth century, since a kiss from them would bestow luck on a new bride. In the nineteenth century in Britain, 'throwing the slipper' was a common custom: people would throw shoes after the newly married couple as they left for their honeymoon, to wish them good luck. Various other superstitions purport to bring good luck to the new marriage, and many are still enjoyed today, even if not taken quite so seriously. The bride should always be carried over the threshold of her new house (or more likely today, honeymoon hotel room) to avoid perils, a possible remnant of the belief that spirits often lingered around thresholds and entranceways. If the couple want children, the bride herself should cut the wedding cake; allowing someone else to do this will mean they will be forever childless. In Britain as elsewhere, the wedding cake has always represented luck. In days gone by it would be broken over the bride's head, and guests would scramble to pick up the pieces as symbols of this good fortune. Even today, pieces of the cake are still often sent to absent friends so that they are able to share in this luck, even when unable to attend the ceremony. In Christian marriage ceremonies there was also a tradition of keeping the top tier of a cake for the christening of the first child. In Yorkshire the bride might throw a plate filled with pieces from the cake from an upstairs window when she returned to her father's house. The guests would gather below to see if the plate reached the ground intact – seen as a good omen. Fortunately, the plate breaking into pieces was seen as even more fortuitous, and the more pieces the better. Cake – in the past a chance to enjoy the unusual luxury of rich, costly food – remains integral to many occasions, from birth to marriage, and its importance and luck-giving properties should never be underestimated! After the marriage ceremony, right up to the Victorian era, the couple would often be accompanied to bed, to ensure the consummation of the marriage. When undressing, the bride would throw her stockings over her shoulder, and whichever maid should catch them was thought to be getting married next. This tradition is echoed in the modern-day throwing of the bouquet at a Christian wedding celebration.

Same-sex marriage was only legalised in Britain in 2013. Homosexuality was, shockingly, still a crime in Britain until 1967, when it was partially decriminalised, and much of the stigma faced is still being battled today as an aftermath. Because of this little folklore has been recorded about same-sex relationships in Britain. One piece of folklore that does exist is the tradition of Polari as a form of slang within the gay community in Britain, which goes back to the nineteenth century, while some claim it has roots in the sixteenth century. It was also used by actors, fairground workers, and by merchant navy sailors, among others, and is said to have been a mixture of Italian, Romany, and London slang. Paul Baker tells us, in his book *Polari – The Lost Language of Gay Men*, that it was used in the first 70 years of the twentieth century in cities with an established gay subculture, yet fell into disuse soon after. It was used by many who found the need for privacy in the face of persecution and prejudice. Words include vada, meaning 'look'; bona, meaning 'good', and eek, meaning 'face'.

> *Before the catching of the bouquet, maids were required to catch the bride's stocking as she undressed.*

13

HOME LIFE

Since the Neolithic Period, about 4000–2500BC, which saw the evolution from nomadic hunter-gathering to farming communities, the home has been at the heart of human experience. At its centre sat the hearth, the vital source of fire, which was – and remains, metaphorically – of central importance in human minds, as a source of food, of life-giving warmth, and also the light that saw our ancestors through the dark, foreboding nights. We know this because archaeologists can identify hearths from the reddening of stones, and remnants of charcoal and burnt bone in the ancient remains of mud floors from the very first houses. So the hearth was always a symbol of home, and this resounds in the many fairy and folk tales from childhood that refer to its importance, and the myths surrounding fires and the home – think of the young heroine who sweeps the ash in 'Catskin', the English version of *Cinderella*. She later uses the ash to disguise her face, but it is also a symbol of her attachment to the family home as she sets out into the world. Fire and the hearth play an important role in folklore, as by symbolising the home they also offer a sense of belonging to a place. A major theme in many of these tales is a fledgling protagonist being cast from their home – which may have become unpleasant or even dangerous for them. Destined to make his or her own way in the world, the protagonist sets out on a treacherous hero's journey.

It is traditional in many regions to light a fire before moving out of a house for the last time, then carry the hot coals from the old fireplace with you to your new dwelling, and rekindle them there in the hearth. It is said to bring luck, and some go so far as to say it means any fairies living in the old hearth will be transported to the next house, to bless the residents anew, since such fairies were often seen as a blessing, offering luck and protection. Superstition also recommends that a small hole should always be left in any house for the pixies to get out. In Lincolnshire, some say it's only deemed acceptable to poke a friend's fire if you have known them for at least seven years.

It's said that good luck is so vital to a home that it should be considered even before building begins. An 1899 account of where to site your house appears to have less to do with bricks and mortar than with keeping the fairies happy:

> Measure it out, and then turn a sod in each of the corners. These should be left for two or three nights, and if nothing happens the site can be deemed safe. A small animal – like a hen – should be killed, and the blood dripped into the four holes. Only then are you able to continue the build. If your house is found to be on a fairy walk, be warned: you should move the site immediately, for if you don't the fairies will certainly replace it!

The quest for good luck was not just reserved for special occasions; it was a thing that ran through all areas of everyday life – sometimes with practical roots. Some everyday superstitions live on – we might still shudder at the thought of putting shoes on the table, or opening an umbrella indoors – but there are others long gone that range from the mildly odd to the incredibly bizarre. For instance, it was considered bad luck to place a deck of cards on the bed, as this might cause a death. In Lancashire it was lucky to find crickets around the house and no one should kill them – there's mention of a farmer's family where someone did, after which their household crickets set about eating away at his best woollen stockings. Some may still remember that, in Suffolk, it was considered bad luck for two people to pass on the stairs, and if a spade were carried through the house it would end up digging a grave. Yorkshire tradition said a cock crowing while facing the front door of a home meant a stranger was due to arrive. Meanwhile, if you dared to leave through a different doorway to the one through which you arrived, bad luck would follow. If someone was leaving home permanently, an old shoe was often thrown across the threshold to wish them success. However, woe betide them if they return for something forgotten, bad luck would ensue unless they sat down inside before attempting to leave again. For those who worry about such things as opening an umbrella indoors, it's reassuring to know that sitting down for a few minutes before going back out, generally takes away the bad luck – a welcome relief for many!

While cleaning the house might be hard work, folklore at least suggests it can be used to ward off bad luck or evil, although sometimes in macabre ways:

> Once the floor has been swept, the dust pile should be left for three days, then covered with a black cloth made of drilling. An elm branch should be used to beat the pile. The witch must assist you, for if she doesn't, then you will also beat her to death with your efforts.

Even so, remember not to take an old broom to your new house when moving – this is very bad luck!

People went to great lengths to protect their homes in the eighteenth and nineteenth centuries, and some people still follow such superstitions today, even if in jest. Often, magical charms – everyday objects, or even animals – were hidden deep under

Throwing an old shoe over the threshold would bring good luck to someone leaving the home permanently.

the floors or hearths of a house, or in the walls or roof. This was thought to ward off malevolent forces. The most gruesome objects have to be the mummified cats found in houses around Britain. One is on display at Lavenham Guildhall in Suffolk, where it had been secreted away in the roof. Other common objects found hidden around old homes to ward off evil and ensure good luck include old shoes and witch bottles. Witch bottles were used to counter witches' curses or as love charms.

For the superstitious amongst us, dining can be an experience fraught with danger. In fairy tales, one must never take food from a mysterious house or stranger, for it represents a lurking or imminent danger – it is probably the food of evil creatures such as witches, ogres or fairies. As you might expect, the danger extends to dining in your own home, and great care must be taken when dealing with food. Sometimes the way in which food is prepared indicates good or bad luck, or shows evil influences at work. Stirring anticlockwise generally means the Devil can be 'stirred in' to the pudding, and many cooks were accused of cursing if caught mixing the wrong way. The only exception is on 'Stir-up Sunday', the last Sunday before the Christian season of Advent, when the Christmas pudding is still traditionally made by many. The pudding should be stirred

anticlockwise, to symbolise the Wise Men travelling from east to west to visit the baby Jesus, and a wish should be made while stirring. And watch out – in Dorset, a kettle that takes too long to boil might be bewitched, and probably contains a toad.

Eating holds similar pitfalls. It is incredibly important to never cross knives at the dinner table, or a quarrel will follow. The person who makes the tea should always pour, for another attempting to serve will surely bring disaster upon the house. If you accidentally break a loaf of bread in two halves, it will rain all the week. A loaf of bread shouldn't be turned upside down once a slice has been taken. And the spoon should always be pushed through the bottom of the shell of a boiled egg once eaten, to let the Devil out. In fact, a childhood rhyme from Humberside recommends it's best to break the whole shell anyway; otherwise a witch might take it, and use it to sail away to sea.

Folklore wisdom on how to conduct our personal care and grooming is also plentiful, and there are many tips for keeping hair at its best

> *It's best to break the whole eggshell to prevent a witch using it to sail to sea.*

– or just for keeping it. It is said a man should shave off his beard to cure baldness, as the beard takes some nourishment from the hair of the head. Others believe that tight hatbands cause baldness. For longer hair, many folk used to advise that singeing hair with a hot poker closes the ends of the hairs, thus keeping the nutritive juices from exuding. Spots on the fingernails apparently indicate good luck, but it's bad luck for anyone to cut their nails on a Friday in Lancashire – a rhyme provides full instructions:

> Cut your nails on a Monday, cut them for news;
> Cut them on Tuesday, a new pair of shoes;
> Cut them on Wednesday, cut them for health;
> Cut them on Thursday, cut them for wealth;

Cut them on Friday, cut them for woe;
Cut them on Saturday, a journey you'll go;
Cut them on Sunday, you cut them for evil.
For all the next week you'll be ruled by the Devil.

In times when doctors and medicine were still unavailable to most, and both of course had to be paid for, many people used 'home remedies' made from common items, such as plants, stones and bones. Even up to the mid-twentieth century a superstition still lingered that one's blood became poisoned over winter, and this poison must be released in the coming spring. A herb called 'boneset' was collected during summer and drunk as a tea in spring to act as a blood tonic and purge all such poisons for the coming year. A method of stopping a bleeding wound was to insert a small human bone: and the bleeding should cease at once. In Oxfordshire, belemnite fossils were thought to be thunderbolts that had fallen from the sky, and hence endowed with magical and curative properties. At the end of the nineteenth century, they were often scraped to make a powder, which was then applied to children's faces to cure the ailment known as 'white mouth' – an eruption of the lips, apparently. Strangely, this cure might have actually worked because of the fossil's chalky consistency. Copious amounts of gin were often seen as a remedy for worms when taken on an empty stomach, although severe warnings were often imparted about the possible side effects being 'a violent inflammatory fever', or – worse – an 'inflammatory excitement of the brain'!

Warts appear to have been a common problem, since countless remedies for them exist. You could 'buy a wart' with a penny to get rid of it, or rub it with a piece of meat and then bury the meat to make the wart go away. Additionally, it could be cured secretly by another person, if a lock of hair was cut from the nape of the sufferer's neck without them knowing – yet, be warned, the assistance of the Devil was required for success! In Lancashire tradition, warts are supposedly cured by rubbing them with a black snail, which must then be impaled on a hawthorn. Or you can rub them with a cinder, then tie this up in paper and drop it where four roads meet; this will transfer the warts to whoever opens the packet. Beware, you will get warts if you put your hands anywhere near water that eggs have been boiled in. A stye on the eyelid can also be cured – by the lick of a dog, being rubbed with a wedding ring or if struck nine times by a tom cat's tail.

Ferrets are surprisingly useful for curing whooping cough in many regions, so it's said. Reverend Hick, of Byer's Green in Durham, told of a boy who came to him with a basin of milk. It seemed his mother believed that the Reverend's family pet could help cure her bairn, or baby of the whooping cough; all that was

> *In Lancashire, warts can be cured by rubbing them with a black snail.*

needed was for the ferret to drink half the milk, and then have the baby drink the other. In Lancashire tradition, the prevention and cure is a little more complicated: whooping cough will never be caught by any child who has ridden upon a bear; but once it has set in, passing the child nine times over the back and under the belly of an ass will cure it.

And finally, shoes to the rescue again – this time as a cure for cramp. In Penzance, superstition had it that slippers placed under the bed with their soles facing upwards would do the trick, while in Lancashire you were advised to place your shoes under the bedcovers with their toes peeping out. To prevent cramp in other regions of Britain, put a bowl of water under the bed, or put sulphur or corks in either the socks or the bed. If the debilitation becomes more serious, and develops into rheumatism, it apparently helps to carry a raw potato. If all else fails, try this all-round cure: an onion fastened to the door prevents all illness.

14

WORKING LIFE

From the Middle Ages to the twentieth century, and – sadly – into present times, many working people have lived in poverty. The poor were considered unimportant in the Britain of the Middle Ages, and their working life was a matter of brute survival, earning enough to fill empty bellies and find fuel to keep warm. A lack of either food or warmth was genuinely life-threatening, and illness and death could bring even more poverty to a family. The elderly succumbed to illness easily, and children often died in infancy. For centuries there was little chance of money or social mobility for the poorer in society. People would scrape a meagre living from any opportunity that they could find, and children were set to work as soon as possible. Many trades were fraught with danger, from accidents in farming and milling, drowning at sea, collapsing mines, and all kinds of dangers in more ordinary jobs, where there were of course none of the concerns with safety that exist in Britain today. Someone might set off in the morning to their day's work but never return, and their death would bring immediate destitution to the family. To falter in your work, or be unsuccessful, was to welcome untold misfortune into your families' life – many folk who undertook even the most common jobs relied heavily on luck, superstition, and honouring the spirits of the land and seas to bless them in their toil, make them fruitful, and keep them safe.'

Many an errant youth set out, wide-eyed, on his first voyage as a sailor, perhaps enticed by the false promises of treasures and mermaids, or simply a regular wage. It was a harsh life of toil and fraught with danger, so it makes sense that seafaring was rife with superstitions. A sailor from north-east Scotland setting out from home on the morning of a voyage, would turn back to his house instantly on meeting a priest, or a woman with either red hair or a squinting eye, to begin the journey again. Both women and priests on board ship were seen as tempting fate, and the ship

It's a bad omen for a sailor to see a red-haired woman on his way to a voyage.

would be seen as destined for disaster. Certain animals were also a bad omen – to some, finding a hare, pig or pigeon on board meant the voyage was cursed from the very beginning, and might leave some sailors loath to set out at all. Specific words, it was said, should not be uttered on a ship – unsurprisingly, all mention of pigs, hares, and the clergy were frowned upon – while the word 'spoiling' was often used in place of 'drowning'. Strangely, it's thought that the sight of a naked woman at sea would ward off danger and appease the raging waves; some believe this is why the figureheads on the prows of many ships are bare-breasted women. In Cornwall, it's said ghost ships are often seen before shipwrecks occur, to forewarn the hapless crew of their fate, as are 'Jack Harry's lights' – lights that appear on a spectral ship that often looks similar to the one that is to be wrecked (many put this superstition down to a real meteorological phenomenon known as 'St Elmo's Fire').

People often sold cauls – a membrane sometimes attached to the head of a child at birth – to sailors for good luck, since they were thought to offer protection from drowning. As late as 1899, in its 19 January edition, the *Daily Mail* recorded that there was still 'some market for cauls among sailors', while signs stating that people had cauls for sale were seen around the docks of Liverpool and London as late as 1950. The going price in 1904 was shown as £3 in one advertisement, currently around £171 in today's money. Cauls were kept for other superstitious reasons too; in Suffolk, a child's caul was hung up in the house and kept covered and it was said it would 'overgive', or weep, whenever the child was ill, and wither away once death befell its owner.

Many seashore churches are dedicated to St Nicholas, as the patron saint of sailors, who had power over storms and tempests. One example in Liverpool has been used as a place of worship since the thirteenth century. At the time when ships still sailed from the docks, sailors regularly left offerings at a nearby statue of the saint to ensure a prosperous voyage, and gave another to the waves for their safe return. Sea witches were often blamed as the cause of a storm or wind rising unexpectedly during a voyage. Indeed, a nineteenth-century woman, Sarah Moore from Leigh-on-Sea, in Essex, was known locally as the Sea Witch. Legend has it that a child of any woman upsetting this fearsome figure would be cursed with a harelip, and any children who broke in to her home would spontaneously combust! Sarah made her living, in part, by waiting on the docks as ships were making their departure, offering to sell any sailor 'a fair wind' for a few pennies. One tale tells of a captain who refused to pay, only to come up against a fierce storm while at out sea, and the crew of course blamed this on the mischief of witches. The captain, perhaps to placate his superstitious crew, rushed to the bow, proclaiming he

would kill the witch, and gave the prow three hacking blows. It was said that Sarah Moore died shortly after the incident, from three strange gashes to her head.

Sighting a mermaid on a voyage would often be a bad omen, heralding bad weather or disaster. It's likely that seafarers mistook seals, walruses or other marine animals for these mythical sea creatures, with the upper body of a woman and the tail of a fish. One of the most famous Cornish legends is that of the mermaid of Zennor. The story goes that a well-dressed woman would attend church

Sea witches were often blamed for high winds during a voyage.

services in the area, enchanting the congregation with her beauty and her wonderful singing voice. Although she kept returning, she never seemed to age, and nobody could work out where she came from. One day she showed an interest in a young man, Mathey Trewella, who also had a marvellous singing voice. He followed her home, and was never seen again. A long time after, a ship came in to anchor at Pendour Cove, nearby. In one version of the tale, a mermaid soon appeared, saying that she was returning home from church and was keen to see her children, but the ship's anchor was blocking her door. The sailors raised the anchor and immediately set sail, as having seen a mermaid was considered a terrible omen. Later, the villagers all agreed that this must be the very same woman who had mysteriously enticed the young man to live with her. Legend has it that they carved her image in oak to commemorate this strange event. Whatever its true origins, the Mermaid Chair, with her image, can still be seen today at St Senara Church when following the Zennor Head walking trail, near St Ives in Cornwall.

Selkies are mythical creatures likened to mermaids, but instead of appearing as half human and half fish, they instead appear as seals in the sea, shedding their skins to walk on land in human form. There are stories of men longing to capture such creatures as selkie-wives, hiding their skins to keep them prisoners on land to bear their children. Many such folk tales end with the wife finding her selkie sealskin, and fleeing to the sea once more. Yet not all selkies are female. In a famous story from Orkney, 'The Great Silkie of Sule Skerrie', a young mother is nursing her baby boy, wondering who the father might be. Suddenly, a figure appears before her, proclaiming to be the father, yet he is a selkie that usually lives on the small rocky island of Sule Skerrie. He gives her a purse of gold as payment for raising his son, and then takes him back to live in the waters. Yet before the selkie leaves, he makes a prediction, that the mother will wed a gunner – a whaler in charge of firing the harpoon – who will one day kill both him and his son, with the first shot he ever shoots. In one version, the final verse describes how the gunner does indeed one day return from his hunting trip, only to show a gold chain found around a seal's neck to his devastated wife. This well-known folk story is the basis for a famous ballad, first recorded in the nineteenth century.

Fishermen faced similar fates to sailors, and the additional burden of having to make a good catch to sell, or else bring famine and hardship for their families and villages. For Cornish fishermen, superstitions include that eating pilchards from head to tail is unlucky, and will drive fish away from the shores. Certain woods would often be used to build fishing boats, and were said to bring good fortune, particularly ash and rowan. In many places, rituals were undertaken regularly to renew this luck. In Burghead, Scotland, 'burning the clavie' was performed every year at Christmas or New Year; tar barrels would be sawn in half, put on poles and set alight, then carried around the harbour. This was to ensure the luck would be carried into the next year and protect the boats from witches. A legend from Holy Island (Lindisfarne), recorded in Balfour's *Northumberland*, tells that a fish once jumped from the water and said, 'Boil my flesh! Roast my flesh! But do not burn my bones!' So, as a result, on Holy Island some people always bury fish, yet never burn them. In other parts of the region many believe that any horsehair kept in water will always turn into an eel, given time.

Cornish fisherman consider it unlucky to eat a pilchard from head to tail.

For fisherman and seafarers alike, weather was of course a major concern. Storms could brew quickly, and winds could rise without warning. It was considered ill luck to whistle on board, as it was said to 'call up a gale'. Other shipboard superstitions included it being unlucky to go near the site of a shipwreck when out at sea, as the voices of the drowned call from the waves, and should a fisherman hear them call his own name, he will surely soon die. No fisherman worth his salt would ever choose to switch tasks aboard ship on a Friday, for this would lead to very dire luck indeed. Fishermen's wives had their own superstitions, that foretold the fates of their loved ones out at sea when communication was scarce, and their husband's fate would be unknown until his return – if he did return. Wives would not turn beds on Fridays – never seen as a particularly auspicious day – in case the boats also turned, and capsized in the waves. In Cornwall cats running wildly about a house were often said to have storms on their tails. One Cornish farmer's wife reported being able to predict sea conditions by the milk in her dairy being agitated like the waves, and feared this would foretell her sailor son's death. An old woman from Hull, with no word from her son's ship for a long time, swore that she was awoken one night by the curtains being drawn aside, and the sailor appearing between them. She declared that this was a sign of his death. Apparently her worst fears were realised, and word came back that the ship he had sailed on was found filled with bodies.

The wives of fisherman would not turn a bed on a Friday in case it caused the boat to turn and capsize in the waves.

Working life on the farm was just as hard, and was undertaken by men, women and children. Here, superstitions related to ensuring a good harvest and the health of the animals, both essential to survival.

In Lancashire, and elsewhere, lucky stones were carried or put in cattle troughs to protect cattle from disease, while a portion of meat from any cow that did succumb to a disease, such as distemper, would be hung within the farm's chimney, to ward off further occurrences. Animal sacrifices to ward off disease were a common practice from the earliest times until at least the nineteenth century in Britain. One story of 1879, from Dartmoor, tells of a farmer whose cattle were afflicted by illness. To rid them of disease he drove a sheep to the ridge above his house and sacrificed and burnt it as an offering to the pixies, whereupon his cattle soon recovered. Hens should only ever sit on odd numbers of eggs in Lancashire, while 11 or 13 eggs are considered especially lucky in the South East. Farmers in Cornwall, when they felt the wind dropping while winnowing the wheat, would traditionally whistle to the spriggan, or air spirit, to bid the wind return. It's also sometimes said that pigs can see the wind, and that unsettled swine are a sure sign of high winds. A commonly known weather prediction, across Britain, is 'Red sky at night, shepherd's delight; red sky in the morning, shepherd's warning.'

Harvest was, and still is, a major annual event for those involved in arable farming. Before industrialisation, gangs of reapers would harvest the corn by hand with sickles or scythes, while women and children followed them to gather it and tie it in sheaves that were left to dry. This backbreaking work would culminate with the annual Harvest Home celebration, where horses and wagons were decorated with garlands, and traditional songs were sung. Often a 'Lord of the Harvest' was appointed to collect money from onlookers. A similar traditional celebration, the

> *Unsettled swine are a sure sign of high winds.*

Mhelliah, is still celebrated on the Isle of Man, while in Cornwall the festival was called *Guldize*. In both Cornwall and Devon a tradition called 'Crying the Neck' marked cutting the last standing corn: the last reaper would cut it, then raise it above his head and shout three times, 'I 'ave 'un!' The rest of the farm workers would then question, 'What 'ave 'ee?', again three times. The tradition would end with the reply: 'A neck!', again three times, and finally everyone would shout, 'Hurrah! Hurrah for the neck!', naming the farmer with their final 'hurrah'. The Old Cornwall Society has revived this tradition in recent years. Corn dollies would be made of these last pieces, some say to house the spirit of the fields, which would be left without a home once harvest had taken place, until the crops returned next year. Corn dollies were often used as favours exchanged between young couples, in North

Yorkshire this would be called a 'corn baby', said to be 'birthed from the harvest', and dressed up in clothes, ribbons, and flowers. At Kilburn, in the Hambleton Hills, it's said that this mell sheaf, or mell doll, would be plaited together after the harvest meal, and take centre stage in the room, where people would dance around it, and drink gin until well into the night. In Yorkshire such celebratory meals would be called a 'kern-supper', or 'churn-supper', because it was customary for the farmer to bring out a full churn of cream and offer great bowlfuls to all who had taken part in the harvest. Slightly different was a 'mell-supper', which was held soon after, once all the corn was brought in and the harvest fully completed. Today, the festival, which was soon adopted in the Christian year, is more commonly called Harvest Festival, and often takes place on the Sunday nearest to the Harvest Moon (the closest full moon to the autumn equinox). In the church it focuses on giving thanks for the harvest, and decorating churches with baskets of fruit and food, often by local school children, that are passed on to those in need. At London's St Martin-in-the-Fields it was traditional for Pearly Princesses to take vegetable bouquets as offerings. The Pearly Kings and Queens Association is a charitable body that is still in existence. Originating in working class late Victorian London, its members wear special suits decorated with huge numbers of mother-of-pearl buttons, and they have held a harvest celebration at St Martins every year since the 1950s.

Harvest traditions today retain echoes of the old beliefs and traditions around farming. The Carshalton Straw Jack parades around Surrey each September until the straw suit is ceremonially burned to celebrate the harvest in the evening. The Whittlesea Straw Bear festival takes place in Cambridgeshire on the Tuesday after Plough Monday, where a man is dressed in a similar straw suit and then led around the town, to be given tobacco, beer and meat. The 'bear' is burned on the Sunday – no man inside by then, of course – so that a new bear can be created from the following harvest. While its origin is unknown, the custom was revived in the 1980s, and still happens annually today. John Barleycorn is probably the most well-known personification of the harvest, thought to be born, die and then be resurrected each year, which ends with his blood being drunk – symbolised by the alcoholic drink made from the crops. The debate still rages as to whether he is a survival of early traditions or a fabricated revivalist idea. An old folk song from the sixteenth century mentions John Barleycorn, so the name has a long history. Many modern Pagans revere him as either a spirit of the harvest, the 'Corn King' or similar ancient deity, or as a memory of ancient kings that were sacrificed each year, possibly to ensure a good crop.

Both blacksmiths and miners are trades further steeped in superstition and folklore. Blacksmiths were seen as magical figures dealing in a form of alchemy from the earliest times, as they take stones from the earth and create something magical from them. In the Bronze and Iron Ages, metal was seen as having special symbolism, and was often given as a ritual offering to the gods. Many metal offerings can be found at sites like Flag Fen, near

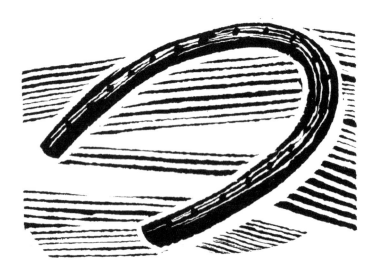

Peterborough, in England, and across the borders of the ancient territories of Iron Age Ireland, and are thought to be offerings to appease the old gods. It is common knowledge in folklore that the fairies are supposed to hate iron, and a well-known tradition that a horseshoe is a talisman against evil forces and witchcraft, and people still sometimes hang them at their door or over the hearth for luck. It's said that horseshoes were first considered lucky after St Dunstan, a blacksmith, managed to shoe the Devil – who begged for mercy and fled, while pledging never to venture near a horseshoe again! Another famous blacksmith story is that of Wayland the Smith, a character said to have his origins in Völund, the mythical smith-god of the Vikings. Wayland's Smithy, a Neolithic chambered long barrow in Oxfordshire, is steeped in legend. It's said that any horse left at the site overnight will be shod by an invisible blacksmith by

For Cornish miners, seeing a black goat or white rabbit was a sign of ill omen.

morning, if a coin is left for the trouble. This legend dates back at least as far as 1738, when it was recorded by Francis Wise, under-keeper of the Bodleian Library in Oxford.

Cornish miners were once called 'tinners', and the Tin Coast of West Penwith in Cornwall now has World Heritage Site status, with its history tracing back at least 2,000 years. For the tinners, seeing a black goat, black cat or a white rabbit in the mine was a sign of ill omen, while some tell of a ghostly hand that followed a man as they descended the ladder – foretelling his death. In Delabole this hand was said to belong to the hand of a miner who had committed suicide. A miner would certainly bring on his own bad luck if he dared to whistle, or accidentally formed a cross with tools against the walls of the mine. To ward off such ill luck, some Cornish miners hung a horseshoe off their machinery, and touched it four times before starting work. A common legend among them was that of the Knockers. These were mischievous spirits who would knock on the cavern walls before cave-ins occurred. While some thought that these sounds were spirits that actually caused the collapses, others thought they were the spirits of miners who had themselves died in accidents giving warning to those underground. It's thought that the sounds might actually occur, and be the more mundane result of beams and supports beginning to break. A similar legend is that of the Seven Whistlers, in which sounds resembling the smothered wailings of children, or the distant cries of birds, were seen as a warning before fatal accidents. In the past, Leicestershire colliers would not venture down a mine if they heard these sounds, as they were thought to foretell a death. It's said they were heard before two fatal accidents at Bedworth Charity Colliery in Warwickshire, in 1874.

15

DEATH AND BURIAL

B ritain's folklore contains many customs and superstitions around death – one of the most feared, mysterious and, of course, inescapable aspects of human existence. Traditions can help to console those left behind, and ensure that a beloved family member or friend is prepared fully to meet the spirit of death, whichever form it may take. The oldest ceremonial burial we know of in Western Europe dates from some 33,000 years ago, in the Upper-Palaeolithic Period. The Red Lady of Paviland, whose body is dyed in red ochre, as was customary, was entombed in a cave in Gower, Wales. Death rituals are age-old, it seems, and no doubt our funerals, wakes and other memorial rituals will one day come to be replaced by others.

In centuries past, when many types of illness were often fatal, predictions of death were considered of great importance. Death omens abound in Britain, and it sometimes seems that every

sound or strange occurrence was viewed as a sign of impending doom. Birds and animals play a large role in traditional predictions of death. Three caws of a crow, or the cries of a screech owl, can announce forthcoming death in the south-east of England. In Northamptonshire a bee entering a house is seen similarly. The ticking of the deathwatch beetle, the crowing of a cock during the night, or the croak of a raven are all traditional portents of death that are common to the whole of Britain. Woe betide anyone who hears the strange tap-tapping of a magpie on a windowpane – another sure sign for most. In the north of England the sight of three butterflies together is an omen, despite their pretty dance. Should you hear the caw-caw of jackdaws or the chattering of swallows from your chimney – beware; either appearing down any chimney signifies that calamity is sure to follow! Always train your dogs to stay quiet after dark, for dogs howling under the window at night in the north-west of England presages an illness or death in the household, while in Northumberland the same omen extends to anyone in the region that is suffering an illness. An old belief in the north-west is that a dog will die when its owner passes away, as the two souls are as closely linked in death as they are in life. It's highly ominous for a dog or cat to walk or jump over a corpse awaiting burial. A nineteenth-century tale from the Borderlands, tells of a funeral cortége pausing for a rest while coming down from a cottage in the high fells. A dog jumped over the coffin when it was laid on the ground, and nobody would continue until the poor creature had been killed for its crime.

Certain plants brought into the house are, it's said, likely to bring calamity or death. Blackthorn blossom and primroses are included on this list, while broom should not be brought in during May, and especially not used for sweeping:

> If you sweep the house with broom in May,
> You'll sweep the head of the house away.

The excitement of seeing the first snowdrop after a cold and miserable winter can entice us, but let us take the following nineteenth-century tale from William Henderson as a lesson. A Sussex woman was heard reprimanding her child for bringing a snowdrop into the house. Asked why she was doing so, she replied that they are obviously a token of death, and look 'for all the world like a corpse in its shroud'. Also, next time you eat a plate of broad beans, try not to consider that, in Yorkshire, they are thought to contain the souls of the dead.

There are of course many night-related images of death. Superstition bids you beware of having nightmares of the Devil, or one's teeth falling out, as they were both seen as sure premonitions of death. Sussex must be a terrifying place to live, as its local superstitions are full of deathly concerns: a strange rattling to a church door, or a heavy tone to the church bell, and a corpse that is unaffected by rigor mortis are sure signs of forthcoming doom. Anyone who sees a will-o'-the-wisp when out at night should consider themselves forewarned, for in Sussex these ghostly nocturnal lights (in reality, probably a natural phenomenon) only flirt with those marked by death. At home, a stopped clock that suddenly chimes is a warning to all, as is the breaking of a mirror – the latter seen as bad luck in most parts of the world. Seating 13 people around a table is said to ensure that one guest will die before the dawn of the New Year, so do be careful when making dinner plans.

In many cultures, the dying are believed by some to possess supernatural powers of divination, and are consulted for prophesies of what is to come. It's thought that they can communicate with the spirits of those already dead, and this power is often heightened in the prudent and pious. A more sinister tale from Windy Walls, near Stamfordham in Northumberland, tells of a ghostly hand that rapped on the shutters of a house predicting the death of a member of the household. Later that evening, a man from the house did indeed fall from a cart and die, just as predicted. In Yorkshire, spirits known as 'fetches'

Seating thirteen people together at dinner is said to ensure one of them will die before the new year.

sometimes appear to forewarn of a death; it's wise to know your fetches from your fairies at such times. According to superstition, people born in the twilight hours, or at midnight exactly, are most adept at seeing spirits and are often able to predict who is soon to die. According to Yorkshire tradition, there is a way for anyone to find out if they will die that year. At midnight, go into the barn carrying some chaff and throw open the doors. Begin to recite a riddle – any sort will do. If you are destined to die within the year, you will see a ghostly apparition of two bearers carrying a coffin appear between the open doors. However, Northumbrian tradition describes a different method. First, take the straw from the mattress or bed where someone has died, and burn it. Look for a footprint in the ashes and measure the family's feet against this mark and – a macabre Cinderella touch – whoever's foot matches the imprint will be the next to die. On St Mark's Eve (24 April), the ashes from the usual household fire can be used in the same way: spread them out at the end of the night, and the next morning look for a footprint that matches that of a family member. It's noted in the *Chambers Book of Days* that a common game was for someone to sneak into the kitchen during the night with a shoe, and make a playful imprint for an unsuspecting family member to find the next day, mischievously 'predicting' their death. Perhaps not one to try at home.

The same book explains the notion common to many regions across Britain that 'a mournful trail of sentenced souls' – those who will die in the coming year – can be seen crossing church greens at midnight on St Mark's Eve. The vigil of watching the church porch between 11pm and 1am was commonly practised from the seventeenth century onwards. A tale from 1631, told by Mr Liveman Rampaine, a minister from Great Grimsby in Lincolnshire, recounts two men from Burton undertaking this, but at midnight they were bewitched, left unable to move and pitched into darkness. Soon, by the glow of invisible torches, they watched as the minister processed into the church, followed by one of their very own neighbours, who was trussed up in a shroud. The shadowy figures entered the church, and the doors slammed shut behind them. The two men outside could hear from within the mutterings of a funeral service, then the rattling of bones and, lastly, the shovelling of earth into a grave. After the ghostly service was done, the same thing occurred five more times, until the apparitions halted, and the moon shone once more brightly in the sky. Both men were so terrified by the ordeal that they were struck down with illness the next day. Ominously, the tale concludes, all of the deaths they saw came to pass within the year.

Traditional superstitions are not limited to those predicting death, but also include those intended to ward off death and danger in many ways. While white pigeons serve as a portent of death in Hull, it's said to be impossible for someone to die on a mattress or pillow containing pigeon feathers in both Cumbria and Northumberland. In fact, a bag of feathers was often put purposefully into the pillow under the head of a dying person, to keep their spirit from leaving their body, especially if waiting for someone to arrive to say their last goodbyes. Be warned though, in the nineteenth century the use of pigeon feathers to ward off the inevitable was sometimes said then to cause a painful lingering death. Just as superstition believed a birth could only happen when the tide was coming in, there was a comparable belief that a death could only occur when it was going out, and so those that held on might live to see another day. In Hesleden, near Hartlepool, there are records from the sixteenth century showing that this belief was held so strongly that the tide was recorded on the parish register when noting each death in the region.

A bag of feathers was often put under the head of a dying person to keep their spirit from leaving their body.

Many customs were observed in the event of a death. Often, in the past, the corpse was kept in the house before burial, and the relatives would wash the family member, and lay them out. This is not so common today, as undertakers often take care of these rituals instead of family members. A custom from the Lowlands of Scotland in the nineteenth century was 'saining' – the blessing of a corpse, which was undertaken at home. William Henderson gives a full account of this practice in his *Notes on the Folk-lore of the Northern Counties of England and the Borders*, summarised as follows. The eldest woman present would light a candle, and pass it about the deceased three times. This candle should be sourced from a witch, a wizard or one who can see into the future. Some say the candle should be made from the fat of a murderer or vanquished enemy. The woman would then scoop three handfuls of salt onto a plate and lay it on its chest, and place three empty bowls (called 'toom') near the fire, as it was thought the soul was like a flame and would flitter around the hearth just after the death. In the western Lowlands a variation was that these empty bowls would be placed on a table, so that that the attendees could place their hands within them as they told fortunes. Perhaps unsurprisingly, it was said that for the corpse to sit up and frown was a bad omen for the one with their hand currently in the bowl. Everyone would then leave the room, and then return backwards, citing this 'rhyme of saining':

Thrice the torchie, thrice the saltie,
Thrice the dishies toom for 'loffie' [i.e. praise],
These three times three ye must wave round
The corpse, until it sleep sound.
Sleep sound and wake nane,
Till to heaven the soul's gane.
If ye want that soul to dee
Fetch the torch frae th' Elleree;
Gin ye want that soul to live,
Between the dishes place a sieve,
An it sail have a fair, fair shrive.

Continuing, Henderson describes how this ceremony is called 'Dishaloof', and if a sieve is placed on the chest, all try to place their hands in it, and the one who manages it will help the soul most; although it's an ill omen for the soul if no one manages to place their hands in the sieve. At this point the windows are opened. Rhymes are sung through the night, and the candle should be kept alight throughout, and a meal of bread, cheese, and spirits shared amongst them, while a game of cards is often played on the coffin itself. After this, the corpse is never left alone until burial, and is watched over by family and friends, called 'a sitting' during daylight hours and 'lykewake' after dark. It's said that everyone present should touch the corpse at least once, to banish nightmares,

and ward off evil, and it was customary for any visitor to houses
in Durham to do similar, to show no hard feelings towards the
dead, and this is thought by some to originate from the belief that
any murdered corpse would bleed at the touch of the perpetrator.
Henderson goes on to describe how similar lykewakes are upheld
in Wales, the Isle of Man, Somerset and Cornwall. He tells that at
one lykewake, a game of hide and seek was played, where a group of
youngsters removed a corpse from the coffin, so one of them could
hide within. The boy was later found dead, and the corpse nowhere
to be found, so was thought to have been taken by the fairies. In
the sixteenth century, Bishop Voysey ordered that such practices
should be halted, and charged curates around the west of England to
make sure that they didn't take place. Other customs associated with
lykewakes include covering mirrors and stopping clocks, a practice
that crops up in other cultures and religions. It's said that mirrors
were shrouded to show that all beauty and vanity has ceased with
the passing, and the clocks too are covered to show that the time
shared with the loved one is no more. In other regions, people say it
was so that the departed's soul would not get trapped inside them,
and it's an old belief that it's bad luck to break a mirror since the
soul is contained within. In both Devon and Warwickshire it's said
that if you look into a mirror in the room where a death occurred,
you will see the deceased over your shoulder, looking back at you
– mirrors are removed from this room to avoid that. On the way to
the funeral, it's seen as good luck to carry the dead clockwise around
the church before entering, which is in the direction of the Sun,
since to go against it is often seen as wishing bad luck or having
evil intentions. In North Wales, a corpse must always travel to the
church on the right-hand side of pathways and roads, and enter
in the north gate. Accounts exist from as early as the thirteenth
century that mention ancient pathways dedicated to corpse carrying.
Some traditional corpse roads crossed what became private land and
farms, but angry mobs were reported to have often forced their way
through, in order to carry the dead along these traditional corpse

roads, also known as bier-balks and leech-ways. The usual highways and roads of villages and towns was seen as unacceptable for transporting the corpse, and it's recorded that men used to 'pinch' at such pathways, thieving the land and trying to keep them as part of their own private property. It's said that after a funeral, a grave should never be left open on a Sunday, or another death will occur within the week. In Hampshire, it was traditional to offer 'Maidens' Garlands' at the funeral of any young virgin with unblemished character – these were white linen or paper garlands, with five paper gauntlets as a symbol of their purity. Garlands dating as far back as 1716 still hang at Abbotts Ann, near Andover, today.

The transition into death is steeped heavily in folklore, and a huge effort is made in paying respects to the deceased. This makes it all the more strange that in Britain there are surprisingly few traditional customs to

It's said that a grave should never be left open on a Sunday, or another death will occur within the week.

remember the dead in the years after their passing. These are usually restricted to leaving offerings of flowers at their gravesides and lighting candles in their memory, particularly on the night of All Hallows' Eve (Halloween or 'All Soul's Night', when the dead are remembered collectively). Superstitions seem to support how easily the dead are forgotten. Cornish folklore, for instance, tells that portraits of the dead are thought to fade. What the dead do leave behind, however, is often used in macabre ways. In Gloucestershire, parish clerks were infamous for squirrelling away old coffin handles found in churchyards, which would later be made into rings, worn on the fingers to rid the bearer of cramp.

AFTERWORD

Death might be thought of as the end, but in folklore life goes on – through the cycle of the harvest and the seasons of the ritual year. Where there is an ending, a beginning must follow. When an 'old chapter' of folklore ends, its memory still lingers on, is changed, reinterpreted by subsequent generations and constantly reborn anew – and with each new birth the stories of folklore are given new life. The traditions, tales and superstitions of folklore are a reflection of beliefs that address what makes us intrinsically human. Each community or culture takes the stories and traditions of their ancestors and makes them their own.

SOURCES
AND FURTHER
READING

GENERAL

Axon, William E.A., *Cheshire Gleanings* (Tubbs, Brook, and Chrystal, Simpkin, Marshall, and Company, 1884)

Balfour, M.C., *County Folklore: Northumberland* (The Folklore Society, 1904)

Baring-Gould, Sabine, *Curious Myths of the Middle Ages* (Rivingtons, 1877)

Baring-Gould, Sabine, *A Book of Dartmoor* (Methuen, 1907)

Bede's Ecclesiastical History of the English People (Oxford Medieval Texts, Clarendon Press, 1993)

Bennet, Margaret, *Scottish Customs: From the Cradle to the Grave* (Birlinn Limited, 2012)

Bray, Anna Eliza, *Traditions, Legends, Superstitions, and Sketches of Devonshire on the Borders of the Tamar and the Tavy, Illustrative of its Manners, Customs, History, Antiquities, Scenery, and Natural History*, Vol. 1 (J. Murray, 1828)

Chambers, R. (ed.), *Hillman's Hyperlinked and Searchable Chambers*

Book of Days: A Miscellany of Popular Antiquities in Connection with the Calendar, Including Anecdote, Biography, & History, Curiosities of Literature and Oddities of Human Life and Character (W. & R. Chambers, 1869). Available at http://www.thebookofdays.com [Retrieved 16/05/17]

Courtney, Margaret Ann, *Cornish Feasts and Folk-lore* (Beare and Son, 1890)

Cowan, J.L., 'Welsh Superstitions', in *Journal of American Folklore*, Vol. 15, pp.131–2, 1902

Daniels, Cora Linn and Stevens, Charles McClennan, *Encyclopaedia of Superstitions, Folklore, and the Occult Sciences of the World* (Yewdale & Sons Co., 1908)

Davies, Jonathan Ceredig, *Folk-lore of West and Mid-Wales* (Welsh Gazette Offices, 1911)

Denham, Michael Aislabie, *The Denham Tracts: A Collection of Folklore by Michael Aislabie Denham, and Reprinted from the Original Tracts and Pamphlets Printed by Mr Denham between 1846 and 1859*, Vol. 1, edited by James Hardy, (The Folklore Society, 1892)

Ditchfield, Peter Hampson, *Old English Customs Extant at the Present Time: An account of local observances* (G. Redway, 1896)

Ettlinger, E., 'Documents of British Superstition in Oxford', in *Folklore* Vol. 54, No. 1, pp.227–49, 1943

Evans, J., *A Tour Through Part of North Wales, in the Year 1798, and at Other Times* (J. White, 1800)

Gilbert. C.S., *An Historical Survey of the County of Cornwall*, Vol. 2 (Longman, Hurst, Rees, Orme, and Brown, 1820)

Glyde, John (1866), *The New Suffolk Garland* (Simpkin, Marshall and Co., 1866)

Gurdon, Eveline Camilla, *County Folklore: Suffolk* (The Folklore Society, 1893)

Gutch, Eliza, *County Folklore: North Riding of Yorkshire, York and the Ainsty* (The Folklore Society, 1901)

Gutch, Eliza, *County Folklore: The East Riding of Yorkshire* (The Folklore Society, 1911)

Hadow, G.E. & Anderson, R., 'Scraps of English Folklore, IX. (Suffolk)', in *Folklore* Vol. 35, No. 4, pp 346–360, 1924

Harland, John, and Wilkinson, T.T., *Lancashire Folk-lore: Illustrative of the Superstitious Beliefs and Practices, Local Customs and Usages of the People of the County Palatine* (Frederick Warne and Company and Scribner and Company, 1867)

Hartland, Edwin Sidney, *County Folklore: Gloucestershire* (The Folklore Society, 1895)

Henderson, William, *Notes on the Folk-lore of the Northern Counties of England and the Borders* (The Folklore Society, 1879)

Hole, Christina, *English Folklore* (B.T. Batsford Ltd, 1940)

Hone, William, *The Every-day Book and Table Book: or, Everlasting Calendar of Popular Amusements, Sports, Pastimes, Ceremonies, Manners, Customs and Events*, Vol. 1 (T. Tegg, 1835)

Jackson, Georgina Frederica and Burne, Charlotte Sophia, *Shropshire Folk-lore: A Sheaf of Gleanings* (Trübner & Co., 1883)

Mackenzie, Osgood Hanbury, *A Hundred Years in the Highlands* (E. Arnold, 1921)

Marvin, Dwight Edwards, *Curiosities in Proverbs* (G.P. Putnam's Sons, 1916)

McPherson, J.M., *Primitive Beliefs in the North-East of Scotland* (Longmans, Green and Co., 1929)

Napier, James, *Folk Lore Superstitious Beliefs in the West of Scotland within This Century* (Alex Gardener, 1879)

National Art Library, *English Forests and Forest Trees, Historical, Legendary, and Descriptive* (Ingram, Cooke, and Co., 1853). Available at: https://archive.org/details/englishforestsa00unkngoog [Retrieved 06/07/17]

Peacock, M., 'The Folklore of Lincolnshire', in *Folklore*, Vol. 12, No. 2, pp.161–80, 1901

Reader's Digest Association (ed.), *Folklore, Myths and Legends* (The Reader's Digest Association Limited, 1973)

Roud, Steve, *The English Year* (Penguin, 2008)

Roud, Steve, *London Lore* (Arrow Books, 2010)

Rhys, John, *Celtic Folklore, Welsh and Manx* (Clarendon Press, 1901)

Simpson, Jacqueline, *The Folklore of the Welsh Border* (Rowman and Littlefield, 1976)

Simpson, Jacqueline, *The Folklore of Sussex* (Tempus Publishing, 2002)

Simpson, Jacqueline and Roud, Steve, *A Dictionary of English Folklore* (Oxford University Press, 2000)

Sternberg, Thomas, *The Dialect and Folk-lore of Northamptonshire* (Russell Smith, 1851)

Tozer, Elias, *Devonshire & Other Original Poems: With Some Account of Ancient Customs, Superstitions, and Traditions* (Devon Weekly Times, 1873)

Various (edited by George Bell), *Notes and Queries*, Vol. III, No. 87, 1851. Available at http://www.gutenberg.org/files/37516/37516-h/37516-h.htm [Accessed 19/9/17]

Warren, Melanie, *Lancashire Folk* (Schiffer Publishing, 2016)

Wright, A.R., *English Folklore* (Ernest Benn Limited, 1928)

CHAPTER-SPECIFIC

Chapter 1

BBC Cornwall, 'All eyes are on Padstow', on bbc.co.uk http://www.bbc.co.uk/cornwall/uncovered/stories/obbyoss.shtml [Accessed 11/10/2017]

Bottrell, William, *Traditions and Hearthside Stories of West Cornwall* (Beare and Son, 1873)

Dodge, Mary Mapes (ed.), *St. Nicholas Magazine* (Scribner & Company, 1883)

Jamieson, John, *An Etymological Dictionary of the Scottish Language* (W. & C. Tait, 1808). Available at https://archive.org/details/

aetymologicaldi00jamigoog [Retrieved 19/07/2017]

Rogers, Nicholas, *Halloween: From Pagan Ritual to Party Night* (Oxford University Press, 2002)

The Padstow Obby Oss Available from https://padstowobbyoss. wordpress.com/ [Retrieved 17/7/17]

Up Helly Aa Committee, *Up Helly Aa*. Web page at http://www. uphellyaa.org/about-up-helly-aa [Retrieved 17/05/17]

Chapter 2

Grinsell, Leslie Valentine, *Folklore of Prehistoric Sites in Britain* (David & Charles, 1976)

Pennant, Thomas, *Tours in Wales* (H. Humphreys, 1883)

Chapter 3

MacBain, A. (ed.), 'Tales of the Water-Kelpie', in *Celtic Magazine*, Vol. XII, 1887. Available at https://archive.org/details/ celticmagazinemo12inveuoft [Retrieved 18/6/17]

Porteus, C., *The Beauty and Mystery of Well-Dressing* (Pilgrim Press, 1949)

Chapter 4

Culpeper, Nicholas, *Culpeper's Complete Herbal: A Book of Natural Remedies of Ancient Ills* (NTC/Contemporary Publishing Company, 1995)

Evans, John, *An Excursion to Windsor in July 1810* (Sherwood, Neely and Jones, 1817)

Greenaway, Kate, *Language of Flowers* (George Routledge and Sons, 190-). Available at https://archive.org/details/ languageofflower00gree [Retrieved 06/07/17]

Hudson, Alison, 'An illustrated Old English Herbal', on *blogs. bl.uk*. The British Library Board. Available at http://blogs. bl.uk/digitisedmanuscripts/2017/04/an-illustrated-old-english-herbal.html [Retrieved 07/07/17]

Morrell, Patricia, *Festivals and Customs* (Pan Macmillan, 1977)

Pearce, J.M.S., 'The Doctrine of Signatures', in *European Neurology*, Vol. 60, No. 1, pp.5–52, 2008

Strutt, Jacob George, *Sylva Britannica: or, Portraits of Forest Trees, Distinguished for Their Antiquity, Magnitude, or Beauty* (Longman, Rees, Orme, Brown, and Green, 1830). Available at https://archive.org/details/sylvabritannicao00strurich [Retrieved 06/07/17]

Van Arsdall, Anne, *Medieval Herbal Remedies: The Old English Herbarium and Anglo-Saxon Medicine* (Routledge, 2002)

Chapter 5

Barras, Colin, 'Iron-age Britons Engaged in Mysterious Pig Trotter Festivals', in *New Scientist*, 2005. Available at https://www.newscientist.com/article/dn28024-iron-age-britons-engaged-in-mysterious-pig-trotter-festivals/ [Retrieved 27/06/17]

Caldecott, Randolph, *The Babes in the Wood* (Frederick Warne and Co Ltd., 1900). Available at http://www.gutenberg.org/files/19361/19361-h/19361-h.htm [Retrieved 27/06/17]

Cooper, Georgina, 'Ghost-like white stag spotted in Scotland', in *Reuters*, Issue 2/12/2008. Available at http://reut.rs/2xkzxVV [Retrieved 30/6/17]

Dio, Cassius, *Roman History*, Vol. VIII (Loeb Classical Library edition, 1925). Available at http://penelope.uchicago.edu/Thayer/e/roman/texts/cassius_dio/62*.html [Retrieved 27/06/17]

Ingersoll, Ernest, *Birds in Legend, Fable, and Folklore* (Longmans, Green & Co., 1923). Available at https://archive.org/details/birdsinlegendfab00inge [Retrieved 27/06/17]

Newman, L.F., Pinchin, M., Rider Haggard, L. and others, 'Ladybirds in England', in *Folklore*, Vol. 49, No. 1, pp.31–6, 1938

University of Aberdeen. *The Aberdeen Beastiary*. Available at https://www.abdn.ac.uk/bestiary/ [Retrieved 27/06/17]

Wallace, R.H., 'White Cattle in British Folktales and Customs', in *Folklore*, Vol. 10, No. 3, pp.352–57, 1899

Warren Chad, Rachel, & Taylor, Marianne, *Birds: Myth, Lore & Legend* (Bloomsbury, 2016)

Chapter 6

Alcock, Leslie, *Arthur's Britain: History and Archaeology* AD 367-634 (Penguin, 1971)

Ellis Davidson, H.R., 'The Legend of Lady Godiva', in *Folklore*, Vol. 80, No. 2, pp.107–21, 1969

Evans, D.M., '"King Arthur" and Cadbury Castle, Somerset', in *Antiquaries Journal*, Vol. 86, pp227–53, 2006

Ford, Patrick K., *The Mabinogi and Other Medieval Welsh Tales* (University of California Press, 1977)

Geoffrey of Monmouth, *Historia Regum Britanniae* [Histories of the Kings of Britain] (Paphos Publishers, 2015).

Gildas, *De Excidio Britanniae* [On the Ruin of Britain], translated by J.A. Giles (Serenity Publishers, LLC, 2009)

Giles, J.A. (ed.), *Nennius: Historia Britonum, Six Old English Chronicles* (Henry G. Bohn, 1847)

Koch, John T., *Celtic Culture: A Historical Encyclopedia* (ABC-CLIO Ltd, 2006)

Rees, William Jenkins (ed.), 'Life of St. Winefred', *Lives of the Cambro-British Saints*, pp.515–29, (William Rees, 1953)

Wright, T., *The Vision and Creed of Piers Ploughman*, Vol. 1 (Reeves and Turner, 1887). Available at http://www.gutenberg.org/files/43660/43660-h/43660-h.htm [Retrieved 27/06/17]

Chapter 7

Anderson, William, *Green Man* (HarperCollins, 1990)

Basford, Kathleen, *The Green Man* (D.S. Brewer, 2004)

Bartrum, P., *A Welsh Classical Dictionary: People in History and Legend up to about A.D.1000*, pp.230–31 (National Library of

Wales, 1993). Available at http://bit.ly/2xOrRNb [Retrieved 27/06/17]

Billington, Sandra and Green, Miranda (eds.), *The Concept of the Goddess* (Routledge, 1996)

Busk, R.H., 'Phenomenal Footprints in the Snow, S. Devon', *Notes and Queries*, s7-IX (213), p.70, 1890. https://archive.org/details/s7notesqueries09londuoft [Retrieved 27/06/17]

Centerwall, B.S., 'The Name of the Green Man', in *Folklore*, Vol. 108, pp.25–33, 1997

Davidson, H.E., 'Milk and the Northern Goddess', in Sandra Billington and Miranda Green (eds.), *The Concept of the Goddess*, pp.91–106 (Routledge, 1996)

Kelly, E.P., 'Kingship and sacrifice: Iron Age bog bodies and boundaries', in *Archaeology Ireland*, Heritage Guide No. 35 (Wordwell Ltd, 2006).

Lobell, J.A. and Patel, S.S., 'Clonycavan and Old Croghan Men', in *Archaeology*, Vol. 63, No. 3, 2010. Available at http://archive.archaeology.org/1005/bogbodies/clonycavan_croghan.html [Retrieved 27/06/17]

Menefee, Samuel Pyeatt, 'Meg and Her Daughters: Some Traces of Goddess Beliefs in Megalithic Folklore', in Sandra Billington and Miranda Green (eds.), *The Concept of the Goddess*, pp.78–90 (Routledge, 1996)

Raglan, Lady (Julia), 'The "Green Man" in Church Architecture', in *Folklore* Vol. 50, No. 1, pp.45–57, 1939

Thackeray, J. F., Apoh, W. & Gavua, K. 2014. 'Adevu and Chiwara Rituals in West Africa Compared to Hunting Rituals and Rock Art in South Africa', in *The South African Archaeological Bulletin*, Vol. 69, no. 199 (June 2014), pp.113–115

The Mowing-Devil: or, Strange News out of Hartford-shire (1678). Transcribed at https://en.wikipedia.org/wiki/Mowing-Devil

Western Times, 'Topsham. The two-legged wonder', *Western Times*, 24 February, 1855. Available at http://www.britishnewspaperarchive.co.uk [Retrieved 27/06/17]

Chapter 8

Briggs, Katharine Mary, *The Fairies in English Tradition and Literature* (University of Chicago Press, 1967)

Chambers, Robert, *The Popular Rhymes of Scotland: New Edition.* (W. & R. Chambers, 1870)

Keightley, Thomas, 'Ainsel and Puck', in *The Fairy Mythology,* (H.G. Bohn, 1887). Available at http://www.sacred-texts.com/neu/celt/tfm/tfm124.htm [Retrieved 08/07/17]

Northall, G.F., *English Folk-Rhymes* (Kegan Paul, Trench, Trübner & Co. Ltd, 1892). Available at https://archive.org/details/englishfolkrhyme00nortuoft [Retrieved 08/07/17]

The Mad Merry Pranks of Robin Goodfellow, (Thomas Cotes, 1639). Available at https://www.bl.uk/collection-items/robin-goodfellow-his-mad-pranks-and-merry-jests-1639 [Retrieved 08/07/17]

Victoria and Albert Museum, 'The Luck of Edenhall: History & Myths' (V&A website, 2016). Website at http://www.vam.ac.uk/content/articles/t/the-luck-of-edenhall-history-and-myths/ [Retrieved 08/07/17]

Chapter 9

Arnot, Hugo, *A Collection and Abridgement of Celebrated Criminal Trials in Scotland, from A.D.1536 to 1784: With Historical and Critical Remarks* (W. Smellie, 1785). Available at https://archive.org/details/acollectionanda00arnogoog [Retrieved 17/06/17]

Davies, Owen, *Popular Magic: Cunning-folk in English History* (Hambledon Continuum, 2003)

Potts, Thomas,'The Wonderfull Discoverie of Witches in the Countie of Lancaster', 1613, in James Crossley, ed., *Remains, Historical & Literary, Connected with the Palatine Counties of Lancaster and Chester*, Vol. vi. (The Chetham Society, 1745). Available at http://www.gutenberg.org/files/18253/18253-h/18253-h.htm [Retrieved 17/06/17]

Towrie, Sigurd,'The Torture of Alesoun Balfour', in *Orkneyjar:*

The Heritage of the Orkney Islands. Available at http://www.
orkneyjar.com/folklore/witchcraft/balfour.htm [Retrieved
17/06/17]

Winsham, Willow, *Accused: British Witches Throughout History* (Pen
& Sword Books Limited, 2016)

Chapter 10

Evans, Sian, *Ghosts: Spooky Stories and Eerie Encounters from the
National Trust* (National Trust, 2006)

Fleming, Abraham, *A Straunge and Terrible Wunder* (1577).
Available at http://quod.lib.umich.edu/e/eebo/
A00943.0001.001?rgn=main;view=fulltext [Retrieved
17/06/17]

Chapter 11

Briggs, Katharine, *An Encyclopedia of Fairies* (Pantheon Books,
1976)

Gripper, Ann, 'Prince William "wets the royal baby's head in pub
over the road from hospital"', in *The Daily Mirror,* 23 July 2013.
Available from http://www.mirror.co.uk/news/weird-news/
prince-william-wets-royal-babys-2079354 [Retrieved 20/7/17]

Hadow, G.E., and Anderson, R., 'Scraps of English Folklore, IX
(Suffolk)', in *Folklore,* Vol. 35, No. 4, pp.346–60, 1924

Rust, James, *Druidism Exhumed* (Edmonston & Douglas, 1871)

Chapter 12

Baker, Paul, *Polari – The Lost Language of Gay Men* (Routledge,
2002)

BBC Archive, *The Parade of the Tutti-Men* (Archive documentary,
1955). Available at https://www.facebook.com/BBCArchive/
videos/400196150353421/ [Retrieved 03/6/17]

Chapter 13

Earl Rath, H., 'Superstition and Health', in *Bios*, Vol. 23, No. 2, pp.154–7, 1952

Leland, D.L., 'Irish Folklore: Method of Starting a New House in the Olden Times', in *Folklore*, Vol. 10, No. 1, pp.118–19, 1899

Timbs, John, *Popular Errors: Explained and Illustrated* (David Bogue, 1856). Available at https://archive.org/stream/bub_gb_itpb6SjlLzoC#page/n3/mode/2up [Retrieved 07/4/17]

Chapter 14

Bottrell, William, 'The Mermaid of Zennor', in *Traditions and Hearthside Stories of West Cornwall* (Beare and Son, 1873). Available at http://www.sacred-texts.com/neu/celt/swc2/swc274.htm [Accessed 19/4/2017]

Child, Frances James, 'The Great Silkie of Sule Skerrie', in *The English and Scottish Popular Ballads*, no. 113, 1882–98). Available at http://www.sacred-texts.com/neu/eng/child/ch113.htm [Accessed 19/4/2017]

Flight, Edward G., *The Horse Shoe: The True Legend of St Dunstan and the Devil* (Bell and Daldy, 1871)

Frazer, James George, *The Golden Bough: A Study of Magic and Religion* (MacMillan and Co., 1890)

Gordon, Dee, *The Secret History of Southend-on-Sea* (The History Press, 2014)

Hamilton Jenkin, A.K., *Cornish Homes and Customs* (J.M. Dent, 1934)

Hamilton Jenkin, A.K., *The Story of Cornwall* (Thomas Nelson, 1934)

The National Archives, *Currency Convertor: Old Money to New* Available at http://www.nationalarchives.gov.uk/currency/default0.asp#mid [Accessed 19/4/2017]

Thurston, Herbert, *Superstition* (The Centenary Press, 1933)

Chapter 15

Johnson, Samuel, *Dictionary of the English Language with Numerous Corrections and with the Addition of Several Thousand Works and Also with Addition to the History of the Language and to the Grammar*, Vol. I (Longman, Rees, Orme, Brown, and Green, 1827). Available at http://bit.ly/2wuSu9z [Accessed 18/05/17]

Radford, Edwin and Radford, Mona A., *Encyclopaedia of Superstitions* (Kessinger Publishing, 2004)

WHERE TO FIND FOLKLORE

Many folklore festivals and events take place in Britain throughout the year. Here are just a few of the most well-known and celebrated.

JANUARY

⊙ **Mari Lwyd**, Llangynwyd, Bridgend: A horse-skull on a pole is carried around the village, as houses are visited for refreshments. 1 January.

⊙ **Burning the Clavie**, Burghead, Grampian: A burning barrel is carried through the village for luck. 11 January. www.burghead.com/clavie/

⊙ **Wassailing** Orchard-visiting wassail events take place around Britain, including Woolsthorpe Manor, Lincolnshire; Cotehele, Cornwall; Birmingham Crescent Theatre. The Chepstow event includes a Mari Lwyd horse-skull tradition.

⊙ **Whittlesea Straw Bear festival**, Whittlesey, Cambridgeshire: The Straw Bear – a man in a costume of straw – is paraded through the town, accompanied by dancers, musicians and street performers, including Molly and Morris dancers, and then burned on the Sunday. Originally the Tuesday after Plough Monday; now the 'bear' only appears during the festival weekend. www.strawbear.org.uk/

⊙ **Up–Helly–Aa**, Shetland: The Jarl Squad marches through the town with flaming torches, along with a galley that is ultimately 'sent to Valhalla': burned at sea. Festivities end in a series of balls and parties. End of January. http://www.uphellyaa.org/

FEBRUARY

⊙ **Imbolc**, various places around Britain: Imbolc is a fire festival that falls on St Brigid's Day, celebrated at Butser Ancient Farm Hampshire, and at Marsden, Huddersfield. Around 1 February.

⊙ **Moonraking**, Slaithwaite, West Yorkshire: A lantern parade to celebrate a local folk tale about smugglers who were caught one night, yet claimed to be attempting to rake a large cheese out of a pond – which was, in fact, the reflection of the Moon – hence escaping punishment for their crimes. Late February. www.slaithwaitemoonraking.org

MARCH

⊙ **Hawick Reivers Festival**, Roxburghshire: A re-enactment of what life was life for reivers, through drama and music. Late March. www.hawickreivers.com/

⊙ **University Boat Races**, River Thames, London: The traditional Oxford-Cambridge boat race. Can take place on any weekend in spring. www.theboatrace.org

⊙ **Tichborne Dole,** Hampshire: One of the oldest doles, or charity festivals, still in existence. Late March.

APRIL

⊙ **Beating the Bounds**, Bodmin, Cornwall: A tradition where villagers check the parish boundaries. Held every five years.

⊙ **Tutti Day/Hocktide**, Hungerford, Berkshire: A Hocktide Jury is selected at the town hall a week before the day itself. The Town Crier summons the people to the Hocktide Court on Tutti Day, when the Tithing Men – accompanied by 'Tutti wenches' – collect their dues from homes around the town: either a kiss or money. Late April.
www.hungerfordtownandmanor.co.uk/hocktide-tutti-day

⊙ **Cuckoo Fair**, Marsden, West Yorkshire: A procession and fair to honour the cuckoo, as harbinger of spring. Late April.
www.facebook.com/MarsdenCuckoo/

MAY

⊙ **Sweeps Festival**, Rochester, Kent: May Day was traditionally celebrated by chimney sweeps in the area from the 1700s, and a festival now revives this celebration with a parade, music, and dancing. May Day bank holiday weekend.

⊙ **Cheese rolling**, Cooper's Hill, Gloucestershire: Dating back 200 years, the annual event sees competitors hurling themselves down a steep slope to catch a wheel of Double Gloucester. An unofficial version of this event takes place in late May after the official event was discontinued in 2009.
www.cheese-rolling.co.uk/

⊙ **Well-dressing**, Staffordshire-Derbyshire border: Locals adorn springs and wells with flower-petal panels depicting scenes from the Bible and other traditional tales. Prominent events take place in Tissington and Bakewell, including an annual blessing of the wells. From May–September.

⊙ **May Day**, throughout Britain: Festivals celebrating traditional

May Day often include a May pole, Morris dancing, music and entertainment. A May Queen and Garland King are crowned at Ickwell Green, Bedfordshire; Jack-in-the-Green appears in Whitstable, Kent; Hastings, East Sussex; Greenwich, Berdmondsey and Deptford, London; Oxford; Bristol; and Knutsford, Cheshire. 'Obby 'Oss festivities can be seen in Padstow, Cornwall. The Dorset Ooser is paraded with the Wessex Morris Men near Cerne Abbas, Dorset.

⊙ **Castleton Garland Day**, Derbyshire: The Garland King is crowned and paraded through the streets, followed by dancing schoolchildren. 28/29 May.
www.visitcastleton.co.uk/garland-day-c19.html

JUNE

⊙ **Appleby Horse Fair**, Cumbria: First week in June.
www.applebyfair.org

⊙ **Midsummer**, many locations around Britain: A celebration of midsummer, the longest day of the year, with bonfires and festivities. The Cheshire Midsummer Watch Parade is a pageant.
www.midsummerwatch.co.uk
Summer solstice celebrations take place annually at Stonehenge, and rituals are led by the Druids, and attended by people from all walks of life.
www.stonehengetours.com/summer-solstice-celebrations.htm
Mid-summer fires can be still be seen around Cornwall. Late June.
www.oldcornwall.net/

JULY

⊙ **Whalton Bale/Baal fire**, Northumberland: An annual tradition since the middle ages, where a fire is built. With Morris dancers. 4 July. www.whaltonvillage.org.uk/news-events/events

⊙ **The Coventry Godiva Festival**, Coventry: While the first

Godiva Procession took place in the seventeenth century, the celebrations now take the form of a free festival of music and entertainment. www.godivafestival.com

◉ **Farndon Rush Bearing**, Cheshire: Procession including schoolchildren, a Rush Bearing Queen and a local brass band.

◉ **Eyemouth Herring Queen Festival**, Berwickshire: Festival to celebrate the herring harvest. www.ehq.org.uk/

AUGUST

◉ **St Wilfrid's Feast Parade**, Ripon, North Yorkshire.

◉ **National Eisteddfod of Wales**: Early August. www.eisteddfod.wales/

◉ **Burryman's Day**, South Queensferry, Edinburgh: A man is adorned with burrs and a garland crown and paraded around the town, given offerings of whisky. Associated with the annual Ferry Fair. Second Friday in August. www.ferryfair.co.uk

◉ **Robin Hood Festival**, Nottingham: www.facebook.com/robinhoodfestival/

◉ **Crying the Neck**, various locations, Cornwall: A traditional celebration of the last sheaf of corn cut at harvest. August/ September: www.oldcornwall.net/crying-the-neck

SEPTEMBER

◉ **Pearly Kings and Queens Harvest Festival**, Guildhall Yard, London: Pa rade with the Pearly Kings and Queens Association, from the Guildhall to St Mary Le Bow Church, with music and morris dancing. Other Pearly Kings and Queens events take place throughout September & October. www.pearlysociety.co.uk

◉ **Carshalton Straw Jack**, Surrey: A ceremonial costume is made from the last straw of the harvest, paraded through the streets, and then ritually burned at the end of the festivities. Beginning of September. www.strawjack.co.uk

⊙ **Abbots Bromley Horn Dance**, Staffordshire: Deer-men don antlers and perform traditional dances, along with a Fool, Hobby Horse, Bowman and Maid Marian, with a procession around the village. Wakes Monday, the first Sunday after 4 September. www.abbotsbromley.com/horn_dance

OCTOBER

⊙ **Spalding Pumpkin Festival**, Lincolnshire: A Grand Pumpkin Parade through the village, with live music, to celebrate local horticulture and harvest. Mid-October. www.sholland.gov.uk/pumpkinfestival

⊙ **Allhallowtide**: Little Moreton Hall, Cheshire.

⊙ **Souling plays**: Traditional folkplays performed by mummers take place at various places around Britain from late October and throughout November. Locations include Halton, Cheshire (www.earlofstamford.org.uk/Souling/); Comberbach, Cheshire (http://www.goosegate.plus.com/mummers/); Antrobus, Cheshire (www.mastermummers.org); Warburton, Cheshire (www.larchfieldhouse.co.uk/Souling/WarburtonSoulingPlay. htm). To find mummers near you, check: www.mastermummers.org/index.htm

⊙ **Hinton Saint George Punkie Night**, Somerset: A candlelit procession of women and children carrying hollowed out 'punkies' or mangolds, to commemorate the search for their lost menfolk on their way back from a local fair. Last Thursday of October. www.facebook.com/punkienight

NOVEMBER

⊙ **Flaming Tar Barrels**, Ottery St Mary, Devon: Weekend of 5 November. http://www.tarbarrels.co.uk/

⊙ **Lord Mayor's Show**, London: An 800 year old parade, in which the new Lord Mayor makes his way from the City to

Westminster to swear allegiance to the crown. With a procession of floats, music, and the traditional statues of Gog and Magog. www.lordmayorsshow.london/

⊙ **Baboon Tossing Night**, Oasby, Lincolnshire: A man in a monkey suit is pursued through the village by mummers and a torchlit parade. Mid-November.

⊙ **Christmas Garland**, Cotehele, Cornwall: A huge garland is constructed by volunteers, and displayed in the great hall from mid-November until late December. https://www.nationaltrust.org.uk/cotehele/features/christmas-at-cotehele

DECEMBER

⊙ **'Smuggler's Night'**, Rottingdean, East Sussex: Children's procession with marching bands. December 3rd. http://www.rottingdeansmugglers.co.uk/smugglers-night-saturday-3rd-december/

⊙ **Krampus Run**, Whitby, North Yorkshire: First Saturday of December. www.facebook.com/WhitbyKrampusRun/

⊙ **Soulcaking**, Chester, Cheshire: A soul caking play from the Jones' Ale Soulcakers. Early December. https://www.facebook.com/Jones-Ale-Soul-Cakers-101793779889669/

⊙ **Midwinter**, various places around Britain: Events include the Druid Ceremony, Stonehenge, Wiltshire. A winter solstice celebration takes place annually. www.stonehengetours.com/summer-solstice-celebrations.htm The Montol procession takes place in Penzance, Cornwall, each year, with guise dancers, mummers, and music. The Sheriff's Riding takes place in York, where the Sheriff parades around the city, accompanied by the York Waits. Late December, 21/22 December.

⊙ **Poor Old 'Oss**, Richmond, Yorkshire: A hobby horse pageant with mummers. 24 December.

⊙ **Derby Tup**, Sheffield, South Yorkshire: A mumming play

involving a replica head on a pole, with ram-like horns, and the snapping jaws of similar horse counterparts from other regions. Around Christmas.

◉ **Nos Galan**, various places around Britain: The Welsh New Year celebration takes place in cities such as Chepstow, Aberystwyth and Chester.

◉ **St Nicholas Hoodening**, Kent: Humorous plays, similar to mumming, accompanied by Morris dancers, and a Hooden Horse. www.hoodening.org.uk/

◉ **The Cutty Wren**, Middleton, Suffolk: Wren hunting ritual, revived by the Old Glory Molly Dancers and Musicians. St Stephen's Day. www.old-glory.org.uk/cuttywren.html

◉ **Hogmanay**, Edinburgh: Traditional New Year's Eve festivities. December 31st. www.edinburghshogmanay.com/

FIND OUT MORE:

Excellent places to find out about folklore events in your area include www.calendarcustoms.com and www.historic-uk.com/ CultureUK.

ILLUSTRATION NOTES

All illustrations by Joe McLaren.

INDEX

ACKNOWLEDGEMENTS

I would like to thank Willow Winsham, for believing that folklore matters and for her advice and editing in relation to witches. Huge thanks are due to the whole #FolkloreThursday team: to the volunteers who have helped bear the workload while I was writing this book, Amelia Starling, Donna Gilligan, Emma Oravecz, Jenn Lanman and Maria Ortado; to the sponsors, writers and guest hosts for their endless support, particularly Ben Gazur; and to everyone who takes part in #FolkloreThursday, for keeping folklore alive in the modern world. Thank you to Peter Taylor and Lucy Smith at Pavilion Books for their support and advice; to Amy Feldman and the team at the National Trust for advice on folklore at their properties; and to Suresh Ariaratnam, and everyone at Sprung Sultan, for tirelessly answering questions and offering support. And finally, heartfelt thanks to my partner, Cyrus Chainey, for endless hours of discussions and proofreading after long days and nights.